The Price of Honor

The Price of Honor

The World War One Letters of

Naval Aviator Kenneth MacLeish

Edited by Geoffrey L. Rossano

Naval Institute Press
Annapolis, Maryland

Library of Congress Cataloging-in-Publication Data

MacLeish, Kenneth, 1894–1918.
    The price of honor : the World War One letters of naval
aviator Kenneth MacLeish / edited by Geoffrey L. Rossano.
        p.   cm.
    Includes bibliographical references and index.
    ISBN 0-87021-584-1 (alk. paper)
    1. MacLeish, Kenneth, 1894–1918—Correspondence.
2. Air pilots, Military—United States—Correspondence.
3. World War, 1914–1918— Aerial operations, American.
4. World War, 1914–1918—Personal narratives, American.
5. United States. Navy—Aviation— History—20th
Century.   6. United States. Navy—Biography. I. Rossano,
Geoffrey Louis.   II. Title.
D606.M3A4   1991
940.4'4973—dc20   90–45844

Printed in the United States of America on acid-free paper ∞

9 8 7 6 5 4 3 2

First printing

The poem "On a Memorial Stone" appeared in *Kenneth: A
Collection of Letters,* edited and arranged by Martha Hillard
MacLeish. Chicago: 1919. Reprinted by permission of the
Estate of Archibald MacLeish.

Now we are names that once were young
And had our will of living weather,
Loved dark pines and the thin moon's feather,
Fought and endured our souls and flung
Our laughter to the ends of earth,
And challenged heaven with our spacious mirth.

Now we are names and men shall come
To drone their memorable words;
How we went out with shouting swords
And high, devoted hearts; the drum
Shall trouble us with stuttered roll,
And stony Latin laud the hero soul;

And generations unfulfilled,
The heirs of all we struggled for,
Shall here recall the mythic war,
And marvel how we stabbed and killed,
And name us savage, brave, austere, —
And none shall think how very young we were.

Archibald MacLeish, "On a Memorial Stone"

Contents

Preface

DESPITE THE WELL-PUBLICIZED HORROR and carnage of the western front, thousands of young Americans who answered the call to arms in the spring of 1917 did so with enthusiasm and determination. Many viewed the war as the struggle of democracy and Christian virtues against the darker forces of militarism and barbarism. Nowhere was this sense of mission stronger than at the country's elite colleges and universities.

Even before President Woodrow Wilson urged that "the world must be made safe for democracy," students by the score had volunteered for service in Europe as ambulance drivers or members of the French foreign legion. Several were on active duty with the air forces of England and France. Other young men had prepared themselves for America's possible military involvement by attending the famous businessmen's training camps conducted at Plattsburgh, New York, or by joining National Guard units in their home states. A few even formed ad hoc organizations, awaiting the moment the government might call for their services.

The First Yale Unit, a detachment of undergraduates who enlisted in the Naval Reserve in March 1917, was one such group. Pursuing flight training at their own expense and with funds and equipment donated by wealthy businessmen, they later formed the nucleus of the U.S. Navy's overseas aviation efforts. Their ranks included such luminaries as Robert Lovett, later secretary of defense, Artemus Gates, nominated for the Congressional Medal of Honor, and David Ingalls, the navy's only World War One "ace."

The First Yale Unit also included junior Kenneth MacLeish of Glen-

coe, Illinois. He was a member of a prominent midwestern family; his
father was a senior executive at Carson, Pirie, Scott and Co., and his
brother Archibald would soon earn a reputation as one of the country's
premier poets. Kenneth's career in naval aviation lasted from late March
1917 until his death in combat a few weeks before the Armistice. Extensive personal correspondence during the nineteen-month period, nearly
three hundred letters, recorded his own varied activities, as well as those
of his Yale comrades and developments in naval aviation generally.

My own interest in early aviation history began more than twenty
years ago when I conducted a series of interviews with veterans of World
War One, pilots and ground personnel alike. In later years I completed
further research into America's formative military aviation efforts, con-
centrating on the joint U.S.-Allied ventures undertaken in 1917–18.

One evening while visiting friends in Oyster Bay, New York, I
happened to mention this interest. My host responded that her mother
had been engaged to a Yale pilot in World War One, a young man named
Kenneth MacLeish who had died in the waning weeks of the conflict. She
then produced two large boxes of letters written to her mother, Priscilla
Murdock, by MacLeish while he was on active duty in Virginia, England, and France.

A quick glance at a few of the letters convinced me of their value both
as historical documents and as mementos of a tragic love affair from long
ago. We immediately began discussing the possibility of publishing some
of that correspondence. Originally envisioned as an article, the project
quickly blossomed into a book-length manuscript as I began to uncover
additional letters and materials from other members of the Yale Unit and
from Kenneth and Priscilla's circle of friends. Further research took me
to New Haven, New York, Washington, and London.

&ca; &ca; &ca;

In carrying this undertaking to a successful conclusion I have received
much assistance and incurred many debts of gratitude. Chloe Bowen,
Priscilla's daughter and the holder of Kenneth's letters, has offered continued cooperation and encouragement. Both she and her husband,
David, have been a joy to work with. I have also received considerable
assistance from the MacLeish family, who provided extensive background information and generously gave their permission to publish
Kenneth's correspondence. Richard McAdoo, Archibald MacLeish's lit-
erary executor, and Donald Belin, MacLeish's attorney, offered both
counsel and advice as I tried to run down investigative leads and to locate

materials. Similarly, Roy Winnick, who edited Archibald MacLeish's published letters, made several contructive suggestions.

In addition to the letters provided by Chloe Bowen, this volume draws on several additional sources. Following World War One Kenneth's mother, Martha Hillard MacLeish, published a memorial volume of letters from her slain son to various family members. A selection of that material has been included to fill in occasional gaps in the MacLeish-Murdock correspondence. David Ingalls's letters to his family, which were written almost exactly contemporaneously with Kenneth's, first appeared in Ralph Paine's *The First Yale Unit* (Cambridge, Mass.: Riverside Press, 1925). *The First Yale Unit,* which was based in large measure on the collected correspondence of unit veterans, also provided comments by many of Kenneth's peers, including John Vorys, Al Sturtevant, Ken Smith, Curtis Read, Frank Lynch, Robert Lovett, Di Gates, and Trubee Davison. Equally valuable were the privately printed war letters of George Mosely (Chicago, 1923). Observations on the exploits of the First Yale Unit by Captain Hutch Cone, Captain Thomas Craven, and Lieutenant William Edwards appeared in William Sims, *The Victory at Sea* (Garden City, N.Y.: Doubleday, 1920).

While no comprehensive study of naval aviation in World War One has yet appeared, two Navy Department publications proved extemely useful in providing context and background. The illustrated *Naval Aviation in World War One* by Adrian O. Van Wyen (Washington, D.C.: CNO, 1969) offered good summaries on a wide variety of topics. *United States Naval Aviation 1910–1970* (Washington, D.C., 1970) provided a concise chronological overview of the period. Reginald Arthur's *Contact: Careers of U.S. Naval Aviators 1–2000* (Washington, D.C., 1967) contained much useful biographical data about Kenneth MacLeish's contemporaries in naval aviation.

Even more than published sources, unpublished materials from public and private collections proved indispensable in filling out the story of Kenneth's wartime service. The staffs at several research facilities greatly lightened my burden, especially curator Patricia Willis (Collection of American Literature, Beinecke Rare Book and Manuscript Library, Yale University), who helped unearth some letters from John Menzies in the Archibald MacLeish papers. The F. Trubee Davison Papers (Manuscripts and Archives, Yale University Library) contain files of correspondence from all the members of the First Yale Unit, especially material from David Ingalls, Di Gates, Robert Lovett, and Kenneth MacLeish.

Archivists at the Public Records Office in Kew, England, led me directly to the Royal Air Force logbooks that detailed Kenneth MacLeish's service with the British in the spring, summer, and fall of 1918, including his final, fatal patrol. A particularly illuminating body of material was generously provided by the family of Robert Lovett, including wartime letters from Lovett to Adele Brown, and an equally informative body of correspondence from Evelyn Preston to Adele Brown. Further encouragement from the Davison and Ingalls families was greatly appreciated as well.

I owe a special debt to Lawrence Sheely, whose uncle, Irving Sheely, flew with Kenneth MacLeish as his observer in the spring and summer of 1918. Mr. Sheely unselfishly offered the results of twenty years' research into his uncle's aviation career, including government documents, family photographs, and a wonderful series of letters and diaries. He made my job both easier and much more pleasant. I am glad to count him as a newfound friend.

Similarly, everyone I spoke with at the Naval Historical Center at the Washington Navy Yard offered encouragement and assistance. Agnes Hoover in the photo archives was a special resource. Roy Grossnick at *Naval Aviation News* donated generous amounts of time and advice. At the United States Naval Academy, the staff at the Nimitz Library were characteristically helpful and cooperative.

Working with the Naval Institute Press has been a particular pleasure. Paul Wilderson, whom I met at a conference on board the USS *Yorktown* in Charleston in 1987, backed this project enthusiastically from the start. Patti Maddocks in the library went out of her way to suggest resources and to make introductions.

No list of acknowledgments would be complete without thanking my wife, Joan, who first introduced me to the Bowen family. Since then she has given unstinting support and encouragement throughout this long undertaking. Sometimes she must have wondered whether I had married her or the word processor. One of these days I hope to make it up to her.

Finally, I must mention my gratitude to John Farwell for taking the time to provide a lengthy telephone interview. A veteran of the First Yale Unit and in his early nineties, he still visits his Chicago office regularly, and it was there that I located him. He is now the last of the First, and as I listened to his reminiscences of Kenneth MacLeish and the rest of those pioneer naval aviators, the letters and photographs I had amassed literally returned to life. To him and to all the men who served with him, this book is dedicated.

The Price of Honor

Introduction

RESTING IN PARIS in March 1918, naval aviator Kenneth MacLeish contemplated his imminent departure for the beleaguered American antisubmarine base at Dunkirk. Though shocked by the recent deaths of several friends in training accidents or over the front lines, he remained largely untouched by the war, and the idealistic fervor that had led him to enlist almost a year earlier still burned brightly. To a friend at home Kenneth wrote, "The Gates of Honor are opened to us, those lucky ones of us who are over here."

Despite the dangers, fears, and frustrations he encountered in the ensuing months, MacLeish rarely regretted his decision, and until his death in combat a few weeks before the Armistice, he compiled an enviable record as a naval aviator. In fact, Lieutenant MacLeish's flying career spanned the entire course of America's participation in World War One, and his voluminous personal correspondence chronicled the growth of naval air power from a military curiosity into a vital weapon wielded against the enemy submarine menace.

When the United States entered the conflict in April 1917 naval aviation was in its infancy. Only a few years had passed since the pioneering flights of Eugene Ely, Theodore Ellyson, John Towers, Patrick Bellinger, Kenneth Whiting, and others. The Naval Flying Corps authorized in 1916 had not yet been established, and the fleet's entire aviation strength consisted of 54 training-type aircraft, 48 officers and 239 enlisted men, 3 lighter-than-air craft, a single instructional center, and a rudimentary expansion plan.

Drawing heavily on the experience of the Allies, military planners explored a wide range of tactics, missions, and technologies. In little more than eighteen months the U.S. Navy built a vast network of training and patrol facilities throughout the United States, while dozens of overseas bases and depots operated in Britain, France, and Italy. A ground school established in M.I.T. in Cambridge, Massachusetts, enrolled nearly five thousand students and graduated thirty-six hundred of them. Similar programs later functioned at the University of Washington and the Dunwoody Institute in Minneapolis. Large-scale flight instruction commenced at Pensacola, Hampton Roads, Miami, Bay Shore, San Diego, Key West, and elsewhere. Other navy flyers trained with the U.S. Army on Long Island and in Texas, or with the Royal Flying Corps in Canada. A Marine Corps aviation program was also begun. Along the coast a string of patrol bases guarded the shipping lanes into major American ports.

Wartime demands and the severity of Germany's submarine campaign forcibly accelerated the pace of development. New equipment was tested and refined, and improved aircraft were rushed to completion. The Curtiss Company, a pioneer in overwater aviation and the nation's premier manufacturer, developed the HS-1 and HS-2 flying boats, as well as the giant NC machines that crossed the Atlantic in 1919. In August 1917 workers began building the Naval Aircraft Factory in Philadelphia. The government-operated plant was completed in mid-October and then greatly enlarged the following year. Large numbers of H-16 and F5L flying boats were constructed there.

The navy's first overseas personnel, 125 officers and enlisted men led by Lieutenant Kenneth Whiting, reached Europe in June 1917, and the initial foreign air station was established at Moutchic, France, in August. More followed in the months ahead: Le Croisic in November, Pauillac in December, and Dunkirk on New Year's Day 1918. Eventually twenty-seven European bases were authorized in Ireland, England, France, and Italy.

Eliminating the submarine menace demanded most of the naval aviators' time and effort. Pilots and aircraft from NAS Dunkirk, though much battered by enemy bombs and shellfire, patrolled the northern entrance to the English Channel and engaged in a long-running duel with enemy forces stationed nearby at Ostend, Zeebrugge, and Bruges. Heavily armed flying boats from the station at Killingholme on the east coast of England scouted far and wide across the North Sea. Bases at Le

Croisic, Brest, L'Aber Vrach, Paimboeuf, and Ile Tudy guarded both the southern approaches to the English Channel and the huge American convoys entering the Bay of Biscay. Several other stations operated in Ireland, patrolling the Channel and the submarine-infested entrances to the Irish Sea. A training unit was also established at Lake Bolsena in Italy, and a patrol base operated at Porto Corsini on the Adriatic Sea. At Pauillac and Eastleigh the navy created small factory cities designed to erect and repair aircraft and engines, while also serving as the principal supply depots for the overseas aviation campaign. Late in the war the Northern Bombing Group based in Flanders commenced sustained attacks against German targets in Belgium. By November 1918 the number of aviation personnel in foreign waters exceeded eleven hundred officers and eighteen thousand enlisted men. Transatlantic flights and aircraft carriers were only a few months away.

The roster of those who contributed to such dramatic growth was long indeed and included seasoned commanders, recent Annapolis graduates, volunteer officers, and legions of enlisted men. One group that stood out, however, was the First Yale Unit, an unofficial organization of college students formed in 1916 at the instigation of F. Trubee Davison, the son of prominent J. P. Morgan partner and Red Cross official Henry P. Davison. Trubee spent the summer of 1915 driving an American Field Service ambulance in Paris and returned to the United States fascinated with the burgeoning field of military aviation. Arriving at Yale that fall, he immediately sought out classmate Robert Lovett, the son of a leading railway executive. The two students agreed that if the United States ever entered the war, they would serve as aviators.

At the urging of officials at the Aero Club of America, a dozen of the Yale boys, including Davison, Lovett, and gridiron standout Artemus "Di" Gates, organized themselves as Aerial Coast Patrol #1 in the summer of 1916. With facilities, equipment, and an instructor donated by businessman and philanthropist Rodman Wanamaker, they commenced training at Port Washington, New York. In late fall the Yale Unit moved its equipment to the naval base at New London, Connecticut, where it conducted several experiments until cold weather precluded further flying.

In March 1917 the United States edged dramatically closer to war, and the Navy Department urged Yale Unit members to join the Naval Reserve Force. At this time several additional volunteers swelled their ranks, Kenneth MacLeish among them. Following a mass swearing in at

New London on 24 March, the entire group journeyed to Florida and further training. After stints at West Palm Beach and Huntington Bay, New York, the Yale volunteers received their pilot's licenses and naval commissions at the end of the summer. A few headed overseas almost immediately. Others performed instructional and administrative duties in the United States. Eventually all but six served in Europe. From their small ranks—fewer than thirty charter members—sprang several squadron and station commanders. Captain Hutch I. Cone, wartime commander of naval aviation forces in Europe, stated that "this group of aviators formed the nucleus of the first Naval Reserve Flying Corps, and, in fact, may be considered as the nucleus from which the United States Aviation forces, Foreign Service, later grew." Lieutenant Commander W. A. Edwards, who headed the aviation desk at London headquarters near the end of the war, echoed these sentiments when he recalled, "I knew that whenever we had a member of the Yale Unit, everything was all right. Whenever the French and English asked us to send a couple of our crack men to reinforce a squadron, I would say, 'Let's get some of the Yale gang.' We never made a mistake when we did this."

During the course of the fighting Yale men served at nearly every important aviation facility and performed every duty from flight instructor and beachmaster to combat pilot and staff officer. One, David Ingalls, became the navy's only wartime ace. In 1929 President Hoover appointed him assistant secretary of the navy for aeronautics. Another Yale Unit member, Artemus "Di" Gates, rose to command NAS Dunkirk in 1918, and during World War Two labored as an undersecretary of the navy. Finally, Robert Lovett helped organize the Northern Bombing Group, the navy's program to cripple the German submarine campaign through concentrated aerial bombardment of port facilities. His appointment as secretary of defense three decades later capped a distinguished career.

By contrast, Lieutenant Kenneth MacLeish, one of the most popular members of the Yale Unit, is little known today. He was born on 19 September 1894 at Craigie Lea, his family's rambling, shingled home in Glencoe, Illinois, a comfortable suburb north of Chicago on the shores of Lake Michigan. His father, Andrew MacLeish, emigrated to the United States from Scotland in 1856 at the age of eighteen. He immediately journeyed westward to Chicago and launched a career as a dry goods merchant. As founder and manager of what later became Carson, Pirie and Scott's Chicago retail store, Andrew MacLeish prospered. He was also a leading layman of the Fourth Baptist Church and helped establish the University of Chicago.

Twice a widower and approaching the age of fifty, MacLeish was introduced to Martha Hillard, a Vassar graduate and daughter of a Congregational minister. Descended from old New England stock that included Pilgrim leader William Brewster and several other colonial notables, the thirty-two-year-old Martha Hillard had taught in both public school and college, and was then finishing her fourth year as principal of the Rockford (Wisconsin) Seminary. They were married in August 1888.

Martha and Andrew MacLeish had four surviving children. The eldest, Norman, was born in 1890, followed by Archibald in 1892, Kenneth in 1894, and a daughter, Ishbel, in 1897. To each of their children the MacLeishes imparted a strong sense of mission and Christian idealism. When not tending personally to the youngsters' schooling, Martha involved herself in the work of the Glencoe school board, the Chicago Women's Club, the Visiting Nurse Association, Hull House, and the National Women's Foreign Mission Society.

Following in the footsteps of his talented and much-admired elder brother Archibald, later one of America's most renowned poets, Kenneth MacLeish entered Hotchkiss School in Lakeville, Connecticut, in September 1910 and Yale University in the autumn of 1914. While at college Kenneth distinguished himself as a talented athlete and was also active in the Yale Home Mission. Spurred by a desire to earn the respect of his family and friends, Kenneth joined the First Yale Unit in late winter 1917, and on 24 March he enlisted in the navy as an electrician, 2d class. He trained with the group at Palm Beach, Florida, and Huntington, New York. On 22 August young MacLeish was ordered to Newport News, Virginia, to act as an instructor, and two months later he received assignment overseas.

In the following months he continued his training at Moutchic, Gosport, Turnberry, Ayr, and Clermont-Ferrand. Along the way he learned to handle a variety of aircraft: French FBA flying boats, Hanriot-Dupont scouts, and Breguet bombers; British Sopwith Camels and D.H. 9s; American-built D.H. 4s. Combat duty included tours at Dunkirk and with two Royal Air Force squadrons. Shifted from station to station, he escorted patrolling flying boats, bombed enemy targets, and engaged in dogfights above the lines. After stints at the Pauillac and Eastleigh supply bases, MacLeish returned to the front in mid-October. He was killed in action shortly thereafter.

Though somewhat overshadowed by more illustrious members of the Yale Unit, Kenneth MacLeish received frequent praise for his work as an instructor, combat pilot, and administrative officer. At one point slated to command a day bombardment squadron, he was later offered one of the navy's night-flying units instead. Unwilling to serve out the remainder of the war tied to a desk, he declined the post, a decision that cost him his life. In a letter of condolence written in early 1919, Captain David Hanrahan, MacLeish's commander from the Northern Bombing Group, remembered that Kenneth was, "without exception, the most popular man in our force. . . . one of the finest pilots who ever flew over the north country. . . . I made special use of [Kenneth] because of his all-round ability. . . . Misfortune overtook him too soon."

In service for nineteen months and overseas much of that time, MacLeish was a prolific correspondent, and his frequent letters to family and friends recorded an enormous range of experiences. Recently a large collection of letters was discovered in the estate of his fiancée, Priscilla Murdock. They first met in 1914 when Kenneth was a freshman at Yale and Priscilla was attending nearby Westover School in Middlebury, Connecticut. MacLeish's aunt Mary Hillard was the headmistress there, and his sister Ishbel was a student. Perhaps Ishbel introduced the young couple.

Their friendship, however, did not blossom into a full-fledged romance until 1917, when Kenneth was training with the Yale Unit at Huntington. Priscilla spent the summer at her family's nearby vacation house at Peacock Point and commuted to the Yale training site to take instruction in wireless telegraphy. In the following months the two of them visited whenever possible. Just before he departed the United States in late October, Kenneth proposed to Priscilla, and she accepted. A few days later he boarded the SS *New York* and sailed to Europe.

Their correspondence, carried on sporadically in the summer and early fall, became their only means of communication, and for the next eleven months Kenneth wrote nearly every day. Much of the material was deeply personal, reflecting the pain and frustration of their prolonged separation and his hopes for the future. MacLeish's letters also included lengthy descriptions of his varied duties, the activities of his Yale Unit friends, and the overall development of naval aviation. He supplied vivid pictures of flight training in the United States, impressions of wartime Europe and European society, a detailed record of instruction at French, British, and American flight schools, lively accounts of front-line service, and pointed reactions to myriad personalities and events. Along the way MacLeish met the leading naval aviation figures of his day—Hutch Cone, Kenneth Whiting, David Hanrahan, Earle Johnson, T. T. Craven. He also came to know many of the famed American flyers on the western front, including Eddie Rickenbacker, Bill Thaw, Laurence Callahan, Lloyd Hamilton, Reed Landis, Douglas Campbell, Alan Winslow, and Paul Baer.

Taken as a group, Kenneth MacLeish's letters provide a very personal view of the progress and experiences of an early naval aviator. Among the letters of the navy's pioneer combat pilots, they are virtually unique in their scope and detail. Back in November 1917 Kenneth had asked Priscilla to keep his letters so that they might serve as a sort of diary. Lovingly preserved for more than seventy years, they offer an intimate record both of the navy's first air war and of a tender romance cut short at the very moment of victory.

1

"Us Sailors Never Reach France Cause!": Training with the Yale Unit

March 1917–December 1917

Kᴇɴɴᴇᴛʜ MᴀᴄLᴇɪsʜ's ᴄᴀʀᴇᴇʀ as a naval aviator commenced formally on 24 March 1917, when he traveled with his companions to the submarine base at New London, Connecticut, to be sworn in as a member of the Naval Reserve Flying Corps. MacLeish was eager to go and had no doubts concerning the soundness of his decision to enlist. But like so many other young men before him, he first had to convince his parents that it was a wise course to pursue. Writing home in early March, Kenneth explained his desire to join the Yale Unit, tried to allay their fears, and asked for their blessing.

New Haven, March 1917

Dearest Mother and Father,

I realize now that when I asked permission to join the [Yale] aviation corps, I hadn't explained it in any sense of the word. In the first place, joining the aviation corps at the present time means only one thing. It means that in time of war they can count on me to be ready to go into action. It does not mean that if I join now I will rush off to some camp and lose part of my college course. One other point: joining the Yale aviation corps does not put me under control of any federal authority. The idea is to join the corps, and after training for a month, if the Advisory Board think it best, to join the Coast Patrol Aviation Corps of the United States.[1] So you see, this corps has nothing whatsoever to do with the federal corps until it is fully trained and ready to go into action.

8

That settles the enlistment. From the above you ought to see that your consent would only allow me to join the corps in case of war. In the second place I have thoroughly made up my mind to join AN aviation corps in case of war. There is absolutely no argument there! That is the branch of the service for which I am best fitted, and in which I could do most. I am only being radical and headstrong because I am perfectly sure that you don't understand the conditions, or else you think that I am the kind of man who can stay at home and let someone else do the fighting. I realize the fact that at least five men are needed at home to support one in the field, but that realization will never, never, never suffice me! I could never stay at home if there was fighting of a real nature. I could never be content at home if the life and honor of anyone dear to me was in danger.

War is terrible, but there are two or three things that are worse. The brutality of Germany with respect to Belgium, the statement by Germany that international law and humanity are mere scraps of paper compared to her needs, the wanton murder of helpless American women and children, the open insults to the honor of the United States—they're all worse than war! There are many things worth giving up one's life for, and the greatest of these is humanity and the assurance of the laws of Christianity. Some people think that the only words Christ uttered were, "Resist not evil." Do you think for a minute that if Christ had been alone on the Mount with Mary, and desperate man had entered with criminal intent, He would have turned away when a crime against Mary was perpetrated? Never! He would have fought with all the God-given strength he had. Religion embraces the sword as well as the dove of peace.

Please think this over and let me know if I can join the Yale aviation corps. Dearest love to both. . . .

1. *In March 1915 Congress established the National Advisory Committee for Aeronautics. In February 1917 this body recommended the establishment of eight coastal patrol stations. At the same time the private Aero Club of America urged the creation of voluntary coastal patrol units, of which the Yale Unit was the first.*

As the likelihood of war grew stronger with each passing week the navy in March 1917 urged the fledgling Yale aviators to join the Naval Reserve Flying Corps. On 24 March the college fliers traveled to New London to be sworn into government service. Trubee Davison received a commission as a lieutenant (jg), and most of those trained the previous summer at Port Washington were made ensigns. The remainder received varied enlisted men's ratings, with promises of future commissions when they passed their aviator qualifying tests. Four days later they all set out for Florida, their destination The Breakers Hotel at Palm Beach.

After a few days to get their bearings, the Yale contingent shifted quarters to the Salt Air Hotel at West Palm Beach, and began training at merchant and philanthropist Rodman Wanamaker's donated flying facilities on the nearby shore of Lake Worth. Instructional staff included David McCulloch, their teacher from the previous summer who served as a test pilot during the war and flew the NC-3 on its 1919 Transatlantic attempt, and Caleb Bragg, a Yale graduate, racing driver, and winter resident of Palm Beach, where he kept an airplane. An expert motorman, Bragg later directed the U.S. Army's experimental work at McCook Field, Ohio. Even more important was the arrival in early April of Lieutenant Edward O. McDonnell from the naval air station at Pensacola, assigned to take command of the unit and whip the college boys into shape. A 1912 Annapolis graduate and one of the navy's pioneer aviators, McDonnell had been awarded the Congressional Medal of Honor in 1914 for his heroism at Vera Cruz.

For aircraft the unit possessed the *Mary Ann,* a veteran flying boat, and a few machines presented by family and friends. Wanamaker also offered the use of one of the Trans-Oceanic seaplanes. Others were purchased with funds donated by the likes of J. P. Morgan and Co. and Harry Paine Whitney.

Palm Beach, April 1917

Dearest Ishbel [MacLeish],

I simply can't tell you how splendid you've been in the past few weeks. I haven't the words in control when it comes to thanking you. In the first place, I thought that I was the only one who really appreciated and understood the conditions. Your spirit and backing have made it very much easier to willingly give my life for a cause that I know is far nobler than any other. You know, honor is the goal everyone wants, and it's wonderful to do an honorable deed and never have it known, but though not as great, it is surely wonderful to have someone very close to you appreciate your attempts to be honorable and to win honor. I can't thank you in words, but if I get into active service I will thank you with deeds. Just now all I can do is obey orders and do the best I can. I am now rated as an expert electrician and get $65 a month. After I have flown alone five hours I will be a provisional ensign, and after forty-five hours more, a full-fledged ensign, drawing about $2,000 a year in service.

As things are now, I have two alternatives: I will either be placed on a sending ship, and act in conjunction with the fleets, or else I will be sent to a point along the coast and act as a patrol, or else instruct pupils—possibly both. So far learning has been slow—I can't get over the fact that I am not in an auto. I can fly the boat in the air, and I can take it off the water, but I can't land and I'm not very steady yet. . . .

Kenneth MacLeish began his flight training in early April and by the end of the month had amassed approximately six hours in the air under the tutelage of instructor Dave McCulloch. Then, finally, on 2 May he embarked on his first solo attempt, a twenty-minute flight in Trans-Oceanic #4. In the next four weeks he logged another ten hours of solo time. But even as he gained experience, the group was preparing to pack up and head north. Rising spring temperatures created unstable air conditions, a particular danger to novice aviators.

Palm Beach, May 1917

Dearest Mother and Father,

Several things have happened in the past few days which are worthy of note. To begin with, I am now flying alone. I was the first one of the new crowd to fly alone, and I also beat four fellows who flew all last summer down on Long Island. I learned to fly in about eleven hours. One is supposed to take at least twelve, so you can see it did come easily to me, and everything is turning out just as I expected. This accomplishment automatically makes me an ensign, and I expect my papers soon.

The plans have been changed so that we will not leave here until June first at the earliest, and we will go from here to Huntington, Long Island. After that, who knows? The idea of our being placed on battleships seems to have been abandoned. Another rumor has it that we will be split into fours and sent to the eight stations along the Atlantic coast for patrol duty. If this falls through, I see but one alternative—to go abroad. Our shipping is in little danger here compared with what is on the other side. Over there we could have our stations along the coast and go out over the ocean for about a hundred miles and convoy ships to harbor.

Several remarks have made me very optimistic. I understand that these F–Boats we are flying are the hardest machines to fly. The boats, of course, will not be used in service. The government machine is a 250-hp pontoon machine with a speed of 85 mph, and a wingspread of 50 feet. They are called the R–3 machine. We expect to have two JN tractor machines, but we will take off the wheels and put on pontoons. The boat will then be known as an N-9 tractor.[1]

I rather quaked in my boots when the lieutenant [Eddie McDonnell] came around and ordered me to fly alone. I was so new at the game that I had very little confidence. I sort of shut my eyes and "let 'er go," and found it highly to my liking to fly the old machine just as I darn pleased and stand no chance of being bawled out by a sarcastic instructor. I took it off the water nicely, and then began to settle back and take things easy. I found that all the nervousness I had previously had come from the fear of making a mistake when the instructor was with me. The next thing I knew I felt myself grinning from ear to ear and trying to whistle, though the wind blew my lips flat and the roar of the motor and propeller entirely discouraged the attempt. I made my first landing alone—a thing I will never forget in all my life. I didn't realize how very dependent I had been on the instructor until I was about to level off above the water! Then something seemed to say, "Here's where you show yourself you can fly, or here's where you bust something." I chose the former and made the most perfect landing ever made. Not until then did I realize how dark it was getting and that I was eight miles from home. I started back and that fool sun went down like a shot. While the rays were still shining on me, below me there was pitch darkness. Well, for once in my life I had a real battle with myself. I finally won out and started to land perfectly calmly and determined that everything should go off smoothly. I couldn't see the surface of the water, but I could faintly make out boats here and there, and I steered my boat between two of them, giving me an absolute reference. When I felt the warm air on the water I leveled off and made a fair landing—nothing to write home about, but perfectly safe. When I got back, they had left in a speedboat with a searchlight to help me, and they had everything round the hangar "lit up." I sure did bawl that lieutenant out for sending me up, and he apologized most profusely and said he didn't know it got dark so fast.

You must excuse my gushing about all this, and I fear it makes you a bit worried, but just remember this: I am apt to exaggerate any tight places, and, furthermore, this flying simply fascinates me, and I fairly dream about it. Always remember that now I have as much confidence in myself and my machine as I have driving the Mercer [automobile]. I am more careful here, and therefore less liable to accidents. I feel absolutely sure that I could get out of anything that could happen to me so long as I fly in this wonderful weather and don't try going up in a storm. I wish you could both have the same confidence in me that I have in myself.

I don't know how safe you felt in the Mercer when I was driving, but I think that I scared you only once, and that was not my fault. I felt perfectly sure that I could miss that car then, and I did. I feel the same way about flying. My instructor said that a pupil learns to fly just as soon as he is perfectly at home in an airplane and I believe he's right.

I wish the navy would pay us—they haven't come through yet! For a good cheap outfit, give me the U.S. Navy at present—they're a bunch of nickel sports. They think nothing of spending a dime or so a month. . . .

1. *The F-Boats used at Palm Beach were small, Curtiss-built flying boats carrying a crew of two seated side by side, powered by a single pusher engine. The Curtiss R-3 was one of a series of two-seat, twin-float seaplanes. The Curtiss JN-4, better known as the Jenny, served as a primary training aircraft for the army. Fitted with pontoons and modified wings and tail, it was used by the navy for similar purposes.*

Most of the time at West Palm Beach was spent flying, or learning engine maintenance, wireless telegraphy, naval etiquette, or aerial gunnery. A rather spirited competition between aircraft crews developed. Each wanted the best machine and the most flying time. MacLeish belonged to a group headed by Di Gates, which also included David Ingalls, Ken Smith, and Robert Ireland. All their work proceeded under the watchful eyes of instructors Bragg, McCulloch, and McDonnell. On one occasion Harry Davison and David Ingalls took off on a predawn flight to watch the sun come up from an altitude of 3,000 feet. Lieutenant McDonnell sternly forbade a repetition of such foolish stunts.

When not pursuing their aviation educations, the men from Yale enjoyed the good life against a backdrop of sandy beaches and palm trees. Some pleasures were simple ones, like a game of pachisi or malted milkshakes at the Seminole Drug Store. Hunting 'gators at night also proved a popular diversion. So did bombing friends' houses with coconuts. Lieutenant McDonnell enjoyed stalking deer, while the rest of the crew sought female companionship. Ken Smith of Patchogue, New York, earned the title of "chief petting officer," but whenever he left the dock with a lady friend, his cohorts pelted him with coconuts.

Palm Beach, May 1917

Dearest Mother and Father,

Not a thing of note has turned up this week. Flying has been very mediocre. I have discovered that the very worst time to fly is when the sun is very bright and there is no wind. It seems that the heat radiates upward in columns like smoke, and the cold air rushes down to take its place. There may be a difference in velocity of 5 or 6 mph between the two air currents, and when you get one wing in one, and the other in the other, you get quite a funny sensation which it is wise never to experience.

In this flying game you have to be very quick and yet not nervous. You have three separate controls to work at once, and if you aren't perfectly cool all the time, it isn't hard to mix them up. One is bound to change quite a bit. I feel perfectly confident in myself for the first time in my life. I never try foolish things, however, because I'm a firm believer in the laws of chance. I believe that a man has only a certain number of chances to take before he fails "to get away with it." If he uses them slowly, he's all safe. There surely seems to be a well-defined and infallible formula connected with all chances.

These F–Boats are as safe as a church. They have a factor of safety of six throughout the whole construction. That means that if a wire has a tensile strength capable of holding 12,000 pounds, only 2,000 will be placed on it. That is one-sixth of its tensile strength. Do you follow me? Over on the other side they have machines that fly 140 mph, but they sacrifice safety for speed. They cut down the head resistance by either eliminating or decreasing the size of their wires and struts. The result is that they have a factor of safety only one or two. The U.S. Navy requires one of at least five.

I got my official orders from Washington, so that I am now in active service, but those cheapskates in Washington only started to pay us on May 3d. We won't get our cash now until June 3d. That puts me up against it for another month, and I'll have to ask for $25 more. Please keep careful account of all the things you buy for me, and I'll pay you back when the much-delayed ship comes in. . . .

At the end of May the Yale Unit packed up shop and headed north. A new site, the Castledge estate, had been selected on the shores of Huntington Bay, New York, a few miles west of the Davisons' home at Peacock Point. A hangar and ramp ways were built, as well as a machine shop and wireless hut. After a week of organizing activities, flight instruction resumed in early June, utilizing N-9 and R-6 seaplanes recently supplied by the Navy Department. The young aviators also had use of a brand-new R-3, and a swept-wing Burgess-Dunne, a gift of financier Harry Paine Whitney.

Most of the men boarded in the Castledge mansion house. The rigors of their stay were further eased by the presence of Whitney's yacht *Whileaway,* lent to the unit and anchored nearby, as well as Davison's yacht *Shuttle.* Baseball games on the beach occupied a few of the rare idle hours, as did weekend parties at the Davisons' estate in nearby Locust Valley. Also present at the flying station were several young women who had formed the Girls' Wireless Unit with the intention of earning a commercial radio license and then enlisting in the navy as wireless operators. It was during these summer weeks that Kenneth renewed his long-standing friendship with Priscilla Murdock. The Murdocks owned a summer home next to the Davison's place at Peacock Point, and the two were able to visit both in Huntingdon and on the weekend.

But the serious work of flight instruction also proceeded quickly as Eddie McDonnell continued preparing his charges for their aviation qualifying tests. By the end of June Kenneth had amassed nearly thirty hours aloft. He was also learning more sophisticated maneuvers, and his final "exam" was scheduled for late July. After that, a navy commission awaited. The one thing that MacLeish feared was that he might be asked to stay on as an instructor and not receive an active-duty assignment.

Huntington, 10 July 1917

Dearest Mother and Father,

This has been a very busy two weeks for me. I have had extra duty because I have been working in the machine shops as well as trying to keep the big R-3 in order. Mother, I hate to brag, and I wouldn't only I feel that it will help your feelings along, when I tell you that I really think I am getting some intelligence after years of fruitless effort! I have been doing beautifully lately with my flying. I learned how to spiral all by myself, and several other tricks that are difficult to explain. I had just got to the stage where I was feeling most confident, and just the period where accidents are bound to occur, when I decided to call it all off, and now I'm as cautious as when I began. Every time I feel sure that I can do something hard, I stop and say to myself that I won't do it, and just go back to the beginning and take absolutely no chances.

They're still picking on me for instruction. I'm just scared to death that they'll make me stay around here and instruct when I've finished my training. It's a regular nightmare for me. But, then, I suppose I have to take my medicine like a man.

Gee! I surely get homesick around here. There are only five of us who don't live right near home. The other four are ensigns and get enough money to go to New York over the weekend, but I have to stick around here. Two weeks ago I was the only person on the place—even the mechanics left. I must close now and get some sleep. I'm first up in the morning. . . .

Huntington, 25 July 1917

Dearest Family,

We take the navy tests this week for our navy pilot's licenses. After that half of us will be sent broadcast over the country as instructors. . . . In two or three weeks I'll be either an instructor or sailing the briny deep. The choice of those who go and those who stay will be entirely on their respective merits. Some can naturally instruct, and others can't. I want to go where I'll be the most service. Here's hoping it's over there. I'll be an ensign in two weeks. I got paid also. Cheers!

Shortly after Kenneth wrote to his parents a near-disaster occurred at Huntington. On 28 July a committee of naval officers composed of Commander A. C. Read, Lieutenant Commander Earle F. Johnson (head of the aviation training section), and Lieutenant McDonnell assembled at the Yale Unit base to witness the qualifying tests. Trubee Davison made the first flight that morning, a flight that ended in a dramatic crash so forceful that his aircraft broke in half. The severely injured Davison was trapped in the wreckage of the slowly sinking airplane, and Lieutenant McDonnell, the first on the scene, immediately dived into the water to free the victim's legs. Jumping into a Marmon roadster, Lovett, Gates, and Ingalls then raced ahead to New York to locate a surgeon. Meanwhile, the stricken Davison was put aboard his father's yacht *Shuttle* and carried to New York were he entered St. Luke's Hospital. He had suffered a broken back. Though he later recovered, his long and painful recuperation prevented him from continuing his naval career. His family and friends were overjoyed that he was alive at all.

Despite Trubee Davison's tragic accident, the navy qualifying tests continued, and the remainder of the Yale crew were duly certified and commissioned. Shortly thereafter the group began to disperse, their apprenticeship ended. A few, like Bob Lovett and Di Gates, were dispatched overseas almost immediately. Others were transferred to the growing naval installations at Bay Shore, New York, or Hampton Roads, Virginia. Those who remained at Huntington for a few weeks witnessed Eddie McDonnell's mid-August attempt to launch a torpedo from an R-6 pontoon scout. The dummy weapon ricocheted up from the water and almost struck the surprised aviator. On another occasion Yale fliers Curt Read and Harry Davison in an R-6 scout armed with a Davis nonrecoil gun were ordered aloft to search for an enemy submarine spotted off the south shore of Long Island.

Kenneth MacLeish traveled first to temporary duty at New London, along with David Ingalls and William Rockefeller. There they participated in maneuvers designed to help submariners detect the presence of nearby aircraft. They also had the opportunity to experience at least one underwater ride.

Newport News, Virginia, was Kenneth's next stop. A group of Harvard fliers had been training at the old Curtiss school there since May under the command of Lieutenant Henry B. Cecil, and plans were under way to increase greatly the naval aviation effort on Chesapeake Bay. In time a half-dozen or more of the Yale men were directed down to the Virginia shore. After a short stay, however, MacLeish was granted leave. He quickly returned to New York and a reunion with Priscilla Murdock, and then headed westward to visit his family in Chicago, where he was forced to bed with a case of blood poisoning.

Chicago, 7 September 1917

Dearest [Priscilla Murdock],

Just a little note before I go to bed. They're sending me to bed early because I developed a case of blood poisoning in my foot on the way out. Budge, if you could have seen me on the platform in front of the train, and heard me, you would have been off me entirely. I was rather mad at missing my train, and I was awfully lonely and blue. I stood there waiting when all of a sudden a voice behind me said, "Is this the Philadelphia Express?" I said, "I don't know, Madam." "What, you don't know? Why the idea! How long have you worked here?" "I've never worked here." "Look here, are you trying to make fun of me, you, an employee? Do you know who I am?" I turned my back.

I no sooner had turned my back when I heard someone trip on the stairs. Down came bags and baggage on top of much fat man. When the dust cleared I was almost knocked unconscious by an attempt made by the same said mass of fat man to climb up me. "Is this the sleeper for Wohumbegunk?" or something equally foolish. Thank goodness you weren't there then. I said some very unkind things. I may have even hurt his feelings. I also said something to the Pennsylvania Railroad. In short, I was at the end of my rope and cussin' mad. And on the first day of my commission. . . .

I'll write you when I know more and feel better. Have you had any misgivings? I'm so worried. You don't seem to believe me wholeheartedly. I can only say again, I love you. . . .

While recuperating at home Kenneth could think of only two things, tracking down his orders and seeing Priscilla again. By now a second contingent of Yale men were on their way to Europe, and MacLeish longed to go with them. He dreaded being left behind in the greatest adventure of his life.

Chicago, 11 September 1917

Dearest,

What's the use? I ask you now, when a fellow has only a few days, why does he have to be in bed all the time? Can you beat it, Budge? I collected this case of blood poisoning on the way home and I've been in bed ever since. To add to my sorrows, my orders were to have been issued on September 7th, and they should have reached me in time to allow me to get to New York by the 11th. When no orders came today I was simply frantic. I just called Ken Smith up at Patchogue and discovered that only a few men had received their orders and that the rest were told to sit tight. That relieved me greatly, but now I have to go back to Newport News because my leave of absence expires on Friday. That may sound harsh, but on the contrary, it's perfectly wonderful to me. It will take four days from the time my orders come and I will be at Newport News when they come. Adding two and two, you and I get four days.

Recovered from his bout of blood poisoning, Kenneth returned to Virginia by way of New York, where he stopped for a short visit with Priscilla. Their friendship, much strengthened during the summer months together, seemed to deepen with each meeting. All too soon, however, it was time to report for duty again. Upon his return to Virginia in mid-September, MacLeish transferred from his former post at Newport News to the navy's newly commissioned (8 September 1917) air training station and patrol base at Hampton Roads.

Newport News, September 1917

My Wond'ful Sorrow,

The trip south was most eventful. And the events began to enact themselves when I left you. I hate to bore you with sentimental drool, but in order to make my story good, you must stand some. When we shook hands I read, or thought I read, something in your eyes that simply made me walk on air. I wandered aimlessly into the station and asked at the Pullman window for my RR ticket, and vice versa, being squelched at both places. Finally located the elusive papers, but found to my horror it was five minutes to nine. I rushed to the baggage room and no one waited on me, so I had to leave my good old trunk that I've lost sitting so long in the New York station. I guess that means weeks of deprivation again.

Then I was still so happy this morning that I walked out of the Pullman without that raincoat of mine. Curt [Read] took me in town then and I haven't done any harm, though my mind still wanders back to the Pennsy Station.[1] What shall I do? They say that absence makes the heart grow fonder, and Lord knows if I get any worse. . . .

This place isn't much now, but it will be splendid in the near future. The government bought the whole Jamestown Exposition grounds, five thousand acres or more.[2] They are erecting the largest and finest navy training center in the country. Aviation is only one camp, but it embraces a camp of two hundred students and nine large hangers. We now have four R-6s, four N-9s, and two F-Boats, with more promised. You see, originally this was a Curtiss school and there are only twenty students here now. Our work really starts when the class of 150 men comes down from the "Tech" [M.I.T.] ground school.[3]

I am very much pleased that I am starting with the school. It looks like a good chance for promotion if I can prove anything. I do so hope that I can make a success of this, but I still feel I would be able to do more in France.

Budge (how do you spell that?), these officers are human! Think of it. Admirals and all. They're slick. We asked them about our insignia and explained, and they said that we most certainly should wear our insignia. They not only said that, but wrote to the Bureau [of Navigation] and cussed 'em for delaying our commissions. I am therefore known here only as ensign. I won't get a leave for three months at least, probably not enough then to get to New York. I hope somebody moves Peacock Point down to the Chesapeake, or the best part of it, and moves it soon, or there will be one less navy aviator.

Well, I must close. Curt's tired and says I'm not safe when I'm alone, so I must go to bed. Write me, won't you?

1. *Curtis Seaman Read, another Yale Unit flier, also relocated to Hampton Roads.*

2. *The Jamestown Exposition grounds were the site of the great 1907 tercentennial celebration of the founding of the original Virginia colony.*

3. *The "Tech" men were recent graduates of the navy's ground school program conducted at M.I.T. in Cambridge, Massachusetts.*

The rapidly expanding naval aviation program at Hampton Roads brought together a diverse group of veterans and volunteers. William "Bull" Atwater of Silver Lake, New York, was one of the most interesting, having previously flown in Japan, China, the Philippines, and India. Following his stint in Virginia, he served at Moutchic in southern France and commanded the detachment of aviation cadets at Lake Bolsena in Italy. Many members of the Yale crowd were also gathered at Hampton Roads, as were several of the Harvard fliers trained at Newport News the previous summer. Of that group, MacLeish was closest to New Yorker Charles Fuller, who later served at the Royal Naval Air Service station at Dundee, Scotland, and U.S. Navy headquarters in London. But all that was far in the future. Instead, MacLeish, Atwater, Fuller, and others went about their duties and tried to figure out what it all meant.

Norfolk, 17 September 1917

Budgey Mine,

. . . I was walking into one of the hotels here when along came one of the other ensigns, a man named [William] Atwater, who used to do trick flying in Japan. I have always been convinced that his previous job was his best one. But nonetheless, he's a good old boy. He said he was on his way to steal a dog and wouldn't we help. He was so awfully funny about it that we finally agreed to go. We planned to keep the owner engaged in a vigorous bull fest while Atwater threw his coat on the pup, then faked illness and rushed out.

Atwater, with his usual farsightedness and determination to get the dog, had prepared for a large evening. He was equipped with a beautiful "bun" and a quart bottle of liquor, and a line that would make William J. Bryan and Billy Sunday stand in awe.[1]

Well, it turned out that we all had a few drinks, and especially Atwater. He took to entertaining like a duck to water. There wasn't a thing he didn't try, from a cakewalk to card tricks. And do you know that he persuaded the family to part with the dog and he didn't pay a cent for it. . . .

Well, to make a long story short, we left at about seven-thirty and came downtown for dinner—Curt, Charlie, and myself. Then began the most serious conversation I have ever taken part in. It began by Curt asking Charlie what his ideas on drinking were, this being the second time in his life that Curt had ever tasted it. Charlie stuck to the good old Harvard doctrine of gentlemanly drinking. That is, if you can't be a gentleman when you drink, don't drink; if you can, go for it. Then he asked me what mine was. I said that drinking and flying were utterly incompatible, and that an aviator was a fool to drink, but that I drank occasionally when I was tired or overtrained and that it had the same effect on me as a musical comedy. It was diverting and pleasing.

Then from the argument a discussion as to whether drinking did any real good and whether it did harm arose. Charlie said that he believed that stimulants often did good, as for instance a beautiful poem like "Kubla Khan," written by Coleridge under the influence of opium. He also cited the work of Bill Thaw the American aviator who was drunk all the time.[2] Then we drifted into a new line. Charlie claimed that his whole idea in life was to help others. He said that if one could aid the community by writing such a thing as "Kubla Khan," even at the destruction of his own manhood, he thought a man should do it. He said he didn't believe in God or anything else. He was the captain of his own soul. He said he didn't believe in anything but the aesthetically beautiful. Of course Curt and I jumped on him at once. Then he asked for our ideas. Curt didn't define his religion, or his conception of God. Then they asked me for mine. I couldn't do it very well, but I said that my religion was a personal religion, and my God a personal god. I have a conscience within me that says this is right and this is wrong. I can't account for that. I have a desire to do the right thing, which I can't account for. I have a feeling that there is an all-powerful influence in my life which I can rely on, can call upon in times of need. In short, whatever there is in me that is wonderful and awe-inspiring and beautiful, is my God. My religion has always been to copy, as well as I can, the perfect life of the most perfect human being.

I know enough about geology to know that the Lord didn't make the earth, and I know enough about organic evolution to feel reasonably certain that no one force ever created life. There is such a thing as natural law, of course, and there is a vast field which the human mind is explaining gradually, but of which there is still a tremendous amount of darkness we call nature. I also admit that there seems to be a divine influence governing all men, not just me personally, for instance, but I can't reconcile myself to a worldly God. I may in the future, but not now. In fact, my whole religion is in an embryonic state. I have lost my child religion, but haven't yet formulated the religion I shall have as a man.

Oliver James says that my orders ought to arrive sometime this week.[3] And if you can stand it, may I spend a few days with you? Don't worry about the wireless class as far as I'm concerned. I would wait years for one evening with you, and anyway, Trubee Davison lives next door, you know. . . .

1. *William Jennings Bryan, thrice-defeated candidate for president and recently resigned secretary of state, and "Billy" Sunday, former professional baseball player turned revivalist preacher, were well-known temperance advocates.*
2. *William G. Thaw (Yale '15) flew with the Lafayette Escadrille in France. Members of the escadrille were known for their antics and hard drinking. The group's two pet lions were named Whiskey and Soda.*
3. *Yale man Oliver James was assigned to naval headquarters in Washington, D.C.*

Norfolk, September 1917

Dearest Mother,

I'm sorry about not writing on Sunday, but I went over to Old Point Comfort and spent the weekend there.

I received a letter from Washington stating that my orders were all jazzed up, but that they should be here in five or six days from today, allowing for all delays in the mail.

I feel now quite compensated for being shoved down here. I told the lieutenant [Henry B. Cecil] that I didn't see how they chose the ones to go abroad and the ones to come here, and he told me Curt and I were sent here because we had the best records of all the enlisted men.

Is Jim still at Craigie Lea? If so, I want you to explain why I haven't written, but I've been flying six and seven hours a day and all of it those nerve-wracking instruction flights, and by night I'm so dead tired that it would be suicide to stay up and write letters. If she's not, please send me her address.

It's so great to feel that the chance of my lifetime is so near at hand. I shall take every precaution going over. That part worries me not one bit. I can swim. Lord help any sub I ever got aboard.

An undertaking as large as the mushrooming air station at Hampton Roads inevitably experienced its share of foul-ups and delays. Many of the Yale men took out their frustrations on Lieutenant Henry Cecil, who had been stationed in the area as officer in charge of training since early spring. In late September Lieutenant Commander Earle F. Johnson, then in charge of the navy's overall training effort, visited the Hampton Roads facility on an inspection tour. Apparently displeased with the pace of operations, Johnson reassigned Cecil shortly thereafter. Cecil went on to compile a fine record, however, serving as commanding officer at naval air stations at Pauillac and L'Aber Vrach, France. While at Hampton Roads Johnson also suffered a minor, but embarrassing, flight mishap.

Norfolk, 21 September 1917

Dearest,

. . . I'm afraid I may get into a bit of trouble around here, but I'm sure it will turn out all right because I know I'm in the right. Do you remember my telling you that Lieutenant [Commander Earle F.] Johnson came down to fly one of our machines, and fell? Well, they had an inquiry about it today to determine the cause. The fact is— Johnson, for some reason or other, didn't level off at all and plunged into the water. Do you know, out of twenty-eight witnesses, not one dared to stand up and say what the cause was? They were all afraid they would get in wrong. Somebody had to be the goat, so I assumed the laurels. I think Johnson is a broad-minded man, and even if our

Lieutenant Cecil did get up on his ear and ask who I was telling a man like Johnson how to fly, I think he'll accept my answer, because he certainly must agree with me himself.

I think this place will be greatly improved. They at last have some system, and the spirit is much better. A day or two ago twenty-two Tech men arrived, all flossed up in their leather belts and shoulder straps. Of course, some of our men got out the dice, and in a few hours' sport, the poor Tech boys were stripped of all their modern improvements. You never saw a "dicier" crowd in your life. They were all picked on, but they're coming through well and deserve lots of credit. . . .

I meant to tell you not to worry about wool. Any kind of sweater, even a lavender one, just so it's made by you, is all a man can ask. Well, dear, I think I'll close now. I do hope to see you before many more days. Give my best to Trubee and tell him the Read brothers and I are holding the fort for Huntington, and not smashing more than a machine a day.

While Kenneth labored at Hampton Roads, Priscilla Murdock continued her study of wireless telegraphy in pursuit of a commercial license. Her companions included Adele Brown, a special friend of Bob Lovett's, and Alice Davison, Trubee's sister who later married Di Gates. When not occupied with his duties, MacLeish thought up different ways to tell Priscilla how much he missed her.

Norfolk, 24 September 1917
UNITED STATES SIGNAL CORPS
WASHINGTON, D.C.

TO: YEOWOMAN PRISCILLA MURDOCK
FROM: COMMANDANT YEOWOMAN'S WIRELESS UNIT
SUBJECT: DESIGNATION AND DESTINATION

1. You are hereby detached from your present duties with your class at Hunter College, New York, and will proceed to the Naval Operating Base, Norfolk, Virginia, and report to the commander of the Aviation Detachment for such duty as he shall assign to you in accordance with your training and qualifications.

2. You have not finished your course as yet, but due to the great

demand for wireless operators this duty is required of you by the public interest.

3. Though your certificate is not due you yet, we will furnish you, by mail, with a tentative license which will answer the purpose.

4. Your salary will be four ($4) dollars a year, which will keep you amply supplied with toothpaste for the year.

5. Aside from your duties as wireless operator, you will also act as companion to Admiral K. MacLeish, who is cold and lonely, and has demanded your premature presence here.

Signed:
Commandant

Norfolk, September 1917

Dearest Mother, Father, and Jim,

Again I write from the hangars, and again I'm officer in charge, and again it's blowing cats and dogs.

I must tell you a peculiar thing about last Monday. After I finished my letter to you, I went up into the watch tower and turned the spotlight on the boats and machines. As I started to climb down the ladder, which comes up under the eaves of the roof and is hard to find, I slipped on the wet roof. When I came to I was lying in the mud, and it must have been fully an hour later.

The funny part about it was that I didn't hurt myself a bit and didn't feel any aftereffects whatsoever. I did have a bump on my head. I must have struck my head up on the roof and fallen perfectly limp. It was a very funny night.

Norfolk, September 1917

Dearest Mother, Father, and Ada,[1]

Well, so very much has happened that I don't know where to begin. In the first place, I haven't received my orders, and I have no idea when they will come. This much I feel sure of—they have been issued and have been in the mail since September 10th, though they may not have left Washington yet. They were made out as follows: "Proceed at once to the disbursing offices at the Fifth Naval District (New York) and get transportation on the first convenient ship. Report to the naval attaché in London and proceed under directions to the naval attaché in Paris, who will direct you to your destination." That means that I won't travel on a government transport, but in style on a passenger boat.

Now for the real dope: Our lieutenant [Cecil] has run this station so miserably that he missed a court-martial by the skin of his teeth. Who do you suppose is relieving him? Our wonderful Lieutenant Eddie McDonnell! The finest man in the navy. He is to be here a month and then goes to France. In the meantime the whole system has been changed, but the only change that would interest you is this: six of us—the two Read brothers (Huntington) and the three officers previously here, and myself—take turns as commanders of the station and first aides to the lieutenant. I've had charge all day, and as luck would have it, a howling northeaster started which will blow all the hangars and machines away if it gets any worse. I have decided to sleep down here at the office, so that if anything happens, no one can say that I wasn't on the job. It's very lonely and frightfully cold down here; besides, the rain just drives right through the walls. I am going to have the guards wake me when they take their posts, and make a tour of inspection with them all through the night to do all I can to keep the machines. I'm responsible for two patrol boats. One of them is knocked all full of holes and about to sink. I'm also having a man sleep next to the telephone at the barracks to make sure that all calls are answered, and I've even gone so far as to get a telephone man down here at this time of night to make sure that the telephone works! If anything happens, I won't be to blame. . . .

1. *Ada Hitchcock MacLeish, Archie's wife.*

Like most of the Yale men stationed in Virginia, MacLeish was cheered by the arrival of Lieutenant Eddie McDonnell, their dynamic instructor at Palm Beach and Huntington. After a successful two-month stint as officer in charge of the Naval Aviation Detachment at Hampton Roads, McDonnell transferred to Washington in November, succeeded by Lieutenant Commander Patrick Bellinger. The feisty lieutenant was credited by more than one observer with getting the somewhat disorganized aviation program there up and flying.

Norfolk, 30 September 1917

Dearest,

. . . What made you think I was supposed to sail last Sunday? If you have any dope on my orders please give it to me at once. I have wired for a duplicate set of orders, but have not heard from my wire. . . . This delay has been deadly. I realize what a perfect nut I've been and how many chances I've missed to make something of myself. You'll never know how terribly disappointed I was in not making a Senior society.[1] I know why I didn't and it almost kills me. I want to get to France and forget the whole thing and start over again. . . .

We were recently graced with the arrival of good old Eddie McDonnell. The former lieutenant, Cecil by name, missed a court-martial by the skin of his teeth for the way he ran this place. The station is brand new now, the men are getting all kinds of flying, and are nearly contented. Also, twenty-two Tech men are amongst those present. They are the saddest bunch I've ever seen. All from South Boston, if that means anything to you. It does to all Harvard men. One of them is a reporter for the Boston *Transcript.* I took him up for his first ride and you can follow the above paper if you want a flowing account of a joyride. I tried to scare him and I feel somehow I succeeded wondrous well.

Harry Davison is down here, came last night, but I haven't seen him yet as I've been on duty out here at the base all day.[2] Curt, Bart [Read], and I are living in Norfolk at the Southland Hotel now. I lost two pairs of shoes in two nights. Guess how? The rats ate the tongues and most of the uppers. Can you begin to approach that? I'd rather lose my shoes than be eaten myself, and the rats out here at the base were getting too familiar when I left.

As you can see, I'm in a perfectly delightful humor tonight. I don't know what the matter is, unless it's that I've been officer in charge all day and have been on duty while Curt and Bart and everyone else were riding around at leisure. . . .

1. *MacLeish had been denied admission into one of Yale's secret societies, of which Skull and Bones was the most prestigious.*
2. *Davison had been stationed at Newport News as officer in charge of enlistments in September. In October he transferred to the facility at Hampton Roads as a flight commander, experimenting with various radio devices, machine guns, and bombing apparatus.*

Ensign MacLeish soon experienced the greatest thrill of his short military career when he went aloft with aviation pioneer Eddie Stinson. MacLeish also found time to visit the army's neighboring Langley flying field. On display were a number of aircraft shipped over from Italy, including a giant Caproni bomber and several smaller scouts and seaplanes. Among the celebrities gathered there was Lawrence Sperry, who was working diligently with the navy to develop a remotely controlled flying bomb.

Norfolk, 1 October 1917

Dearest,

I'm so thrilled I can't speak, so I'll write you a line or two. One of my ambitions has been fulfilled. I went up with Eddie Stinson this afternoon, the greatest American flier. I looped all by myself. I got out of a mean right- and left-hand tailspin alone. I did vertical banks galore (until I thought I would get seasick, in fact). And I ended up by coming down in stalls. Talk about a circus. When Stinson came down everybody clapped, so you can just picture the ride I had. I was so mussed up inside that I honestly was in doubt whether my wonderful luncheon would do me any good. Oh, Budge, am I happy! At least I've had my hands on a machine that will do tricks and not be suicidal doing them.

The worst sensation of them all, however, was the tailspin, because you never know whether you will come out of them or not. Even Stinson didn't want to put me into them, but I was set on it and so he did. He says they're dangerous, and when he says a thing is dangerous, I am inclined to believe him, because he hasn't the faintest idea what fear is.

. . . And on top of all this, we went to Langley Field this morning and saw the Caproni that carries twelve people fly, also the Macchi boat (115 mph), also a 280-hp Pomelio that flies 120 mph, and an SIA which climbed out of sight in five minutes. Aside from that the day was dull. Next Sunday, if I'm still here, I may get a chance to fly in that Pomelio, and if I do, the Italian pilot said he would put me through a barrel roll and fly upside down, the only things that an aviator can do that I haven't already done. Also, a flock of us may get a chance to ride in the Caproni, if Lawrence Sperry sticks around for a while. . . .

Lover, you and I have got to see each other soon and straighten this out. The stories which you choose to call "awfully funny" about me are, no doubt, absolutely true. I give you my word, that day has been, and always will be a perfect nightmare to me. Can't you see me, a measly ensign, holding a commander's wife, and a 250-pound one at that, on my lap with her husband sitting next to me, with his daughter on his lap. Picture me if you can, and then add that she will never see fifty again, and took great delight in holding my hand and then screaming with laughter at my livid countenance. Pardon me, but My Gawd! It was fierce! If all navy ladies were as flirtatious as Mrs. Methuselah and as heavy, may the good Lord spare me from such. She really weighed 150 pounds, because I weighed her on the scales. She thought I was kidding, but I wanted to see what paralyzed my legs.

The men of the Yale Unit were among the first qualified naval aviators (Di Gates was #65, Bob Lovett was #66, and Kenneth MacLeish was #74). They were quickly parceled out to the various flight schools then being organized. Inexperienced pilots themselves, they were pressed into emergency duty as instructors and played an important role in training the next generation of military fliers. Despite Kenneth's complaints about his trainees, fellow officers were impressed with the record he compiled. Bart Read later recalled that MacLeish easily "won the respect and friendship of the students and worked with them exceedingly well."

Norfolk, 4[?] October 1917

Dearest,

. . . The sweater came today and it's beyond words. It's exactly what I wanted and it's knitted perfectly wonderfully. I'm so much in your debt now that a few words of thanks would only be the same old stuff, but I shall treasure the sweater as something you made, and you will never know what that means to me.

Talk about flying, I'm getting sick of it. I put in almost six hours yesterday, and only a bit less today. I just stepped to the window to see the fire next door. Lots of noise, but nobody hurt, not much fun.

I have the funniest class to instruct you ever saw. They're all from South Boston. Where they got a college education or its equivalent I dare not guess from fear of displaying my ignorance. They can't even speak the old mother tongue. One of my men is pretty good, but the other five are hopeless. I honestly believe I could take them up and fly upside down and they wouldn't know the difference. They have no sense of lateral balance and I've been forced to hit two of them already to make them let the controls go.

So, Trubee wants to know whether those tricks were in land machines? You tell him that my ride with Stinson was in a Curtiss JN-4, but that two days later Mr. Atwater, a man who was in my class when I first came down here, and I climbed to 10,000 feet in an R-6. On the way down we looped three times, got into a right-hand tailspin, and came the rest of the way in a vertical spin. Tell him also to keep this under his hat, as the lieutenant gave us orders NOT to loop, and I have everybody but Harry [Davison] thinking we didn't. You see, we were above heavy clouds, but somebody saw us upside down through a hole in them, and the people at Newport News saw us get into a tailspin. You may also tell Trubee that I'd rather die than loop that hotel again. I thought the thing would stay upside down forever. The gas ran out of the tank and made me sick to my stomach.

Two days ago one of my noble class got into a tailspin in an N-9 climbing on a left-hand turn, just exactly what happened to Harry.[1] I was about 1,500 feet up and got out all right. Well, I must close. Oliver [James] wired that my orders would be here in six days. Shall I believe him? Also, German submarines are expected in U.S. waters in ten days; confidential! . . .

1. *Davison had experienced a "spectacular crash" at Huntington the previous July while flying an N-9, but escaped with only cuts and bruises.*

By mid-October Kenneth was ready to move and impatiently awaited orders from Washington. Several Yale colleagues had already been dispatched overseas, including Lovett and Gates, who departed in mid-August, and John Vorys and Al Sturtevant, who sailed a month later. MacLeish's most reliable source of information was Yale classmate Oliver James, serving in Washington as an aide to Lieutenant Commander Earle Johnson. This was the very same Johnson whose flying MacLeish had roundly criticized just a few weeks earlier.

Norfolk, October 1917

Dearest Aunt Mary,[1]

My orders are scheduled to arrive in six or seven days from now. I shall probably sail from New York and will be given five days before sailing. I intend to pay Ishbel a visit at Vassar and you one at Westover. If I don't have any time I will wire you. At present there are not enough instructors here and I have been putting in six or seven hours a day in the air, which is twice too much. I am getting tired of water machines and long for the time I shall be flying fast scout machines. I had a glorious ride with Stinson, the great American flyer, a week ago. I told him I had never been in a land machine and that I wanted to loop, tailspin, stall, do flipper turns, and fly upside down. He balked a little about the tailspin, because he said they are dangerous, but I insisted and we started. He was bent on making me sorry for it, too. He showed me how to loop, and I did it four times; then he showed me tailspins, and I did three more which nearly set him crazy, after which I don't know what happened. He did every crazy wild trick known to man, and when I came down I felt as though I had been turned inside out and back again about five times. . . .

1. Mary Hillard, Kenneth's aunt, then headmistress of Westover School in Middlebury, Connecticut.

Finally the long-awaited orders arrived. Directed to proceed to New York, and thence to London and Paris by the first available liner, MacLeish headed northward in late October. Both his mother and sister came to visit in Manhattan before he sailed. Kenneth also reserved a few days for Priscilla Murdock, and while visiting at Peacock Point he proposed. Priscilla accepted. Two days later he departed for Europe.

Transatlantic crossings were always an adventure, and never more so than during World War One. The discomfort caused by bad weather paled before the risk of submarine attack. German U-boat assaults had drawn America into the war, and the threat they posed was very real indeed, accounting for 300,000 to 550,000 tons of Allied shipping each month in the second half of 1917. Evelyn Preston, a close friend of Adele Brown and Priscilla Murdock, crossed over to Europe in September aboard the liner *Rochambeau,* reporting that everyone on board seemed to be on a mission, but as they neared the danger zone she quickly lost her "habitual calm." Passengers engaged in frequent lifeboat drills, hoping they would never put their newfound knowledge to the test.

Kenneth MacLeish and his companions traveled aboard the SS *New York,* the same liner that had carried Admiral Sims to England earlier that year. The week-long crossing was enlivened by a continuous round of dinners, entertainment, and gambling. MacLeish's shipboard acquaintances were a varied lot, but united by their participation in the war effort. Among the notables was Sir William Wiseman (1885–1962), victim of an early gas attack, who was then serving as chief of the intelligence service attached to the British embassy in Washington, D.C. A confidant of President Woodrow Wilson's intimate adviser, Colonel

Edward House, Wiseman frequently carried sensitive messages between Washington and London. Also present on board the *New York* was Conigsby Dawson (1883–1959), an English author who had moved to the United States in 1905 and later served with the Canadian army in 1916–18. At least two Yale men accompanied MacLeish to Europe, George Catlin ('01), assigned by the navy to study the construction and use of paravanes, and John Farrar ('18), a lieutenant in the air service beginning an inspection tour of aviation camps in England and France.

SS New York, *Sunday, 28? October 1917*

My Beloved,

I have developed a most remarkable plan. I shall try to write you a page every day out, and I wish you would keep this letter until I return, because I foolishly packed my diary in my trunk, and if you can stand it, my letter to you will serve as my diary until the latter shows up.

The trip has been uneventful so far. Tonight there is a brilliant full moon and the air is crisp. As I walked the deck in the moonlight, I recalled every moment of the walk to Davison's my last night, and it seemed to me those last few hours were the most beautiful in my life. We will be happy, won't we.

There are several people of interest on the boat. My first acquaintance was a little Scotsman whose accent was suspiciously broad, and when he gets excited his intonations verge towards the gutteral, and he apologizes for his pronunciation, saying that he has been in Mexico for fifteen years and speaks Spanish as well as he does English. He is very curious and inquisitive, and when I told him I didn't know where I was going he said, "Oh, in other words, you won't tell me." I'm not crazy about him and he is being watched closely.

There are numerous and sundry army officers, mostly majors in the Engineering Corps, and several lieutenants in the Sanitary Department. My special friends are Johnny Farrar and Bill Kimble [an interpreter], who teaches John and me French.

We have a very cheerful doctor at our table. He belongs to the ship, but you might think things were the other way round to hear him talk. I think he has melancholia, or else the worst grouch I ever saw. He keeps telling John about how they were torpedoed, or struck a mine, and sat in open boats in a snowstorm. He told us that a hole was torn right under his chair, and that John's chair was thrown up through the skylight. He keeps telling us what a common thing it is to see a U-boat, and that he doesn't see how the ship has made so many safe trips, and that this one is surely the last. All of which is getting under our skin.

Conigsby Dawson, the English writer, is on board, much in uniform, and sharing ownership of this tub with Doc. We're not very good friends. He said to me the other day, "I say, what rank are you, anyway?" I told him and asked "And what are you?" He gave me one look that I wouldn't trade for another in the world. I don't like him anyway. He's in the war merely for the experience of it. With him, everything is self, all his stories explain how HE felt under certain circumstances; not once does he forget himself and serve the cause.

This must suffice for the day. You see, we darken ship and can't open portholes at night, and the air is so stuffy I can't breathe. Good night, my beloved. Pray that God gives me the chance and the strength when it comes.

Monday

Monday, but not nearly so wonderful. It's much too rough. Poor John is on his last legs after a game night, and either I ate too much fruit or else the tide is turning on me also. I'm not sick yet, but I refuse to boast.

Today we had a boat drill, fire drill, and finally gun drill. Of the latter I can say very little except I'm pleased and full of hope. I met a lieutenant commander [Rollie Riggs] who is going to Rome as a naval attaché.[1] He says the war will be over surely by the fall of 1918 or the spring of 1919, and possibly before unless we develop a defense against submarines. The big drive this spring may end it, but if it doesn't there is absolutely no hope of starving the Huns, and they are sinking ships three times as fast as they can be built. He gave me a thrill when he said the war might be won in the air. Once the Huns lose that supremacy, they'll tumble. Unless we can curb the subs or gain complete supremacy in the air, the war will be over and the race will be in Germany's favor. Why doesn't America wake up?

I folded you in my arms and kissed you just now. Did you know it, lover? Good night, dearest.

Tuesday

We passed this day without drills. The weather is still perfect, but it's blowing up a bit tonight. I met a young Englishman who lost sight in one eye and has been unable to enlist, so he has traveled all over the world. He is very interesting. He says that New York today is like London three years ago. That is hopeful, because it's the first sign of awakening. We have four more days before we sight land, and probably three more before we pick up our convoy. The largest school of porpoises I ever saw passed us today. They jumped clear out of the water, unlike any I ever saw before. It was a beautiful sight.

Wednesday

Say, listen, a joke is a joke, but this is going too far. I'd rather enjoy playing this rolling game if I could stop when I wanted, but this boat has the habit. Yesterday John was afraid he would die; today he's afraid he won't. Both the upper and lower decks are awash, so there isn't any exercise to be had. I heard a good story on our friend Josephus Daniels.[2] He was raised out in the middle of the country, and probably knows how to raise corn. When he first went aboard a battleship he astonished everybody by bending over a hold and looking down. He turned with wide eyes, saying, "My God, it's hollow!"

I don't know whether I like Conigsby Dawson any better or not. And you tell Mrs. Runyan that her friend [George Catlin] is a fine boy, but an awful poker shark. You see Dawson and Catlin cleaned Lieutenant Hull[3] and myself out of about $50. We won first at Klondike, but when we changed to Jackpot we weren't so well off. Dawson is the funniest man alive. I guess I do like him, and his looks are very sentimental because he doesn't expect to live long.

We reach the danger zone day after tomorrow, and even if we have to take to the lifeboats, I'm going to keep this letter. I'm coming to believe that we haven't a chance to get away with it, but, as I said, I'm an absolute fatalist in a case like this. In an airplane I have lots of faith, and I'm not worried in the least.

Thursday

It's November first to everyone in the good old United States, but just plain Thursday to me. Oh, I am homesick and I do miss you. But what's the use of crying now? The milk's all over the floor and I have myself to thank for it. Our love has made such a difference to me, and in such a short time.

Lieutenant Commander Riggs tells me that my best bet is to try to

get down to Venice to the naval school there for my advanced training.[4] He's a wonder and he says he'll do all he can to try and help me,
but I think I'd be of more service in northern France, and I'd just as
soon fly in the cold if it will do anybody any good.

We may pick up our convoy tomorrow, and we may not pick it up
until Sunday. We should dock about Monday, I think. The water is
much smoother now and we're making better time. It was sure rough
for a couple of days. I got drenched yesterday. No one ventured on
deck except little Willie (Kenneth MacLeish], and I hadn't been there
more than five minutes before I discovered why. The reason was
about a shipload of green water that washed over the whole ship. I
hung onto the rail and got drowned, but that's better than feeding the
sharks. What's more, I haven't missed a meal yet. Hear me cheer!

I had some money changed today and got $200 worth of the
darndest-looking tissue paper you ever saw. I miss you, my beloved,
oh so much. Good night.

Friday

That man Dawson keeps winning from me, but the more he wins
the better I like him, all of which proves my contention that the mind
works backwards. Mr. Sisson, the editor of "Cosmopolitan" fame,
was my companion in goatdom tonight.[5]

All the army men and the fifteen Boston Tech balloonatics[6] have to
stand watch and I don't. I'm in the navy, haw, haw. Really, there are
some characters on this boat. Three old majors who fought in the
Spanish-American War. You realize at once that they aren't men who
came over for the experience. They're too old for that, they just came
through sheer sense of duty. If you haven't done so already, you
should read Conigsby Dawson's *Carry On*. There are parts that I fear
may draw tears to your eyes, but it gives a most vivid picture of what I
shall have to contend with, and the courageous spirit with which men
do carry on.

Tomorrow we pick up our convoy, or perhaps tonight. Thank the
Lord, it's an American convoy, which means that we will be on time.
Nothing would please me more than to wake up in the morning to the
sight of a destroyer.

I've been wondering how I'll feel when I get near my first Boche.
There's a spirit over there that I'm sure I must catch. It's easy enough
to take a big chance when all your pals are doing the same thing, still, I

anxiously await my first experience. I'd feel much better if I could dig up some animosity towards the Huns, or better yet, develop a firm resolution to win. The latter, at least, I'm sure of developing, perhaps both, who knows.

Saturday

Our convoy finally reached us. It came sneaking along this after-noon. It was greeted with many a sigh of relief, too, I can assure you. All day long men and women paced the deck with anxious eyes continually searching until it became a physical effort to look any-more. Our first sight was head on and the narrow beam of the de-stroyer gave it the most striking similarity to a submarine at close range. We couldn't make out what it was until it was alongside because its camouflage was so effective. A second destroyer appeared shortly after from the same quarter.

Sir William Wiseman is on board, and seems very nice except he simply cannot unbend. He finally sat down and had a chat with us. There are about a dozen secret service men on board. No one explains their presence, but no one tries. We are overladen and our draft is six feet more than normal, which keeps our imagination quite active.

That boy Catlin is a prince. He's loads of fun. There is also a Scotsman named Cook who has been in Mexico for some time. He has a dry humor. He couldn't see that camouflage was effective because one could see the destroyers when they first came over the horizon. Catlin explained that the idea was not to hide them but to make them look like something else. Cook then said, "Why don't they cam-ouflage the coal so you can't see the smoke?" Then he turned to us, and pointing at the destroyer said, "It's a four of spades, you're deceived." Catlin kidded him along. He kids the life out of Dawson and Dawson doesn't quite know what he's being kidded about.

Sunday

Well, we dock tomorrow if all goes well. But an awful lot can happen before tomorrow, even though it's five A.M. now. I guess I won't linger in that vein, however. I cleaned up on the whole gang for once, and now Dawson has to take us to dinner in London, and that crazy Scot has sworn to take me riding. I told him it would be funny, so now he insists.

I certainly am the goat. A young fellow has been posing to me as an

English naval officer in plainclothes. I fell for it until today, when the Scotsman asked me what I was trying to do chatting with Sir William Wiseman's valet. Can you beat that? All the Americans gave me the blot, but Dawson and the Scot got real mad when I remarked that he looked like one anyway. We have a circus together. Dawson, Cook, Catlin, and a senior lieutenant in aviation from Pensacola named Hull, great-grandson of Isaac. No one else on the boat is even interesting except Lieutenant Commander Riggs and friend John. I admit that I am just a little bit shy about bed tonight. We're in the Irish Sea, the scene of many mishaps. It's a nice, clear night with calm water. What more could a sub want. We rigged out minesweepers today. Catlin is over here to study them. They're ALMOST 100% effective.

Good night and goodbye, my own.

1. *Lieutenant Commander Roland R. Riggs (1884–1970) was a Naval Academy graduate, class of '04.*

2. *North Carolina's Josephus Daniels (1862–1948) was a well-known newspaper editor and Democratic politician who served as secretary of the navy during World War One.*

3. *Lieutenant Carl T. Hull, naval aviator #46, graduated from Annapolis in 1913 and later received flight instruction at Pensacola.*

4. *Plans were being developed to have American aviators train with Italian forces. Some aviators were already under way to the Italian naval aviation school at Lake Bolsena, northwest of Rome.*

5. *In a remarkably varied career, Francis Sisson (1871–1933) served as a newspaper reporter, magazine editor, advertising executive, and bank director. During the war he was actively involved in railroad finance and regulation.*

6. *The "Boston Tech balloonatics" were either air service balloon companies who received preliminary training at M.I.T., or a group of naval balloon men on their way to European schools.*

After landing at Liverpool, MacLeish journeyed overland to Manchester and then down to London to report to naval headquarters. He had not visited the British capital in many years and was amused, puzzled, and intrigued by all that went on around him. In his naiveté he hoped to witness an air raid to see what all the fuss was about.

London, 7 November 1917

My Beloved,

Here we are, so far. Three of us seeing London together: Lieutenant Commander Riggs, who is bound for Rome, a lieutenant who is to be military attaché at Stockholm, and my little self. We saw almost all of

London last night that we could see, but we are going to stay here until Friday.

The embassy[1] treats us royally wherever we go, and for once I'm riding the gravy train. We went to a show at the Gaiety [Theatre] last night, and I thought it was a dress rehearsal for a Keystone Komedy. It turned out to be English humor, but it really was pathetic. It would be raided in New York.

We are hoping that they give us an air raid tonight before we go, but they say they only have them when there is a full moon. A bomb dropped in Picadilly Circus, and I never knew there was so much glass. I thought the air raids weren't very dangerous, but they seem to be demoralizing here.

Whoever told me that you couldn't get a thing over here was a lowlife. I haven't found anything yet that wasn't better than all American stuff, and 20 percent cheaper. I have half a mind to sell my outfit and get a good one for less money.

There isn't another thing to write about, except that London is gayer than ever, and very dark at night. I ran into a "jazz band" chorus. Talk about an evening. They won't let us dance, and they won't serve us drinks, but we're having a circus in spite of that. . . .

1. *The U.S. embassy also served as naval headquarters.*

London, 8 November 1917

Old Pal,

Just this late line to show you that we have arrived over here. I've just been to the embassy to see about orders and transportation, and can get positively no information about my destination and, what is more, I couldn't impart the same if I knew it.

It may interest you to know that we have some real men in the embassy, especially the navy. Admiral Sims is beyond compare, and the pay inspector is a corker. Commander McBride is the finest officer in the navy, so you see we're well represented.[1] The [American Officers'] Club is an enormous mansion, the city house of a wealthy English nobleman, and it's too beautiful for words. It's absolutely ideal.

I have talked a great deal with men who know, and I've become very pessimistic about the war. . . . I'm not any too pleased with my prospects. If any aviator makes more than thirty flights without being hurt, he apologizes for being alive. My case is different, and I'm willing anyway, but it's not cheerful. . . .

1. *Admiral William S. Sims (1858–1936) commanded American Naval Forces in Foreign Waters. Captain Lewis B. McBride (1880–1940), naval constructor, headed the Repair Section at London headquarters. The reference to "pay inspector" may be to paymaster Captain Eugene Tobey.*

After a week in London Kenneth crossed the Channel to France and proceeded to Paris to receive further orders. The young ensign quickly discovered that travel in wartime Europe was no luxury excursion. A lack of fluency in French further complicated MacLeish's journey.

Paris, 10 November 1917

My Beloved,

This stage of the trip was the worst. Crossing the Channel is never delightful, but in a crowded packet boat where one has to stand all the way and where everyone else is sick it is FAR from pleasant. We landed late in the evening and took a night train to Paris. There were no first-class compartments left and we had to travel second class. There was a man in the compartment who was joined later by his wife, and when we were nicely settled in—lying full-length on the seats—we were forced to move by the arrival of two corpulent peasant women who talked all night and annoyed us by eating raw onions and drinking too much wine. After a frightful night we came here [Hôtel Eduoard VII] and went to bed, and we've just gotten up. I haven't reported to the attaché yet, and I haven't gone over to CPS & Co.[1] I wonder if I will find a letter from you there. I hope for your sake that you haven't missed me as much as I've missed you.

If it weren't for Rollie Riggs, the Lieutenant Commander, I very much fear that I should still be at the dock trying to make them understand that I wanted to go to Paris. You know, I nearly laughed myself sick. I was struggling along with a porter, trying my level best to explain why my baggage should be sent through customs, when I heard a little kid jabbering French. I audibly remarked, "My Lord, even the little kids can speak French!" much to Rollie Riggs's amusement.

The French people are simply superb. I have never in my life met anyone who is anti-French, whether or not they are violently pro-German, and I have only been able to understand that since I've been here. They are the most polite people in the world, they are clever and systematic, and they are extremely resourceful. I think that my devotion to the French people and their cause will develop a heartfelt animosity for the Huns. I have traced John [Vorys] and Al [Sturtevant] so far, but I think I've slipped it over on them several times, finding clubs, etc., that they didn't. . . .[2]

1. *Carson, Pirie, Scott and Co., the Chicago department store, whose office in Paris served as Kenneth's home away from home.*
2. *Vorys and Sturtevant, fellow members of the Yale Unit, sailed for Europe a few weeks ahead of MacLeish. In November 1917 they were at Hourtin, near Bordeaux, and then St.-Raphaël on the French Riviera.*

Ensign MacLeish reached Paris in early November 1917 and reported to naval headquarters to receive further instructions. There he met Commander Kenneth Whiting, the daredevil aviation pioneer who led the navy's First Aeronautical Detachment to France in June 1917. Among his many exploits, Whiting had once been shot from the torpedo tube of a submerged submarine. While visiting the American embassy MacLeish also encountered some survivors of the *Alcedo,* a converted yacht pressed into antisubmarine duty on the Bay of Biscay, and later sunk by a U-boat. When not on official business, he toured the sights of Paris, visited the opera, and tried to catch up on the activities and whereabouts of his Yale Unit colleagues. He missed a rendezvous with Di Gates by a day or two.

Paris, 10 November 1917

My Dearest Ones,

I fooled the USNRFC [United States Navy Reserve Flying Corps] as you see. They used to translate it as "Us Sailors Never Reach France Cause!" But here I am, and my little bells are tinkling. And Paris! Oh, it's far better than even the wildest tales picture it. It's as much as your life is worth to go out to dinner here. There are literally thousands of girls who say they will show you around Paris, and it's a two-fisted fight to shake them off! Rollie Riggs and I are together, and I never laughed so hard in my life. I can't speak a word of French, and Rollie gets jazzed up once in a while himself. We finally got out on the street, where one enjoys comparative safety. . . .

I saw Commander Whiting, to whom I am to report, and he said that I would be sent down to join the Huntington crowd [at Moutchic-

Lacanau]. That is west of where Archie [MacLeish] is, but I shall get in touch with him at once. I wonder if I'll find mail. I rather hope I shall; that is—well, if I don't I'll be mighty sad. It's a long, long time since I've heard from home.

We are going to see *Manon* this evening and *Madame Butterfly* tomorrow, if I'm here. I have no idea when I'm leaving, and I think I will go to Moutchic, down near Spain—of that I'm not sure.

I met a couple of naval officers at the embassy who were on the *Alcide* [*Alcedo*] when she was torpedoed. One was asleep on his bunk, and knew nothing until he woke up on a raft—alone and badly hurt. The submarine came alongside and asked him what boat was sunk— he didn't even know his ship had been torpedoed.

I must close now and get ready for dinner. I'm happier than I've ever been, and prospects are bright for the next month or two, at any rate.

Paris, 13 November, 1917

Beloved,

I've seen about enough of Paris, and I move on tonight to join the gang. The trick men are at Moutchic-Lacanau down near Spain, and the steady men are at Le Croisic. John and Al are at St.-Raphaël near Italy. Some of the men are to be sent up to Dunkirk where they will actually get busy. They, at least, will be busy dodging bombs, because the place gets bombed every few days. By the way, I go to Moutchic.

The English Tommies are the greatest lot you ever saw in your life. They're such a stolid bunch, nothing ever worries them. They can't speak a word of French yet they get along beautifully. An English officer told me a queer story. He sent his batman, a man who couldn't speak a word of French, back to a farmhouse to find out about getting a bath. The Tommy came back with a long story about how the woman of the house was washing clothes today, and would be ironing the next, but that if the officer went over Sunday, he could have hot water. How under the sun do you suppose he did it?

All the officers say the Scotchmen are the real fighters. They say they don't turn a hair when a shell hits them. All Tommies are alike. They do exactly as they're told to do, no matter whether they see any reason or not. This little story is typical of them. An officer saw a Tommy beating the life out of a horse. He yelled, "Don't beat it, talk to it, talk to it." The Tommy, seeing no sense to the order, but realizing that orders were orders, addressed the horse as follows, "Hello, I coom from Manchester." You have to be in the right atmosphere to appreciate the story, or it isn't funny otherwise.

The Hindus are a funny lot too. They can't use them in raids or surprise attacks because they behave just like little children. When they go out in the dark, and if they happen to get separated, one will cough or make noise, just to see if his friends are near him. This infantry captain had a bunch of Canadians with him on a raid, and he said that a Boche patrol passed within ten yards of his men and never saw or heard them. The Indians would have jazzed the party for sure if they'd been there.

You never hear an officer brag about what he has done. They don't make any bones about saying they were scared either. It's the men who have never been in trouble who talk as though they were never scared. It takes a brave man to "carry on" when he's so scared he can't see straight.

The boys at Moutchic are flying FBAs, the same kind of machine as Caleb Bragg's, that one we saw Caley and Bill Thompson in.[1] They are being trained in bombing at present, which sort of hints at the kind of flying they will be engaged in. I doubt very much if any of us will be sent back to the United States as instructors because they say that once a man gets over here, he hasn't a prayer of getting back again.

I heard a wild rumor that Hobey Baker had been killed practicing, but it was denied at headquarters.[2] There are more Americans in Paris than in all England.

I have to sit up all night tonight on the train, so I guess I'll try to get some sleep now. The train service all over is a mess. There are practically no sleeping cars. The only ones there are are used by officers on the main lines. The number of trains a day is cut down to two, for instance, between Paris and Bordeaux. There is no such thing as a dining car.

I heard unofficially that 180,000 Italians were captured, either deliberately walked over to the Germans or were ordered by their officers to retreat, and that all communications had been cut.[3] I can scarcely believe that, can you?

There was no mail for me at CPS & Co. It is too early for mail, I guess. I think you had better send my mail directly to CPS & Co. at 42 Faubourg Poissonière, Paris. Miss [Emma] Guthrie says I will get it much quicker that way. They are well known here and their mail gets immediate attention. . . .

    1. William P. Thompson (Yale '18) served at the navy's M.I.T. ground school and at Hampton Roads. The obsolescent FBA, or Franco-British Aviation reconnaissance plane, carried a crew of two, and cruised at 68 mph, with a range of approximately 185 miles.
    2. The rumor was untrue. A renowned athlete at Princeton, Baker fought with the Lafayette Flying Corps, transferred to the U.S. Army's 103d Aerosquadron, and eventually commanded the 141st Aerosquadron in the waning weeks of the war.
    3. In October and November 1917 the Italian army was routed at Caporetto on the Austrian front, losing nearly three hundred thousand prisoners before reestablishing its lines behind the Piave River.

The navy's training base at Moutchic–Lacanau, situated on a small inland lake near Bordeaux on the Bay of Biscay, had been selected by Lieutenant Kenneth Whiting during his June tour of French aviation facilities. The first American pilots under Lieutenant John L. Callan, a member of the navy's First Aviation Detachment, reached the site in early July and a few flights were undertaken. NAS Moutchic was established 31 August 1917 as a flight and ground training station. Enlisted man Irving Sheely from Albany, New York, who later became Kenneth MacLeish's observer, arrived at Moutchic in late August and found a facility just beginning to take shape. He immediately went to work placing flooring in tents, digging a well, and erecting hangars. The first two were up by late September. Yale Unit veteran Robert Lovett, recently arrived from flight training at Tours, oversaw the fabrication of two FBA flying boats, the first of which he piloted on 27 September. By early October five planes were operable and more hangars were going up, as were accommodations for the men, including a YMCA building and mess hall. Sheely noted, however, that life at Moutchic resembled camping in the north woods—sleeping in tents, cooking food over a fire on the ground, bathing and washing clothes in the lake. Nonetheless, the station was ready to begin regular instruction of both pilots and enlisted men in ground and flight courses. Several members of the Yale Unit passed through the school. Kenneth MacLeish reached Moutchic in mid-November, just missing Lovett, Di Gates, Henry Landon, Samuel Walker, Ken Smith, Dave Ingalls, and Reginald "Poosh" Coombe, who had recently departed for other duties.

My Beloved (I censor myself! Haw haw, I'm an ossifer),

I didn't neglect writing you this past week, in fact I felt quite ashamed, but really, I was so blue and lonely that I thought no letter was better than a blue one. You see, my worst fears are realized. When I got here the crowd [the Yale Unit] had finished and gone, and now I feel completely out of it, and see no hope of ever catching up with them. Not only that, but there wasn't any room at the station, so they sent me over here to a hotel. Why they call it that I'm not sure because there isn't even a bathtub in the town, and no heat, and only a candle for light. No one here speaks English and I don't speak French. Oh Budge, Budge, I was lonely.

I got a flight today and will get another tomorrow, which will finish me up on stick control. I have to be careful on these machines (FBAs), so I can't have any fun. Seven Frenchmen were killed in one week flying them, and I'm not crazy about them. They do queer little tricks due to the gyroscopic action of the rotary motor, and the controls aren't very sensitive.[1] They aren't like Caleb Bragg's, they're not half as good.

Everyone here is pretty blue about the outcome of the war. I have met several people who are willing to discuss getting licked, but I absolutely refuse to even consider it. The French are well "fed up" on the war, but they will never, never quit. I don't think that the present war will last long, what I fear is another worse one.

The German prisoners around here are very interesting. They are so tickled at the wonderful treatment that they get here that they work like slaves, twice as hard and twice as well as the French, and they aren't even guarded most of the time. German discipline is something that you and I cannot understand. It's absolutely iron-bound. There are two officers around here, both prisoners, and they are in charge. One keeps his men spic and span, and the other lets his men dress shabbily. The strict one told the other one that if he didn't keep his men in good shape he would report him when they both got back to the fatherland.

I ran into an English officer in Paris who told me some interesting things. He said he saw some German prisoners lying on the ground, so badly wounded that they couldn't get up and march to the hospital. They put a German officer over them, and he walked over, barked out a short command, and the whole outfit jumped to their feet like rockets and stood in formation. Two of them were so badly wounded that they rolled around like tops, but they were even afraid to let themselves faint.

The soldiers may hate their officers, but they realize their authority, and they also realize they simply cannot get along without them. A good German officer takes care of his men, and the men know it, even though they may hate him. The German prisoner can't understand the Allies' authority or discipline and we can't understand theirs.

My name was sent to Paris as one of four men to be sent up to England to fly these new "America" seaplanes used for bombing and for defense against subs.[2] I hope I'm not sent because though I don't mind dirty work, I don't like such a monotonous job, no risk at all. I want to join Bob [Lovett], Dave [Ingalls], and Di [Gates] at Dunkirk. That's where they fly land and water machines, and that's where the "fun" is at present. I may also be sent to Tours, the land flying school, in charge of a draft of enlisted men who will be trained there.[3] That will mean plenty of land flying, but no action. Well, we can't all have what we want, and by the time I leave this place, I'll be willing to settle down and take anything they give me, and be thankful for it. . . .

1. *The cranky FBA was powered by an air-cooled 130-hp Clerget rotary engine, which imparted considerable torque, making it a dangerous machine for unskilled pilots.*
2. *The H-12 "Large America" flying boat employed by British forces for antisubmarine duty was a successor to the H-4 "Small America" developed by Curtiss in 1914.*
3. *On 1 November 1917 the U.S. Army assumed control of the French aviation training field at Tours.*

While on leave in New York just before departing for Europe in late October, Kenneth had proposed to Priscilla Murdock, and she had accepted. He had not yet told his parents, however, feeling they would disapprove. When the MacLeishes did learn of the couple's plans, they urged delay, questioning the wisdom of wartime marriages. In fact, the engagement was not announced until the following August, a source of much frustration to Kenneth and Priscilla.

Moutchic, 23 November 1917

My Beloved,

You should have seen me registering surprise this morning. There was a letter from you dated October 30th, but mailed November 1st. That's pretty good time, isn't it? I've been so tickled all day long that it has passed like a minute, and I've read and reread your letter till I know it by heart. At last we're in communication with each other.

But now, to ease your mind. Mother, to my great surprise, was not suspicious in the least. Ishbel was the dangerous one, but she's such a brick that one wink was enough to end the whole affair. I didn't get one second alone with Mother, so I didn't think it necessary to tell her. If you wish it now, I will write to her about it. I'm crazy to tell her, but you didn't seem too enthused at first. As for Mother hating you, you silly girl. Don't you think that for one single second. She said more fine things about you than I can count. I sat back and smiled, just aching to tell her that I loved you more than life itself, but not quite daring until I heard from you again. So the way things stand now, Mother is not suspicious, she is very, very fond of you, and I didn't tell her that I kind of liked you myself a bit.

I wish you all the success in the world in your wireless exam, but I have a nightmare every time I picture you at the station with those heartbreaking aviators. Don't you dare forget me and play too hard with those boys. I'd fly clear across the ocean at you if you did.

Wasn't it funny the way I found little brother Archie tucked away up here at Limoges, and I was only a few miles from him. It's a small world. Our boss is up at Paris attending some big pow-wow and when he comes back, he'll bring my orders, I think.[1] I wait with bated breath, whatever it is.

The French are so funny. I haven't succeeded in getting a drink of water since I've been in France, and I have to go thirty miles for my bath once a week. It seems you can't persuade them that water may be used externally at night, internally at meals, and is not merely the stuff to push under bridges and keep fish in.

One fact seems to impress itself on me more clearly every day. The initials USNRF, which used to mean U Shall Not Reach France, have come to mean Us Sailors Never Risk Fighting. In other words, unless the navy changes its tactics soon there won't be any doubt about my returning home safe and sound, because I will never see any active service. All my requests to go to Dunkirk where the real fighting is taking place have been laughed at, and I shall probably have to be content chasing subs most of my military life. I'll feel like such a fool after the war if I don't get some active service. The old saying "You're in the navy now!" holds a world of significance.

Well, hereafter have no fears about the censor. There ain't no such thing, and if this letter reaches you by Christmas, just remember that I send you my love, such as it is, and promise to make it worthy of yours.

1. *Lieutenant Grattan Dichman sailed to Europe with Kenneth Whiting in June 1917 and assumed command at Moutchic in late October.*

Moutchic, 23 November 1917

Well, Henry [an unidentified friend],

I just got your wonderful letter today. . . . It's colder than all-fired blue blazes in this part of France, and I'm lonely, and nobody loves me, and there aren't any worms this time of year, and, besides that, there isn't even the proverbial garden. Also, I speak no French and the hotel keeper speaks no English.

My career will evidently be devoid of all hairbreadth escapes, etc. I came here with the idea of flying like a fool, so that they would be sure to send me to the front, where I can have some fun, but after my first exhibition I was beached for a week, and told that I would probably be given a patrol on the Irish coast, as they didn't want any d——d fools at the front.

I don't think I'll stay at this station very long because I was only sent here to learn how to fly a stick-control machine, and also to see what kind of flyer I was. I thought the crazier they were the better chance they had of seeing active service, but my dope was wrong, evidently. I did notice, however, that after the boss called me down, he asked how I did some of the tricks, so there may be some hope yet, and he may just be kidding me.

They asked me to try out a new machine [FBA] the other day. It was a lulu. I never flew a rottener contraption in my life. It was a flying boat with a rotary 130-hp motor in it. Well, it was fast enough, but when one turned to the left, the gyroscopic action of the motor put the machine in a dive, and vice versa on a right-hand turn. Also, it has a perfectly flat bottom, so that unless you landed tail first you bounced some two or three times. When one bounces three times the French call it a "Capitaine de Frigate." The above-named gent wears three gold stripes on his sleeve, hence the smile. . . .

Moutchic, 25 November 1917

Dearest Family,

. . . A pleasant surprise arrived today, I received orders to move on. I don't know where it means this time, but every step these days is an ominous one, and you may be sure that I am making the most of every opportunity to fit myself out for what is coming. . . .

I wish I could place that brother of mine. I got into communications with him at Limoges, and later read that he was in Paris. I can't make out whether he intends to stay there or return to Limoges. Maybe he never even left. At any rate, I'm going to wire Arch this morning and stop there on my way to Paris.

I have moved up from my summer resort by the sea and am now at a station where there are two of the old Huntington crowd.[1] After a good, hot bath in Bordeaux I feel like my old self again. There's a stove up here—you people don't know what happiness one old sixteenth-century stove full of burning coal can bring! It's like a square meal after two days' diet.

Speaking of cold and hunger, do you remember the boy named K[en] S[mith] I called up about my orders. He lived at Patchogue, Long Island. I'm sure Father remembers, he paid the bill. Well, he gave us an awful scare the other day. He was on patrol duty over the ocean when his motor broke down. The rest of the patrol didn't see him fall out. The next day one of his carrier pigeons returned with a note saying he had motor trouble and giving the approximate location and direction of the drift. The day after that his other pigeon came in without any note. He was finally picked up after drifting fifty-odd hours without food, water, or heat. . . .[2]

1. *Freddy Beach and Chip McIlwaine served at Moutchic until 21 May 1918, when they were ordered to the army's day bombardment school at Clermont-Ferrand.*
2. *Smith was stationed at Le Croisic carrying out antisubmarine patrols in Tellier flying boats.*

Moutchic, 26 November 1917

Beloved,

My orders to move on came. I don't know where I'll be sent, all I know is that I report to headquarters. I think I'll run into Bob, Di, and Dave, who have not gone to their station because of several diseases which have broken out there. I have a hunch that I will join them and go to their station. If you know where it is, I don't. It may be in Italy for all I know. . . .

John [Vorys] and Al [Sturtevant] are on their way to England for instruction in these young hotels [flying boats] I mentioned in my last letter. Freddy [Beach] and Chip [McIlwaine] are here at this station now. I moved up from my summer resort on the ocean, and after a good old bath in Bordeaux, I'm beginning to chirp up and feel normal. As far as news from the outside world goes, however, I'm still lost.

I think I'm settling down into the best frame of mind philosophically that I can possibly get into. I'm beginning to feel that the war will be a long one, and that there will be plenty of action somewhere and sometime. Yet the function of my organization still seems slightly foolish. The subs are now operating over seventy-five miles from shore. One thing is very gratifying, we have been given precedence over the whole army because it is conceded that the subs must be cleared out before troops can be sent over. The army is inclined to take this medicine harshly, and most especially the Signal Corps, who appear to be frothing at the mouth. . . .

By the end of November MacLeish had returned to Paris, his work at Moutchic completed. The next phase of his naval career required training on small land scouts, preparatory to assignment at the antisubmarine base then organizing at Dunkirk near the Belgian border. In fact, fellow Yalie Di Gates was already on his way there to assist Lieutenant Godfrey Chevalier in readying the site. In a letter home to the injured Trubee Davison, Bob Lovett reported that "Dave, Ken MacLeish, and I will proceed with aerobatics, en route to Dunkirk, where we will rejoin Di, but that's a long way off."

Paris, 29 November 1917

Beloved,

The American mail goes out tonight, so I am writing just a note to tell you that Dave and Bob and I are to fly fast scouts,[1] and Di, who left last night for a certain station [Dunkirk], is to fly bombing machines because he's too big to fit into a scout. Bob and I are being sent to England for final training. The ultimate station where we will be sent is the one I have longed to be sent to. It's where the real action is taking place.

Di is the first of our group to reach the front. I saw him off last night and admit that the handshake and goodbye were more sincere than ever; I think we both were wondering whether we should meet again.

You see, this station was given up by the French and British because it was considered impractical due to the heavy bombing raids carried out almost every night. We have new dope on the situation and are going to experiment. The commandant was very cheerful. He said he expected us to be shot down like birds, but I don't think it's that bad.

Here's a little Christmas poem from Bob and Dave:

> No matter how stormy the weather
> No matter how the wind may sigh through the trees
> And the foamy waves break on the hungry rocks
> Remember always that there's a B in boat.

Bob sends his very cordial regards, all terms of endearment, and a breath of Paris. . . .

1. *Possibly a reference to either Hanriot-Dupont scouts, or SPADs converted to seaplane duty.*

The uncertainty of mail service caused the navy fliers in Europe to send their Christmas letters as early as possible. Bob Lovett penned a special holiday greeting to old friend Priscilla Murdock.

Paris, 30 November 1917

Dear Chub [Priscilla Murdock],

Just a line to send you my Christmas greetings and to tell you that Kenneth is with me now and that we are in the pink. We anticipate bully fun at Dunkirk after our acrobatics are over, and we miss Di terribly. Ken and I are standing back to back in the Paris baths and we have won out so far, hooray! We leave in three days, I think, and when things look up I'll write more.

Yesterday we saw a streetcar with "complet" on it so we got aboard and thought we'd find out where the place was. Don't know yet what happened. Funny country this. They all speak French horrid. Love to all the family, and with all good wishes, believe me, unconditionally,

Bob Lovett

Visiting in Paris, MacLeish frequently observed the leaders of the war effort going about their business. Late in November he stopped at the famed Crillon Hotel, where he spotted most of the top American brass conferring with the Allies. Among those present that day were Generals

John Pershing and Tasker Bliss, Admirals William Sims and William Benson, Marshal Joffre, Lloyd George, the British prime minister, and Raymond Poincare, the president of France.

Paris, 1 December 1917

Beloved,

    Well, to begin with, I'm sore. First for writing that last letter [29 November 1917], which was awful and should never have been written. Conditions aren't nearly as bad as I pictured them, and I'm sure we'll get away with it. Secondly, I'm so damn mad at Aunt Mary that I could choke her. Do you know what she's up to? She thinks I'm crazy about Elizabeth Clark, and now she's started matchmaking with Elizabeth, which will end up with little Willie [MacLeish] held in contempt and called fickle again. Can you beat that?[1] Here's an extract from Aunt Mary's letter to me: "The picture that I'm sending to Detroit to E. C. looks the observer straight in the eye, so I don't think you'll be forgotten." Well, I don't want Clarkie to have my picture. Where under the sun do you suppose that Aunt Mary got the idea? Do you think it's a product of her fertile brain? Lord, I'm mad!

    Another wonderful letter from you today. You've been splendid about writing, and I do appreciate it so. You see, you are my source of information from the States, and I'm counting on you to send me all the gossip and news from my friends.

    Did Erl [Gould] fall in an N-9 or an Aeromarine, or an R-6? I know it wasn't a boat or he would have been hurt.[2]

    I told you, didn't I, that Dave, Bob, and I are going to Gosport or Oxford in England to train on scouts and then go to Dunkirk? Di left night before last for the latter station. He will fly bombing machines up there, but not until we arrive, because we are to convoy the big machines. I wish we could get busy and have it over with. I hate to have to look forward to it for a couple of months. Bob's nerves are going back on him, I'm afraid, he's very high-strung. You needn't repeat this, however, I shouldn't be surprised if they shifted him and gave him a station instead.

    I visited the factory where they are making our machines. They sure are wonders. They go about 120 mph, and handle beautifully. The only disadvantage being that the Boche machines go 130 and handle better, and are driven by the best pilots in the German army.

    Crock [Ingalls] is in the next room with one awful-looking

Frenchwoman. Now and then I hear Crock's stock phrase which he uses on all occasions, "Qu'est-ce que vous avez dite." It's a scream.

Say, if Adele [Brown] is so crazy about Bob, why doesn't she show him. The poor boy is love _____. I don't know whether it's over Adele or his future cheerful work, but Adele could cheer him up I think.

Crock and I had tea with the marchioness de Chambrun this afternoon, ahem! She's an American woman and mighty nice.[3] Yesterday we saw Major Generals Pershing and Bliss, Admirals Sims and Benson, Lloyd George, Marshal Joffre, and President Poincare all over at the Crillon Hotel.

Lots of ex-ambulance men are going back to the States this Saturday.[4] I wouldn't trade places with them for a minute, but just the same, I'd sell my soul to go back for about a week.

Your mail is never censored, you know. Isn't that rather nice. I censored my own until now. Whether this is opened or not I couldn't say. Certainly not by anyone you or I know, so I can brazenly proceed. But seriously, Budge, I miss you terribly and I wish this war would come to an end. I can't see myself chasing off half-cocked for another one.

1. *Elizabeth Clark was a Westover friend of Ishbel MacLeish, Kenneth's sister.*
2. *A charter member of the Yale Unit, Erl Gould was stationed at the navy's Bay Shore, New York, patrol base. In the autumn of 1917 while flying an R-6 pontoon scout, he crashed from a height of 75 feet but escaped unhurt.*
3. *The marchioness of Chambrun was married to the Marquis Pierre de Chambrun, who had represented the French legislature on a unity mission to the United States in the spring of 1917.*
4. *These were veterans of the volunteer American Ambulance Field Service.*

Paris, 2 December 1917

Dearest Family,

. . . I shall probably spend Christmas in London. Have we any friends there? I hate to spend the day in a hotel, but I guess I'll have to be content and remember "c'est la guerre."

I wish Bruce [MacLeish] could have been with me yesterday.[1] I went out to a field where they test new machines.[2] I saw all the latest types of fighting machines, and one monoplane that I simply haven't words to describe. A SPAD and a Sopwith Camel, both capable of about 130 mph, were playing up there when this monoplane came along. It went by them as though they were going backwards. And climb! Wow! Why, the pilot pulled up into a zoom, which is a jump upward. The SPAD zooms about 200 feet and then dies out, but this darn monoplane can climb at that angle. It was more than 45 degrees and held it all the way up. He climbed out of sight in four minutes.

They can't be used because they can't be handled easily; they're very tricky in heavy air; and they can't land under 110 mph. So only about ten men in the world can fly them. But they'll be perfected soon, I guess. The man who flew this machine is the best the French have. He and Guynemer had a bet, and he stuck to the latter's tail for fifteen minutes.[3] Guynemer couldn't shake him off, so you see he's fair enough—n'est-ce pas? . . .

I must close now and go back to the office. I don't know when this will reach you—perhaps before Christmas. If so, the merriest kind of Christmas to you, and may it be the last one without all of us there with you.

1. *Bruce MacLeish was Kenneth's older half-brother, who lived in Chicago.*
2. *The Aviation Acceptance Park at Orly.*
3. *Ace Georges Guynemer flew with France's Les Cigognes Escadrille and scored fifty four victories before he was killed in November 1917.*

Paris, 2 December 1917

Beloved,

We've just been out to the camp where they send all the machines to go to the front. There were hundreds of them, and machines of every conceivable type. But the ones that caught my eye were the SPADs.[1] They are, without exception, the neatest arrangements I've ever seen. Bob, Crock, and I are moving heaven and earth to get them instead of fast seaplanes, and I think we shall work it.

I went for over an hour without seeing a single drunken army officer disgracing his uniform. Honestly, Budge, if you could only see some of these young boobs who have been given commissions because they look well in officers' clothes, parading around the streets of Paris, drunk as lords, with a vile-looking "chip" on each arm, it would make you sick. I think the navy is bad enough, but I have only seen two naval officers make a scene in public. They baby the army too darn much, anyway. Wait till they see some real fighting. The Marine Corps has it all over the army and is better than the navy. The French government has given over Bordeaux and Paris to the marine police, that's an honor, but those marines are the boys who can fill the bill. Every one of them is a gentleman, a wonderful soldier, and a great big hunk. If you could only see some of the things that wear army uniforms you wouldn't blame the French for saying that the American draft took "tout le monde sans choisant."

Bob got a letter from Adele today, no use going into details, but he wasn't arrested. Crock sent nothing (censored). Bob sends Parisian greetings and I join him in saying he can't send more. Bob says we saw a machine today that looks like you: fast, trim, speedy, well-built, good at high altitude, slow landing speed, and single control. Loads of love.

> 1. *Probably the SPAD XIII, a tough, powerful-machine introduced in the spring of 1917, following the successful SPAD VII. It was a favorite of Eddie Rickenbacker's "Hat in the Ring" squadron, though at least one pilot noted that the plane had "the gliding angle of a brick."*

Paris, 4 December 1917

Beloved,

I'm beginning to understand why so many American soldiers and sailors go wrong in Paris. Of course the temptations now in Paris are perfectly frightful. I have never been out walking in the evening that at least two girls didn't come up to me and grab my arm. They're so darn persistent that they're repulsive to me, but just lately some ideas have entered my head that scared me. Of course, what has always kept me straight was the thought that I owed it to my family, and the girl I would marry, and to my own pride and education. But what if I never see my family again? Danger demands its rewards in excitement. The greater the danger, the stronger the desire. Why should I refrain? These are some of the thoughts that have arisen lately. They aren't very powerful with me because I have decided to live, while I live, in a way which would make you happy and, if I must die, in a way which would make you proud. But I guess there are many men in our service who aren't as lucky as I am. Perhaps the girl they love has turned them down; perhaps their families have turned them out. I don't blame them nearly so much now. I'm inclined to pity them. They don't need to have what remnants of their religion remain to them collected and strengthened. Their crying need is something practical and tangible which will drive the old saying, "Eat, drink, and be merry for tomorrow you may die," out of their heads. That's why I think people and churches back in America are on the wrong track.

England has suffered terribly because of a frightful mistake the War Department made. They didn't give the men leaves of absence at regular intervals. The result was that wives went two years without seeing their husbands. They went wrong. When the husbands finally came back, well. . . . Conigsby Dawson told me that there were two hundred applications for divorce in the British headquarters every week. And that's why I'm afraid. Our government won't give us leave because it's too far to go. Do you think conditions will ever be that awful in the States? Lord, I hope not. . . .

My next letter from you should contain news of the arrival of my first letter to you. I wish I knew when we left. I want to get out of this city.

Kenneth MacLeish spent most of his time in Paris awaiting new orders and the arrival of Yale friends from home. Both Curt and Bart Read were due any day, after being ordered overseas from their duties at Hampton Roads. Another group of expected Yale men included Erl Gould, Allan Ames, Wellington Brown, and William Rockefeller, who had been assigned to the naval air station at Bay Shore, New York. They would not reach Europe, however, until late 1918.

Paris, 6 December 1917

My Beloved,

We're still here in Paris and there's no prospect of us getting away for some time, either. Curt and Bart ought to be drifting through before long now. I suppose that means Thorne Donnelly and his Bay Shore outfit. . . .[1]

Did you know that you have become known as the "Slim Princess" among Bob, Di, Dave, and myself? No, of course you didn't. But don't you think it's pretty nice? We've decided, but I insist, that you should be here to keep our spirits up. These European women are "no bon," as they say in Paris.

I had an awful fight the other night with about five drunk Canadians. I got banged up about the mouth, and also came near being choked to death. They tried to pull me out of a taxi and use it for themselves. Some friends guarded my right and left wings and we staged a small edition of the Battle of Paris before we were interrupted by the military police, but it was great while it lasted. The funny part was, no one lost his temper, we were all laughing.

I do hope to hear from you soon, Budge. Bob and Crock have discovered your picture. What shall I do? They've tried to steal it from me every night since.

    1. *Aviator Thorne Donnelly, a native of Chicago and graduate of Trinity College, headed a detachment of fliers from the Bay Shore, New York, naval air station.*

Among the many Yale men converging on Paris was football All-American George Mosely, like MacLeish a native of Chicago, who had joined the French air service in July 1917 and trained at Tours and Pau. After serving with Escadrille N. 150, he transferred to naval aviation in December, informing his family, "We [Mosely and Stuffy Spencer] are thinking of joining the navy again. We will be put on the fastest hydro-aeroplanes they have, SPADs with little pontoons under them, and be sent to Dunkirk, where we will be in an escadrille under Chevalier." Also in Paris where men from the Second Yale Unit organized by Ganson Depew [Yale '19], which had trained at Buffalo, New York, during the previous summer and fall. Among those ordered overseas in November 1917 were Edward DeCernea, Edward "Shorty" Smith, and Stephen Potter.

Paris, 9 December 1917

Beloved,

    I've just been rereading your last letters and now I'm all cheered up. Dave and I have been in bed for two days with rotten colds and feeling low. Bob and Dave made me put your picture up on the mantelpiece, and I wish you could hear some of the conversations you carry on with us. You are consulted as to the probable weather for the day, what we shall eat, and countless times you act as judge in a quarrel. But I always win the judgment because if I don't, I won't let them talk to you anymore.

    Who do you think woke me up out of a sound slumber yesterday afternoon? Curt, Bart, and George. They came with six Buffalo men I knew at college. I sure was glad to see them.

    Bart said he had no messages for me. Curt said so too. Aren't you just a little bit ashamed of yourself. Bart says he forgot to say goodbye to you and he's sorry. Curt says to send any messages that I think discreet. I let him send his very best. Bob sends all terms of endearment and all his usual pet phrases, and if you see various friends of yours that she believes him very cordially. His admiration for you is only exceeded by his wonder, and his wonder only surpassed by his unquenchable love. Curt adds, "By his good looks."

I just got a letter from Di. He says the weather has been so bad [at Dunkirk] that they haven't had any raids so far, but after the letter I happen to know that they had a frightful bombing party. He says it's as cold as blue blazes where he is.

I got a bunch of mail from home, and a perfect wonder from Arch. He has shifted to artillery, and though I don't think he ought to, I suppose I must support him.[1] He put the whole thing wonderfully. He says the only way to be cheerful is to think I'm going through this for you. He knows I'm in love, but I didn't tell him who it was. But he has the right idea.

Must go now, we're going to lunch. I hope to hear from you soon.

1. *Archibald MacLeish had been serving with a hospital unit but in December 1917 transferred to the field artillery.*

Finally, on 9 December Kenneth received orders to proceed to England for further instruction. Though he was eager to continue his training, the overall atmosphere in the French capital was dispiriting. The Italian front nearly collapsed at Caporetto. Britain's fall offensive achieved little but additional casualties, while the French army seemed totally spent. American combat units had not yet made an appearance. MacLeish conveyed these feelings in letters to his family.

Paris, 9 December 1917

My Dearest Ones,

At last the order to shove off has come, after what seems an interminably long time in this awful hole. Three of us go to England, as I said before, to fly fast land machines. One of the boys [Lovett] will drop out to take command of a station, leaving two of us to go on from there.

The outlook is very, very dull and gloomy. There are no bright spots. Even America's awakening is more or less of a good dream. You people over in the States simply cannot conceive the horrors these men go through. A fine young lieutenant played around with me when I was here last, only a month ago. Today I saw him and didn't recognize him. The lines in his face had deepened and he had become very, very thin. He was very quiet and sad. He was at Bourlon Wood and he is the only survivor of his machine gun corps.[1] You can't imagine the filth and chilling cold in the trenches. I can't—I haven't seen them—I've only heard. This lieutenant has a D.S.O. and the Cross of Belgium. He said, "You mustn't blame us if we curse you and call you airmen embuscades because you live and eat well, but when we see you over our heads we all wish you damn good luck."

The other night we went to a show and there were some Tommies there fresh from the trenches, with the trench mud fresh on their boots. The orchestra played "Tipperary" for them. It cuts me to the quick to see a girl cry, but to see men cry is frightful. . . .

1. *A salient between Amiens and Cambrai seized by British troops in the fall of 1917, Bourlon Wood fell to a powerful German counterattack in early December.*

Paris, 9 December 1917

Dearest Sister [Ishbel MacLeish],

We move on in a couple of days to finish up the last links in the chain of preparation, and then we're off for the front. And we shall have the honor to be the first to see active service, which is only fitting, as we were the first to enlist. But my flying education has been somewhat flighty in spots itself, and I sometimes have misgivings. However, I shall learn to shoot with a machine gun, and shoot straight, and that's what counts, I presume. How they hit anything from an airplane will continue to be an unsolved mystery to me. Let's hope the mystery isn't solved at my expense—that wouldn't be so humorous. . . .

2

"Weather Fit for Ducks and Sea Monsters": Flying with the RFC in England and Scotland

December 1917–March 1918

ENSIGN KENNETH MACLEISH'S transfer from French to British flight schools and from lumbering seaplanes to nimble scouts initiated a new and exciting phase of his aviation career. News of this development quickly reached friends and acquaintances at home. Evelyn Preston, a confidant of Adele Brown and several others of the Long Island crowd, met the young navy aviators on their way through Paris and soon passed the word along. "Bob [Lovett], Dave Ingalls, and Ken MacLeish are the ones chosen for acrobatic work," she wrote. "Do you realize that they are the only three out of the whole naval aviation that were chosen, and all of them the outcome of Huntington?"

A few days later she added a postscript, "I had to say goodbye to those nice creatures . . . . They left for England Wednesday morning . . . looked in the pink."

The trio reached London in the second week of December. Contrary to expectations, the U.S. Navy ordered Lieutenant Lovett to the RNAS station at Felixstowe on the North Sea coast. Lovett was being groomed to command an antisubmarine patrol station in France, L'Aber Vrach, with temporary duty at Felixstowe designed to provide an in-depth look at an operational facility.

MacLeish and Ingalls, soon joined by fellow Yalie Edward "Shorty" Smith, were assigned to the RFC aerodrome at Gosport on the English Channel near Southampton. Edward Traver "Shorty" Smith of Patchogue, New York, and Port Antonio, Jamaica, was the younger brother of Ken Smith, a classmate of MacLeish and a member of the First Yale Unit.

After the outbreak of war in April 1917, Shorty joined the Second Yale Unit which, like the First, was a privately sponsored organization designed to produce naval aviators. The group trained at Buffalo, New York, from April until the following November, when they passed their flight tests and received commissions as ensigns. Several members were then ordered overseas, Smith among them. Edward Smith was, in fact, of slight stature, occasionally got lost, and suffered acutely from airsickness. These traits earned him a nickname and a fearsome amount of ribbing, but he endured it all with good spirits. He finished the war as a lieutenant (jg) and received his honorable discharge on 25 September 1921.

During MacLeish's short layover at London's Savoy Hotel his interests revolved primarily around sightseeing, visiting other Americans, and eagerly anticipating the possibility of a late-night raid by German bombers. He had yet to experience the terror and destruction these attacks inflicted. Less than a week later, on 17 December, Kenneth rode down to Gosport to commence instruction on Avro trainers. He was thrilled at the prospect and began performing acrobatic stunts his first day at the field. In a letter to Priscilla he exulted, "Talk about happy! . . . there's nothing in the world like your first solo."

MacLeish was also pleased to report that companions Dave Ingalls and Shorty Smith had reached Gosport about two weeks ahead of schedule. Work at the field lasted only a few days, however, because of the Christmas holidays. With time on their hands and no specific duties, the Americans returned to London and joined a joyous reunion of naval aviators. The holiday conclave afforded the opportunity to catch up on news from home and exchange reports on recent activities. The spirit of the season was somewhat tempered by Kenneth's enforced separation from Priscilla, his failure to receive mail, and the incongruity of celebrating the Prince of Peace in the midst of war.

A few days later flight operations resumed at Gosport. Temporarily, at least, the Americans were the only students at the base, much to their delight. Paired with a British instructor, MacLeish made rapid progress. Within a week he was soloing in a Sopwith Camel, one of the most dangerous aircraft on the western front. Kenneth was both amazed and awed at the machine's performance. Mounting a powerful rotary engine and exhibiting a dangerous tendency to spin, the Camel enjoyed an unhealthy reputation as a pilot killer. No matter, MacLeish gloried in it.

After his first flight he wrote Priscilla, "Those Camels will do a thing so darn quickly that you barely have time to decide upon it." A few days later, perhaps feeling more confident than circumstances warranted, he spun his aircraft down from 5,000 feet, managing to pull out a few hundred feet above the ground. Scared and dizzy, he waited a few minutes, then took off and repeated the maneuver. When David Ingalls attempted the same movement a few days later, he admitted, "Very foolishly I did six or seven tailspins before coming in. . . . I felt rotten for two or three hours afterward."

Dreadful flying conditions often slowed the training process. David Ingalls told his father that "the weather has been rotten. Wind, clouds, snow, and worst of all, fog." MacLeish seconded these thoughts, observing, "Rain and hail have lost their fascination. Snow is quite the thing to fly in." In mid-January the weather grew so bad that flight instruction was again temporarily halted, and the aviation cadets received three-day passes to London. While at headquarters MacLeish met with Captain Hutch Cone, chief of naval aviation in Europe. Kenneth also took the opportunity to make arrangements for his military insurance, almost letting the news of his secret engagement slip out in the process.

In the weeks that followed the trio of naval aviators continued their instruction in a program punctuated by dramatic flights and near-disasters. On more than one occasion MacLeish and Ingalls fought mock battles in the skies above southern England. At other times they undertook cross-country flights that tested their endurance, ingenuity, and navigational skills. The rapid pace of instruction and abominable weather led to frequent training mishaps. In early January Shorty Smith was nearly killed when he lost control of an Avro trainer while looping at 2,500 feet. That same day Dave Ingalls flew into a web of telephone wires but managed to land his damaged plane. Two weeks later Kenneth smashed the propeller and undercarriage of his Camel while stunting with his instructor.

With increased confidence came aerial hijinks. At one point MacLeish observed, "There's no game like this in all the world. You're always taking such wonderful chances, and it's a grand feeling to get away with them." Kenneth especially enjoyed buzzing less experienced pilots, the "Huns" he called them, or looping within a few hundred feet of the ground. He also loved "bush-bouncing," zipping along a few feet above the ground, then hopping over trees and houses. David Ingalls witnessed a similar phenomenon, noting that with each passing week the pilots grew cockier, sometimes landing within a few feet of the hangars. One afternoon he and Shorty Smith went out on a cross-country flight, zooming as close to the ground as possible, "giving the people and animals a great scare. It must have been very exciting to see [four] Camels tearing along just over the ground."

Though Kenneth MacLeish frequently took chances while flying, pushing himself and his machine, he also studied the training process with cool detachment, carefully analyzing its strengths and weaknesses. During the weeks at Gosport he began collecting notes about the British method of flight instruction, hoping to use the information to improve the American system. The result was a report that he forwarded to navy headquarters in Paris in which he recommended that seaplane pilots first be taught on land machines. He also stressed the important part played by an instructor's attitude and motivation in successfully communicating with his students. Finally, he endorsed the British method of training mechanics.

In early February MacLeish, Ingalls, and Smith completed their course at Gosport and received orders to report to the RFC gunnery school at Turnberry, Scotland. For Kenneth this represented something of a homecoming. His father had emigrated from Scotland many years before, and the entire family had returned for an extended visit a decade before the war. Situated on the Firth of Clyde southwest of Glasgow, the Turnberry school offered concentrated instruction in the use, mechanics, and maintenance of automatic weapons. Days were filled with lectures and demonstrations, with the evenings devoted to copying notes and studying. Very little flying was attempted. The nature of the course and the perpetual fog and drizzle precluded active operations. As Kenneth noted, Scottish weather was "fit for ducks and sea monsters only!"

Difficulties caused by poor flying conditions and the grueling, exacting instruction schedule paled before the ire aroused by the arrival of the "roughnecks" or "Hard Guys," a complement of navy enlisted men trained at flight schools in France and now ordered to Scotland to complete their work. MacLeish ridiculed their supposed lack of breeding and education, and their unwillingness to conform to the British system. Kenneth's uncharitable comments concerning these men say more about his own prejudices than about any shortcomings on their part.

With the work at Turnberry completed in a few weeks, MacLeish and his companions moved on to the nearby School of Aerial Fighting at Ayr. Here the task of producing combat flyers was completed. Among the many students at this RFC finishing school could be found pilots from England, Ireland, Canada, Australia, and South Africa. In addition to the small navy contingent, dozens of Army Air Service pilots were there, part of the "Lost Battalion" of American aviators dispatched to England in the fall of 1917 and later memorialized in Elliot White Springs's classic *Warbirds*. Future aces Springs, Laurence Callahan, George Vaughn, Reed Landis, and many others trained in Scotland.

At Ayr the men flew front-line aircraft, mostly Camels and S.E.5s. They engaged in frequent aerial battles and often employed camera guns to determine the winner. As the days passed individual encounters gave way to group operations, mimicking the tactics employed at the front. After only two weeks of advanced work at Ayr, the navy pilots were judged proficient and ready for combat.

Straining to graduate pilots as quickly as possible, English flight schools rushed the men through their course, with the inevitable result that scores were killed or injured in training mishaps. While stationed in Scotland, MacLeish learned that Yale friends Fred Stillman and Lyman Cunningham had both died in recent accidents. On one occasion he counted twenty-three crashes within a four-day period. But the expected German spring offensive simply would not permit a more leisurely pace as Britain mobilized every resource in preparation for the onslaught.

Though far from centers of activity at London, Paris, and Dunkirk, Ensign MacLeish kept himself well informed about the exploits of his Yale compatriots. Di Gates's travails at Dunkirk elicited sympathy, while Bob Lovett's assignment at Paris headquarters as the chief assistant to Captain Hutch Cone drew applause. In a letter to Priscilla he explained, "That boy [Lovett] has a better head and more ability than any two men in the service, and I'm glad they're beginning to appreciate the fact." On a more somber note Kenneth received word that Albert Sturtevant, another First Yale Unit member, had been shot down in flames over the North Sea. Two weeks later came a report that one more friend, Curtis Read, had died in a flying accident at Dunkirk.

Flight training at Ayr ended in early March. While awaiting further instructions, Kenneth used the short break to visit his Scottish cousins, pleased with the opportunity to discuss his relationship with Priscilla without fear of revealing secrets. That sojourn lasted only two days, however, followed by a return to Ayr and then travel orders for London.

By 12 March 1918 MacLeish and the other navy flyers were back at
headquarters, en route to Paris and then Dunkirk.

After a final round of social calls, they crossed the Channel in mid-
March. While waiting in Paris MacLeish visited with Mr. Henry
Davison, the chief sponsor of the Yale Unit, then on a tour of Red Cross
facilities in Europe. Kenneth spent the evening of 20 March writing
letters, anticipating his trip to the front due to begin the following
morning. In a note to an old friend he again outlined his thoughts about
the war, and the possibility of dying for a cause in which he believed
passionately. Early the next morning Kenneth MacLeish set out for
Dunkirk.

London, 13 December 1917

Beloved,

Wow! What an evening. To begin with, there's one of those London fogs out. It's so thick the taxis nearly had to be led around with a
guide. It was sort of creepy walking around in it because you couldn't
tell what you would bump up against. Then we went to the *13th
Chair*. Nuff sed! If Crock hadn't been leaning on me in the dark, I
would have accused him of murder.

Crock is the most amusing man I've ever met in my life. Bob and I
have kidded him to an inch of his life. He's so enthusiastic and good-
natured. But once in a while he makes one of the funniest remarks I've
ever heard. He's getting quite touchy now because we've kidded him
too much about that passionate laugh of his. He's a scream.

I won't know until tomorrow where we go from here, but I'll write
you when I know. I've read and reread your letter so many times I
know it all by heart. On second thought, I think I shall make my
letters to you my diary, so steel yourself for some frightful ordeals.
That might even mean a letter a day. Bob and Crock send love. I guess
I can say that, but I send a thousand times more.

In London the trio of Yale aviators learned that despite earlier plans,
they would soon be splitting up. As Evelyn Preston reported, "At the
last moment [Bob Lovett] got orders to go to a different school to learn
the duties of a C.O." Rather than accompany MacLeish and Dave Ingalls
to an RFC school for aerial acrobatics at Gosport, Lovett went to Felixstowe, an English seaplane base in East Suffolk. From this station near
Harwich the Royal Navy patrolled across the North Sea toward Holland,
searching for enemy submarines and surface raiders.

After Lovett set off for Felixstowe, Kenneth MacLeish remained behind in London for a day or two, attending the theater and anticipating
one of the evening bombing raids he had heard so much about. At this
juncture a replacement for Lovett joined the Gosport-bound flyers,
Edward "Shorty" Smith, a member of the Second Yale Unit trained at
Buffalo and recently arrived in Europe.

London, 14 December 1917

Beloved,

Here's looking at you while I write, and I am, too. I don't know
what I'd do without that picture. If a show written by Barrie and called
Dear Brutus ever comes to New York, and if Gerald du Maurier[1] takes
the leading part, see it if you never see another show in your life. It's all
about what people would do if they had a second chance in life, and it
made me wonder what I'd do if I had a second chance, and I decided
that we would have been married some four years ago—what do you
think?

Now that we're all here in London we find that they can only take
us one at a time every week at the station we planned to go to
[Dunkirk]. Bob is really leaving us to take command of the station
[presumably L'Aber Vrach]. It's pretty soft for the "sticker," isn't it?
He's sure to get home now. "Shorty," Ken's brother, has taken his
place with us. He was at Buffalo with John Farwell.[2] He's a good flyer
and a damn fine boy.

Last night was a slick night for an air raid, and the searchlights were
playing on the clouds and open sky for some time, but we were
disappointed again. I'll get bombed all I can stand in a few weeks,
however. Poor Di. He's getting a frightful thumping up there. The
Huns absolutely framed the station next to his, and one bomb fell on a
brick wall which covers the dugouts. I don't think Di lives any closer
than he has to, and I'm sure he's not on active service yet. He's waiting
for us, but it's an awful place to wait. Keep this news under your hat

[censored paragraph]

to you! So if you hear a lot of bad news from the rest of us, just smile
knowingly, but don't tell anyone why you're smiling. As a matter of
fact, the conditions here put me in mind of a line Bob read to me the
other day, "And those who are the first on the field of battle must pay

for the miscalculations and delays of their government with their lives." That isn't a noble thing to die for, and that's my one regret, but there are plenty of brighter things to think about so let's try them instead.

I got a perfectly splendid letter from Arch. And though it's blue and I said I wouldn't think about such things, this may come in very handy sometime, so pardon this bit of inconsistency. "Whatever happens to you, dear old boy, you can always know that I am back of you heart and soul. If you make your mark, I'll be the proudest man in the army. If you are unfortunate, I will understand. If anything happens, I'll remember you as I've always thought of you, as one of the _____ etc.

_____. And I won't grieve because I know that you made a great sacrifice gladly for the sake of things you stand for."

Isn't that great? And do you wonder that I wanted you to benefit by it. He's just gone into the artillary; he was right about going too, for what we need more than a thousand men is a good officer, and a man. He is the latter, and he will be the former. Well, beloved, more anon. I have missed my luncheon in order to talk to you, but it was well worth it. I take to dreaming more than ever these days.

1. *Sir James M. Barrie is best known for his play* Peter Pan. *Actor/manager Sir Gerald du Maurier was a popular performer of the day.*

2. *Chicago native John Farwell trained with the First Yale Unit and in September 1917 was assigned as an instructor with the Second Yale Unit in Buffalo.*

London, 16 December 1917

Beloved,

I haven't had any mail from you for some time, and it will be days before I get any, too, because when I came to England I didn't know where I would end up, and I've only just cabled my address now. Aunt Mary [Hillard] sent me an identification tag with a little place to put a picture. It's only so big _____. Now, be a good girl and finish the job, would you? I'll give you a ride on my chest if you will. Lord, I feel so simple that I'll have to stop before I make an awful break.

I am going to Gosport[1] tomorrow, and I'm sorry to say that I'm going all alone. Dave and Shorty have to wait in London or thereabouts for one or two weeks before they join me. It's a shame that we have to split up this way, but I guess in the end it will be better, at least it will hasten matters.

I ran into a boy named Laurence Callahan from Winnetka, Illinois.[2]

He's here in England training. I think it's to be a drunkard, but he says it's to be an aviator. Honestly, Budge, some of the fond parents in the States will be damn sorry that they ever let their sons get into this war. I almost lost my faith in human nature in Paris when I saw boys like Wally Winter and Alan Winslow raising the devil.[3] It's a darn shame, too. They have the idea that they'll never see home again. I hope I never get that blue.

1. *Gosport was an RFC training field on the Channel coast near Portsmouth and Southampton.*
2. *Callahan, a member of the Princeton contingent of air service pilots, reached England in the fall of 1917, and later flew with #85 RAF and the U.S. 148th Aerosquadron.*
3. *Both Winslow and Winter trained and flew with the French. Winter was shot down behind enemy lines in March 1918. Winslow transferred to the U.S. 94th Aerosquadron.*

The dismay MacLeish expressed at the "shocking" behavior of both U.S. troops abroad and the war-weary European citizenry was widespread among American observers. Evelyn Preston echoed Kenneth's observations, confiding to Adele Brown, "The boys come to Paris on leave and have a hell of a gay time (excuse my language, but you know what I mean)—I used to get terribly depressed about the whole idea. . . . Of course I've given up trying to understand it, how nice, respectable boys can suddenly break loose and find their fun in that way." Even Di Gates, captain-elect of the Yale football team, had little complimentary to say about Frenchwomen. After a dinner in Paris with some American friends he reported, "It certainly seemed good to see some real American girls once more, instead of these painted French beauties whose characters are always doubtful, even beyond that, practically a certainty." Perhaps so, but Victorian morality was one of the war's first casualties. American "innocence" followed soon after. As a favorite song inquired, "How ya gonna keep'em down on the farm . . . ?"

London, 16 December 1917

Dearest Family,

I am going to Gosport, England, in the morning, which is quite good news. It was only necessary to stay in London three days this trip. I wonder if I shall hear from you in time about any friends or relatives in London. Christmas is not far off, you know.

I met several boys in Paris who had just come from the States, and one of them, Bart Read, had a package for me which his brother Curt had put in his trunk. He didn't know where it came from, but I could give a fair guess, and it surely was welcome. If you can possibly work it, please send me some sweet milk chocolate—like Hershey's, or something of the sort. Also, all the large, heavy woolen socks in the world would be more than welcome, and one of those woolen helmets that fits my head, and is large enough, yet very warm, wouldn't go amiss if sent my way. Wristlets are of no use to anyone—tell all your friends, it's just a waste of wool.

I haven't had any American cigarettes for so long that I really don't remember what they taste like. You can't really appreciate the difference between a good smoke and one of these French smokes till you've coughed yourself blue in the face over the latter. Do you suppose you could find it in your heart to send me either Fatimas or Murads or, even better, some Deities. I don't think the package would be opened if it was sent through C.P.S. & Co. In the regular mail the clerks invariably like cigarettes better than you do, with the result that you never get them.

The war news is getting gloomier every day, isn't it? It surely looks bad at present. I wonder if the Americans really will wake up and send over the promised ten thousand aviators and machines. I'm almost certain that there won't be over five hundred trained aviators out of ten thousand unless they have a finishing school in the States. As for the machines, I have hopes. We're all counting on that Liberty motor.[1] It's either got to come through or we're done for. Can't we benefit by France and England. Must we make blunders to satisfy our morbid curiosity?

1. *In May 1917 the American Aircraft Production Board ordered development of a new power plant. Engineers J. G. Vinson and E. J. Hall set to work, and the first test models were ready by early July. Thousands of eight- and twelve-cylinder examples were produced during the war.*

While Kenneth MacLeish was undoubtedly depressed by the war situation, the resumption of actual flight training did much to restore his spirits. He lived to fly, and at Gosport on the Channel coast he would soon be getting all the air time he could handle. With permission to begin solo flying again, his enthusiasm knew no bounds.

Gosport, 19 December 1917

My Beloved,

Talk about happy! After four flights I finally persuaded my instructor to let me solo. Oh, Budge, there's nothing in the world like your first solo in a machine, and it's twice as wonderful on a land machine. These buses (Avros) go about 80–85 mph, climb like the deuce, and handle beautifully.[1] I tried all morning to tailspin, but she wouldn't stay in one. This afternoon I caught the knack, and did about six or seven, mixing loops in wherever I could, and ended up sideslipping a few hundred feet. I was so tickled that I couldn't see, and to add to my glee, Shorty and David arrived today, two weeks early. Isn't that almost as good as it could be for one day. It still insists on being cold, but as long as it's clear, I don't worry a bit. I think I shall make out a report on this station and show it to the men at headquarters. It's the most ideal sport in the world. You get up when you please, about nine A.M., you fly when you please and as much as you please, and you get the best training in the world. As long as they accomplish results, why is it necessary to be uncomfortable?

Dave and Shorty were in that air raid last night. They were in a taxi when they heard a BOOM! The taxi driver went frantic. It was over shortly and they got to the theater, but they had to duck up an alley first. I always just miss those darn things. I suppose I'll get plenty of them before I'm through.

One of those ten men who came over was killed yesterday. His name was [Ensign Phillip] Page, I think.[2] He had been at Squantum and came from Norfolk with Curt and Bart. He was flying those Young Americas (H-12s) down where Al, John, and Bob are [Felixstowe]. He stalled the machine on his first solo. Bad luck, wasn't it? He was an awfully nice chap. They haven't found his body yet, but they all saw the crash.

The proximity of Christmas is somewhat appalling. And the worst of it is that I'm sure I don't know how I'm going to get out of here. One can't travel on the railroads from the 20th till Christmas, and this place doesn't close until the 21st. I don't see any chance unless I fly up.

1. *The Avro 504J was a primary British training aircraft introduced in 1916, with a top speed of 90 mph.*
2. *Ensign Phillip Page, naval aviator #170, was killed during a test flight at Felixstowe on 17 December 1917.*

Whether by train, automobile, or airplane, MacLeish and his companions journeyed up to London for the Christmas holidays. Several members of the Yale Unit were in town, including John Vorys and Al Sturtevant at the Grosvenor Hotel. Vorys called it "a joyful reunion" with a great deal of "gossip about what the various boys from Huntington were doing." A similar Christmas Eve gathering of Yale men occurred in Paris.

London, 25 December 1917

Beloved,

Today is Christmas, and it would be hard to realize it except for something that happened last night. You know there is a difference of five or six hours between London and New York. Well, I was sleeping soundly and it must have been about half past one or two in the morning when I had a restless feeling, and woke up calling your name. Do you suppose there is such a thing as mental telepathy? Were you thinking about Christmas Eve about six o'clock? I can't explain it, but I had such a wonderful feeling of nearness and companionship. Most of the officers here are of the opinion that I wouldn't be able to send you a cable wishing you a Merry Christmas, so I didn't even try, but my little experience last night compensates that thought.

I had a funny time at Gosport the day I left. I went up alone, and after doing a few loops, tailspins, and sideslips I got up enough nerve to "roll" the Avro. Well, I got around once beautifully, but I didn't know they would only roll once. The result was that I got into a spin with my motor full on, and before I could cut it, it went "dud." I was 2,500 feet up and quite a distance from the aerodrome with a stiff breeze in my face. I nearly had a fever before I got down. I just skimmed over some telegraph poles and wires and fell into the field. Gee, it was fun for a while!

You know at Gosport they expel you from the school if you limit yourself to straight flying, you must do stunts all the time. It's seventh heaven. Poor Shorty gets airsick all the time. When his instructor rolls him around, he gets seasick and has to come down. My instructor was shot twice through the chest, crashed in no-man's-land, and crawled in at night. His machine burned up right on top of him, and it didn't hurt him. He was under shellfire for six hours while it was light.

All the people send Christmas greetings to you, and I send more. I send you that promise, and I send you a pure, strong love. It makes me the happiest man in the world.

One drawback to the closeness of the First Yale Unit was that everyone seemed to know everyone else's business, and that information crossed the Atlantic via multiple channels. After sharply criticizing the behavior of others, Kenneth soon found himself called on to defend his own actions from the accusations (lightheartedly) leveled by his "friends" Bob Lovett and Dave Ingalls. In the coming months the progress of several romances—MacLeish and Priscilla Murdock, Bob Lovett and Adele Brown, Di Gates and Alice Davison—attracted as much attention and analysis as the fighting in Europe.

London, 27 December 1917

Hello Old Top [Priscilla Murdock],

I am writing this note in self-defense because both Bob and Dave say they've written home about this experience of mine, and that I better defend myself. I don't think I need to, but here it goes. Do you remember me telling you about a certain party in Paris that I had with two English officers [6 December 1917] when one of the Englishmen tried to steal every taxi he saw, and six Canadians tried to take one away from me, leaving me pretty well "beaten up" with several marks that I couldn't explain on my smiling visage? Well, that same pair of men, the Britishers, were arrested by the provost marshal, but not until they had picked up two awful-looking French chips, and they benevolently bestowed them on me and told me to take them home. I nearly had a nervous breakdown trying to figure out how I could leave mine and get home. I finally got up the nerve, pushed her in the door of her flat, and ran like a fool. I was congratulating myself all that night and the next day, until we went to Ciro's[1] and I ran into her again. Can you beat that? And she used to write notes to me every single day trying to make a date. I got nervy again and went over and told her to stop writing, that there was nothing doing, but it didn't do one bit of good. Every time we went to Ciro's we ran into her, and Bob and Dave just kidded me blue in the face. I've never been so embarrassed. That's more of the tale than Bob and Dave know, so I guess that's enough, but never again! Will you forgive me for that and still trust me? It wasn't my fault. Lord, what a poor night for me.

1. *Ciro's was a fashionable Parisian club and restaurant.*

Inevitably, Christmas leave ended and the work of training for war resumed. With the brief holiday left behind, the pace of instruction at Gosport accelerated. If weather permitted, aviation cadets spent hours aloft, gaining self-confidence and perfecting their acrobatic techniques. First MacLeish soloed, then Ingalls and Shorty. And all the time Kenneth kept wondering, where was his mail?

Gosport, 29 December 1917

Beloved,

I'm puzzled. I have received newspapers and bills from Paris, but not a single letter since December 10 or 11. That's almost three weeks and I surely am worried. You last letter was a wonder, but three weeks is a long, long time.

I hope I get a letter from you before very long. Crock has a good scheme, that is, he thinks it's good. He has a girl in every port. In London over vacation we didn't even see him but once. Al and John got a bit mad, and I did too. He hadn't seen John or Al in several months and probably won't see them again for some time, and he only stuck around long enough to say hello, and didn't even say goodbye. I don't know who the girl is. She's an American acting as a stenographer down at Royal Navy headquarters. I think her name is Alice Bowler. Crock was so tight with her that he wouldn't even take us around to see her. Perhaps the reasons were very good, who knows?

Dave and Shorty both soloed this morning and the three of us are going up together this afternoon. We're going to have an aerial battle, or something like that. Dave is almost surely off somewhere. He drives me and Shorty crazy. You know what a spoiled kid he is anyway, well, on top of that, he has lost all the manners he ever had, and now he makes the most disgusting noises you ever heard, and he's so darn nervous and fidgety that we're gradually going crazy.

This winter flying is not so very much fun. I went up this morning and flew for about an hour, and I've never been so cold. I had lots of fun, though. The clouds were only 2,000 feet up today and I amused myself by getting up as much speed as possible, just below them, and then pulling back and looping into them, or diving in and letting go of the controls, and then I'd come crashing and spinning out of them. I got one fine old thrill. I came down, made a landing, and was just getting off again, turning as I climbed. All at once my motor began to sputter and I started to sideslip into a large brick house. I just pulled out in time to avoid the chimneys. It was only oil pressure and I was able to fix it without having to land. My old heart was pumping at an awful rate for a second or two. Lord, there's no game like this in all the world. You're always taking such wonderful chances, and it's a grand feeling to get away with them, because you gain such self-confidence. I'm getting to feel quite at home now. I used to get lost in vertical banks and spins, but I know just where I am all the time now.

I wish this war would end. I want to get home. You don't appreciate America till you are forced to stay away from the place against your wishes. The English and French girls are nice enough, but for a real prehistoric, good old "gool" girl, give me the American maid every time. Also, one can keep warm in America in winter, but not here. I don't believe that there are more than two furnaces and heating systems in Europe, and I haven't had the good luck to see either of them yet.

This noise about the war being finished in the air, I have come to believe, is pure "bunk." It will be finished on land, and only after the sub[marine] is cleaned out, unless, of course, it is finished the other way round in the next six months. Here's hoping the sub is forever blotted out.

Gosport, 30 December 1917

Dearest Family,

The weather is bad this afternoon. This morning I had a couple of good rides, and between rides I learned a good lesson when I saw a poor devil fall a few hundred feet in a tailspin. My instructor here is a perfect wonder. He served some time in France until he crashed in no-man's-land with two bullets in his lungs and crawled to the English side that night when it got dark.

I'm getting to feel quite at home now in almost any position. The hardest stunt yet for me is the vertical spin. You're in so tight that you simply cannot lift your leg off the floor. It's all you can do to lift your hand due to the tremendous centrifugal force. You can guess how your "innards" feel.

I have no idea how much longer I'll be with the Royal Flying Corps. Not very much longer, I judge, from the progress I've made so far. The next move will be to get practice on a machine gun. After that the fun will commence at Dunkirk, and I shall be ready. The question of shooting the Huns never bothers me at all. It's the old story of survival of the fittest. What I wonder is, how will I behave under fire? Whether I'll keep my head or lose it, lose it in both ways, unless I keep cool. The one consolation is that the Hun will probably be just as scared as I am. No, the question of conscience about killing a Hun never enters my mind. I don't look at it that way.

Far from home, cut off from familiar faces and sights, Kenneth MacLeish, like countless other soldiers overseas, eagerly anticipated letters from family and friends. A prolific writer himself, his spirits rose and fell with the rhythm of mail call. He could never understand why his good friend Bob Lovett seemed so reluctant to take pen in hand.

Gosport, 30 December 1917

My Beloved,

At last! Three wonderful letters from you all in one bunch. I think those people in the Paris office wait until they have enough mail to make it worthwhile, then they send it in a bunch. I'll explain this censoring mail business, in case you failed to get your mind off it. Di used to censor all mail written by enlisted men. The officers' mail at those stations is not censored except by the author, who is supposed to use his own jurisprudence, or something like that that officers have.

I don't know whether my sympathy goes out to Bob or Adele. When I see Bob he moans about never getting any letters, and when you tell me about Adele it's always the same with her. Somebody is making a big mistake somewhere. I told Bob to sit down and write a note every single day till he got an answer, which would be in a month at the outside. I think they both want to hear from each other, but neither one will sit down and write unless he or she happens to have received a letter.

New Year's Eve offered the barest break in routine, an evening of frivolity in the midst of war. The next morning, New Year's Day, meant a return to flight instruction, taking advantage of whatever fair weather was available.

Gosport, 1 January 1918

Beloved,

I just finished welcoming in the Noo Year. I wish they'd do it more often. I love Noo Year. I was having a wonderful time with a little tissue paper hat on my head, and somebody had to go and spoil it by setting fire to my hat, and I didn't know until my hair was on fire. Dirty trick. I'm almost bald. But seriously, it wasn't so bad. We had a New Year's party over in the officers' mess. They had those paper surprise packages that go bang when you pull the ends off. The party was real entertaining until they began throwing glasses and bottles at each other. . . .

I got a note from some cousins of mine in Scotland inviting me up there for Christmas.[1] I got it on December 31st. Some mail system! It was mailed on December 15th; sixteen days for a letter to go from Glasgow to Gosport, a distance of not over four hundred miles. I could walk it in half that time.

I never had a better flight than I did today. It was glorious up, and the air made one feel like a perfect, brainless nut. I did things I'd never think of doing on regular days, such as looping within 200 feet of the ground, and climbing into clouds and coming out in a tailspin. I was singing to myself and just having a wonderful time, chasing what we call Huns here, men who are just learning to fly. It sure is sport to sneak up on them and just miss them by a few yards. . . .

An RNAS man arrived today with the worst news yet. It really is getting to be quite a strain on my nerves. It isn't a joke anymore. He has been at Dunkirk and says they have made up an average. One percent of their men get home again. About 85% are killed and the rest lose their nerve. I wish we could get started and have it over with. This lingering death is awful. . . .

By the papers you must be having a darn cold New Year.[2] Fourteen below zero is fair weather for New York. I wonder if you feel the cold there as much as I feel a paltry 32 degrees here in this place. Lord preserve me from a climate like this. It's so cold that I shiver in the morning and never fail to cut my face while shaving. There's no such thing as a heated house in England; you put your faith in a fireplace, I personally have none!

What are the chances of you girls getting a job with the navy soon?[3] I hope you get a good one. I'm not too stuck on the idea of having you shipped off to some godforsaken station all by yourself. Not that you couldn't get along all by yourself, but the class of men entering the Naval Air Service now are by no means like the first bunch. For instance, the [enlisted] men who will complete our flights are good examples. Two came to us in irons; they had been in the brig. Four had diseases. Four were just thugs from the East Side of New York, and the other four were pretty nice boys. They will all be shot down the first time out, of course, but the question is, can we flight commanders get back, or must we be shot down too?

1. *Cousins James and Jane (MacLeish) Yule, who lived in Dunlop, Scotland.*
2. *The winter of 1917–18 was the coldest on record in the century.*
3. *Priscilla, Adele Brown, and Alice Davison all tried to join the navy as wireless operators. Rebuffed, they worked instead as Signal Corps inspectors in New York–area factories.*

Contemporary observers were keenly aware of the rigid class system maintained in Great Britain. These social distinctions carried directly into the military sphere, with the army segregated into "other ranks," non-comissioned officers, line officers, and staff officers sporting red cap bands and lapel tabs. Similar attitudes prevailed in the Royal Navy. Kenneth MacLeish's upper-middle-class background and private school education produced comparable views.

Nowhere was this more evident than in his uncharitable attitude toward the enlisted men chosen to receive flight instruction, the "Hard Guys." These sailors, part of Lieutenant Kenneth Whiting's First Aeronautical Detachment, trained at French schools at Tours and St.-Raphaël. After completing primary instruction, several continued on to the RFC finishing school in Ayr, Scotland. One group was slated for eventual duty at Dunkirk.

Gosport, 3 January 1918

My Beloved,

Today was quite an eventful day for me. To begin with, I went around and got my official time. I had two hours and five minutes dual time and three hours, forty-five minutes solo time. I went out to the aerodrome expecting to fly an Avro. I did. I went up with my instructor and we did some forced landings in little fields by sideslipping into them. Then we did some cross-wind landings, which are fairly hard as you have to be banked way up on one side and land on one wheel and your tail skid. I was simply rotten at the sideslipping. I lost my eye for distance and altitude altogether. I was fairly disappointed and thoroughly discouraged when we landed, and guess my surprise when he said, "Well, you're ready to go up in a Sopwith Camel." I almost fell over backwards. A Camel is quite a step from an Avro because a Camel is the hardest scout to fly. He was either doing his damndest to kill me, or he had an exalted opinion of my flying ability. He gave me a few pointers and I started. He told me that it climbed best at 60 mph. I pulled it up into what I thought was a good climb and looked at my airspeed meter. I received shock number two—I was going 95 mph. I pulled the nose up into what looked worse than a stall before she read 60. Then I looked down at the carburetor adjustment and set it. When I looked up only a moment or two later I was at 3,200 feet. Then I fixed my glove which was flapping around, and when I looked again I was at 6,000 feet. By that time I wouldn't have been the least bit surprised if the machine had started talking to me.

Nothing, I thought, could surprise me after all this. I was ready for anything. I nosed down a bit to what I thought was flying level and throttled my motor a bit. I was thoroughly enjoying life when I noticed I was over Southampton. That's about thirty miles away. I looked at the airspeed indicator and it said 110 mph.

My instructor had told me not to try any tricks under any circumstance, because the machine went into a tailspin so easily and because it spun so fast that very few men can stand more than six revolutions without losing their head. He also told me to use full left rudder in a right-hand turn or the nose would fall and I would spin. I tried a left-hand turn, banking the little bus up vertically, and everything went beautifully. Then I banked up to turn to the right, but she wouldn't turn, so I thought I would start with a little right rudder and then give her full left. Just about the time I made up my mind to push the right rudder I had been around twice. I never went so fast in my life. I was next door to a spin, with my motor full out. That put the wind up, as they say here, in English, or rather American. I was scared pea green. Then I decided to spin the thing if it wanted to spin so much, and just about the time I decided on this momentous action, I realized that I was already in one of those bloody things. Honestly, those Camels will do a thing so darn quickly that you barely have time to decide upon it. How or when I came out of that spin will always be a mystery to me. I'm still a bit woozy. I gave up the idea of tricks and started to come down. It occurred to me it would be a good idea to fool with my motor and get used to it, so I throttled down from 1,200 to 800 revolutions. Then I decided to see how fast I would be going when my motor was turning up to 1,200 again, so I nosed down. When I saw the needle at 1,200 I looked at the airspeed indicator and guess what I saw? The darn thing said 205 mph. I soon stopped that. I made a perfect landing, but couldn't catch my motor again after I landed, and a poor mechanic had to run clear across the field to crank up again. I had two more rides in the bus this afternoon, and each time I got away with it. The last time I was just making a perfect landing, when my wheels hit a ridge when I was still going about 90 mph, and I bounced so high that I thought I would never hit again, but I made a second landing from the bounce which was fair.

Shorty had a close call yesterday. He was looping an Avro, and the strap in the front seat fell over his joy stick, holding it back as far as it would go. The machine came down 2,000 feet, first stalling and then diving. Just as he got near the ground, he thought of sideslipping, he did it, and made a perfectly beautiful landing, only he went through a fence and smashed a wing and his undercarriage. Crock upheld the reputation today. He was sideslipping in a tiny little field and he crashed into six telegraph wires that he hadn't seen and carried away his aileron on one wing. He got down without crashing, however. When I was in that spin I remember leaning my head against the cowling with a sickly grin on it, and thinking that I, at least, would make a good, clean smash-up for the Americans.

One of these Camels would fit into your library in the house at Peacock Point without any difficulty. You can touch the tail planes from the pilot's seat, and the motor is practically in your lap. It's as small as a Baby Nieuport.[1] It's called a Camel because there is a funny hump between the pilot and the propeller which covers the machine guns and makes them streamlined. They are tremendously over-engined, and as a result are so tricky that they're the hardest fighting machine to fly. One trick is characteristic—in a loop, unless you put on full left rudder at the top of the loop, it will do a couple of rolls. It's the same as a spin, only you are going horizontally instead of vertically down.

1. *The small, agile Nieuport 11 "Bébé," powered by an 80-hp LeRhone rotary engine and armed with a single Lewis machine gun mounted on the upper wing, was introduced late in 1915.*

Only nineteen feet long, the Sopwith Camel made extraordinarily quick turns to the right because of the great torque generated by its rotary engine. This same characteristic caused uncounted spins, many with fatal results for inexperienced pilots. Dave Ingalls echoed MacLeish's observations, calling the nimble scout "the trickiest and hardest to fly" and claiming that "the darned little machine spins at a terrible rate." He felt the effects of the wild gyrations for several hours afterward. Nonetheless, the Camel, named for a humped faring that covered its twin machine guns, became the most successful Allied fighter in the war, downing almost thirteen hundred enemy aircraft.

Gosport, 6 January 1918

Beloved,

I heard some of the weirdest tales today. One was about a little French girl who lived behind the lines and kept a pigeon loft for these homing pigeons. One day she saw one coming during a terrific attack. She rushed out and caught the bird, thinking that it had a marvelous bit of news upon which hung the outcome of the attack, and, as she couldn't read English, she rushed over breathless to this British officer. He opened the note, and guess what it said? "Fed up carrying this damned bird!"

Another story. An American who was flying with a French escadrille crashed in an English aerodrome. He got out of the machine and asked a mechanic where the commanding officer was. He was shown to an important-looking, refined Englishman. He walked over and said, "Say, are you the big push in this outfit?" The officer said haughtily that he happened to be the C.O. The American went on unabashed, "Well, I spilled my gasoline kite all over your lawn, and I'd be much obliged if you'd sweep it up."

ﻋﻤ ﻋﻤ ﻋﻤ

After an interval of about six hours I will resume my letter writing, but more seriously, because I've been scared to death and also because I've been frozen to death in the interval. You see, I was flying the Camel and I felt real devilish, so I spun her. Instead of coming out, I held her in. I started to spin at 5,000 feet. At 4,000 I kicked over the rudder, but nothing happened—she kept on spinning. By this time I was pretty well fed up on it because I was so dizzy that I didn't know where I was. I was absolutely all in and pretty well scared. I began to look around and found that my stick was back. I pushed it forward and came out about 800 feet above the aerodrome, so darn dizzy that I couldn't sit up straight. I was weak, but I managed to land somehow. I sat there about five minutes before I could go back up again. I spun her again so I wouldn't lose my nerve and came out all right. Then I went out with my instructor and we went up north about fifty miles to visit another aerodrome. By the time we got back it was dark and cold. I never have been so cold. At 3,000 feet it was nearly zero, and at 10,000 it was 25 below. The other day at 17,000 feet it was 54 degrees below zero. I'm still so darn cold I can hardly sit still long enough to write.

Shorty went up in a Camel this afternoon and got away with it. He hates it just the way I did at first, but he'll swear by it pretty soon, you see if he doesn't. You can't beat them under 10,000 feet. Dave is waiting for the one in his flight to be fixed. He sends his best, and I send more than I can write. Read between the lines.

Though the fledgling naval aviators were eager to fly as often and as long as possible, they also welcomed opportunities to visit London. Good food, warm baths, and diverting company offered a pleasant respite from the dreary dampness of the Channel coast in winter. In mid-January Dave Ingalls and Kenneth MacLeish received three-day passes, which they used to fight what Ingalls called the "Battle of London." Bunking in at the American Officer's Club they dined out, went to the theater, and discussed the military situation with the "many very interesting officers, army and navy, who are always on their way to and from France and America."

London, 12 January 1918

Beloved,

. . . We had another "washout," hence we came to London again. We will be finished down at Gosport in about a week, and then we go to Turnberry, Scotland, for some machine gun work and aerial fighting.[1] We will be there about two weeks, and then we go to Dunkirk. . . .

1. *The RFC gunnery school at Turnberry, Scotland, was located about fifteen miles southwest of Ayr on the Firth of Clyde.*

Among the officers MacLeish encountered in London were Admiral William Sims and Captain Hutch Cone, the chief of naval aviation in Europe. Captain Cone urged the young flyers to complete their training as quickly as possible. Kenneth wasn't sure what that meant, speculating that a trip home as an instructor might be in the offing. Dave Ingalls interpreted Cone's remarks very differently. He predicted that additional naval flight personnel currently undergoing instruction at French schools would soon be finished with their courses. Then both groups would be combined for duty at Dunkirk.

Gosport, 15 January 1918

Beloved,

Captain Cone, father of naval aviation over here, sent word down that we're to hurry up and finish our course. What do you think he's up to? I know nothing about aerial fighting, and I can just about hit the corner of a large barn door. If I went over now, I'd be keeping company with a serious accident. I just wonder, has he given up the idea of Dunkirk, and does he want us to go back to the States to instruct?

. . . It's been doing all sorts of funny things here lately. Day before yesterday they had what they called a blizzard, and we couldn't get any coal, or mail, or papers, or food. All this over four inches of snow. The countryside went wild and they said it was the worst snowstorm in history. It melted the first night it was out. Then it took to raining today. It did that very well for England, it poured by gosh!

Rain and hail have lost their fascination. Snow is quite the thing to fly in. Captain Brearly busted my Camel.[1] He landed it on the framework of a new building. I admit, it was thoughtless to put the building right where he wanted to land, but at the same time, he was cruel to my Camel.

I used my head today and now I own a fine new pair of flying boots. You see Crock, Shorty, and I wanted to get some knee boots, sheepskin-lined, for flying. There were two pairs, both secondhand. Crock won one pair on the size of his foot. Shorty and I couldn't even enter the race. Then it was a go between Shorty and me for the other pair. They fitted us both; Shorty won, but only temporarily, for this is the conversation I cooked up:

(Me) "Where do you suppose they got those secondhand boots?"
(Sh) "I don't know."
(Me) "I guess they must pull them off the poor devils that get killed flying here."
(Sh) "No! Really?"
(Me) "Sure, see how the heel has been crushed. Look inside, see if there's any blood."
(Sh) "Hell, I don't want these boots."

(Me) "Neither do I. Here, I'll take them back."
(Sh) "All right."

Exit K. MacLeish and Boots. Not a bit bad. What do you think?

I almost made a serious break when I was up in London the other day. I went in to see about my life insurance with Crock. The sergeant in the office said, "Oh, you're the man I want to see. You can't make out your insurance to your fiancée." I think I blushed. No, I'm sure I did, and if I remember, Crock howled. I told the sergeant he must have made a mistake, meanwhile looking daggers at him, kicking him in the shins, and shaking a fist concealed from Crock. The sergeant saw his danger and said, "Oh, yes, pardon me, it was Smith," and I got away with it, but that's the truth. . . .

1. *Captain N. Brearly, D.S.O., M.C., enlisted at Liverpool in October 1915, was mentioned in dispatches three times, and transferred to aviation in February 1917.*

Though Priscilla and Kenneth considered themselves "engaged," they had issued no formal announcement. Kenneth was concerned that his parents might object, and the young couple kept their plans secret for several months. The government-sponsored life insurance described above paid the beneficiary $10,000 in 240 equal monthly installments, and cost the subscriber $6.67 per month.

Gosport, 18 January 1918

Beloved,

. . . One letter from you was the funniest thing I've ever read. Where under the sun did you pick up those Christmas verses? The letter came yesterday morning when I was still in bed and I almost passed away laughing. I read the verses to Crock and Shorty and we three lay in bed and roared. Crock, by the way, is sitting here by the fire sucking his gum and inhaling it with such mingled and audible disgusting noises that I can't keep my mind on what I'm saying.

Since last Sunday (five days ago) we've had one fairly good afternoon of flying and not another minute. I'm so fed up on this place I can hardly see, and there's no chance of getting away until I get some more time on Camels. The Camel being completely wrecked, I shall have a pleasant wait. . . .

I wrote Trubee a long dissertation on how to train aviators yesterday. It probably bored him to death. I'd like to do my time over here and then go back to the States and get a school there. No aviator can last more than six months here and be any good, with a few exceptions. They get too cautious and don't take the chances they should, or they lose their nerve entirely. I'm fairly high-strung and I don't expect to last more than three months at the outside. The trouble is, I don't think they'll let me go back to the States. It's too far. They'll let me rest up over here and then send me back to work again. A pilot usually lasts about nine days of actual fighting at Dunkirk, so I may be through in short order. There won't be much fighting till spring, however.

Poor Di! He surely has been treated about as badly as anyone in our bunch. They promised to let him fly scouts at Dunkirk and then reneged because he was too big. But they sent the poor boy up there just the same, and he's been in that hole all winter long. It's a thankless job, and he's been bombed about every half hour almost every night he's been there. It's bound to take the pep out of a man and I don't know how he can stand it. I sure will be glad to see the old boy again.

The winter of 1917–18 was one of the coldest on record, while heating and bathing facilities in England often proved inadequate by American standards. John Farwell, another member of the Yale Unit training in Britain that winter, later recalled that basins of water set out in the bedrooms would be frozen by morning. Though Farwell's lodgings were located in a great manor house, fifteen or more cadets frequently shared one bathroom. MacLeish capitalized on every possible opportunity to secure a warm bath, rhapsodized over the sheer pleasure of it.

Gosport, 19 January 1918

Beloved,

. . . I had my first bath in two weeks tonight. Lovely! I feel so clean! I feel about ten pounds lighter, about eight pounds of that is in the head. The water was almost warm, too, and I lay there luxuriating for an hour.

Shorty got a "book" from his girl. It was handwritten, too, twenty pages in all. He spent all morning reading it, and all afternoon and evening answering it. He says he's glad she only loves him a little bit, because if she wrote him every day, he couldn't spare time for flying.

Dave and I had a battle today, two of them in fact. Not the kind of battle we're going to have someday. No, it was an aerial battle. I was in an Avro (speed 80 mph) and he was in a Camel (speed 110 mph), and he tried to get behind me and keep pointed at the tail of my machine. But by very skillful manipulation of the controls, he couldn't. When he got too close, I shut off the motor, and he would almost run into me. He got mad and wouldn't play, he even started to go down. That was when I won the battle. I opened up and sneaked down on his tail. He didn't know I was still playing, and I stayed behind him all the way down, because he didn't look around. I got down and bragged about how I drove him down and forced him to land. Now do you see any reason why he should get mad and call me a d____ and poor _____ and _____! And he even said _____! I almost lost my temper.

I smashed a machine today. Not very badly though. I only fell about twenty five feet. I was out with my instructor. We were doing forced landings in little fields all around the country. I did pretty well, I guess, because he said I was O.K. and didn't need any more instruction. Then he took to kidding me. We were climbing out of a field over some trees and telegraph wires. Just as we got almost over them he yelled, "Do you like flying, Mac?" I answered at the top of my lungs, "Yea, Bo!" accentuating the "Yea" with a violent push downward on the controls, and the "Bo" with a yank back. On the downbeat we got mixed up with the top of a tree, and on the "Bo" part of it we got more so, with the result that we drove straight down. I pressed my face lightly on the cowl, leaving a dent two or three inches deep in the aluminum, and leaving a crump on my jaw to fit it. We smashed the undercarriage and bent some other stuff that isn't supposed to be bent, such as the propeller. . . .

Given the risks he took, and his delight in pushing both himself and his machines, it is surprising that MacLeish did not suffer more injuries and crashes than he did. Many other cadets, including several of Kenneth's friends, were involved in severe training accidents. The lucky ones lived to talk about it.

Gosport, 24 January 1918

My Beloved,

What do you think? Arch is a second lieutenant in the field artillery. He's so tickled that he doesn't know what to do. Poor Ada, it must worry her, but she's the bravest girl in the world. She told me in a letter that though her cowardly self cropped out now and then, and argued against added risk, she was just as happy most of the time because she had the memories of a perfect year of happiness, and she said she wouldn't trade places with anyone. Very few have a year of perfect happiness in a whole lifetime.

I amused myself yesterday with a new trick I learned. When you pull a Camel into a loop, if you pull the joy stick too fast the machine tends to turn to the right going up and on its back, so that you need full left rudder to keep going straight. Well, I wanted to see what would happen if you pushed right rudder instead. What do you think the fool bus did? It rolled on top of the loop. Talk about a funny situation, that is one. The worst of it was that I practiced it for half an hour, and every time I came out on my back. When I got down I discovered that every single wire in the machine was loose, so it must be a strain, and I won't do it anymore.

There was the densest fog yesterday that I've ever seen and it came over like a shot. I was about 10,000 feet up when I first saw it, over the Isle of Wight, and by diving at about 130 or 140 mph I could just skim over the aerodrome before it settled. Captain Brearly wasn't quite so lucky. He got caught in it at about 2,000 feet. He flew by instrument until he got to 100 feet, then he had the pupil look out over one side while he looked out over the other. The first thing they knew their undercarriage was just grazing a greenhouse and they were entirely surrounded by trees. He zoomed and opened his motor and got away. He flew above the mist and then flew south for a while, hoping to land in the Channel somewhere near shore. When he came down again he found himself directly over the beach, so he landed on the sand and perched there an hour and a half until he could fly home.

Another instructor in our flight crashed into the top of a tree and the machine stuck there. He says he came near being shot as a pheasant by some hunters under him. Another instructor in "A" Flight did a vertical turn ten feet off the ground which saved him from crashing into some wireless masts over at Portsmouth, and then got stuck in the mud. So you see, flying yesterday was what they call "dud." Lord help me if I had been caught in the Camel. An Avro lands at 40 mph, but a Camel doesn't stop under 70 mph unless you're clever with the controls.

I put it all over on Crock today. I've got a new trick that he can't figure out. Whenever we get going in a circle around each other I pull the nose up and take off almost all the bank, and nearly stall the machine, but I keep the rudder hard over. The result is that I can make a much smaller circle, and at the same time climb right away from Crock. I get up aways, level off, and dive on him. I got him cold about six times straight, and he never got near my tail. Another advantage is that if he tries to put his nose up without taking off any bank, he'll spin for sure.

Dave Ingalls described the mock combat in more restrained terms. To his father he wrote, "I had one thirty-five-minute fight with Ken. Somehow or other I unfortunately broke the rudder bar—on which one's feet rest, and also the motor is in bad shape and is being overhauled; my Camel has been laid up since." Ingalls also noted that as training progressed many of the pilots were getting rather "frisky." Everyone, it seemed, wanted "to show off a bit . . . landing very close . . . within about fifty feet of the hangars."

Gosport, 26 January 1918

My Beloved,

. . . We had a great time yesterday. Shorty offered to fly a Scotchman from here to Bournemouth.[1] Of course, Dave and I couldn't let the demi-man slip any cross-country work on us, so we came along. The clouds were only 600 feet up and, all in all, it was the worst day of flying we've had yet. We had a head wind going over, and though our airspeed was 80 mph, our ground speed was only 40 or 50. We flew in formation all the way to Bournemouth. We ran into a very, very low cloud there, and when I came out in the middle of the city only 300 feet up, I decided it was too much of a good thing. Suddenly Shorty pulled back and went up into the clouds. I couldn't exactly see his idea, and I proceeded a little way before I pushed down and headed for the beach in case my motor went out. I lost Crock there too. The mist settled and I had visions of sticking in the top of a tree, the way the instructor did, or running into the masts of a wireless station. The vision nearly became a reality. I just cleared two tall masts. I was down in about 200 feet then, and decided that home was as good a place as any, so I went out over the water again and made tracks which, with a tail wind, gave me a ground speed of about 130 mph.

I got back to the aerodrome without any more trouble, and about half an hour later Crock drifted in. We waited until dark, but Shorty didn't show up. We didn't get any word from him until about eight o'clock, and by then we were pretty well scared. We finally heard that he had a forced landing this side of Bournemouth and wouldn't be home until today. Crock nearly hit two stacks over the city and Shorty landed just for fun. Give me those two Smith brothers for two boys who can get themselves into trouble. I used to think it was hard luck, but now I know it's just a lack of horse sense. . . .

1. *Bournemouth, thirty miles west of Gosport, is situated on the Channel coast at the entrance to Poole Bay.*

While Kenneth MacLeish made his way through the fog back to the aerodrome, wondering what had become of his companions, Dave Ingalls and his mechanic landed in a muddy field near Bournemouth. They attracted a large and curious crowd of men, women, and children who asked if the downed flyers needed an ambulance. Declining assistance, the two aviators and their growing retinue dragged the plane to a small patch of dry ground. Their takeoff was impromptu but effective. "By the time we hit the mud," Ingalls informed his parents, "we were almost flying. There was then an anxious second and we were off, missing surrounding people, trees, and wires equally closely."

Back at Gosport MacLeish and Shorty Smith were preparing to attend a local dance. The "sophisticated" Yale men found the entire affair humorous. Kenneth observed that "the girls don't dance to music . . . they dance according to instructions, three steps, then a hop. After every seven evolutions, they turn. . . . They are still dancing the Grizzly Bear, and for an amusing spectacle give me an English couple performing said dance."

The social affair also gave young MacLeish another chance to stand up for the navy by criticizing the army. "Trust the army to disgrace the uniform and the country," he told Priscilla. One officer got "boisterously drunk . . . made everyone sick by his talk." The army cad maneuvered a girl into a cozy corner "and what happened I can only guess at, but screams issued forth."

Gosport, 28 January 1918

Beloved,

Hello again. How are you since the last time I asked? You ought to be merry and bright because it's Crock's birthday. He's not quite a man and not quite a boy—he's just nineteen. He's got nineteen hairs on his upper lip, too—pathetic spectacle. I have that many on each side, but you can see mine, you have to feel Crock's.

We may fly up to London tomorrow, and then go up to Felixstowe to see the boys. It's about 120 miles in all, and we should make it in a little over an hour in Camels. If I don't get there or back you'll know it's because for the last three nights there have been thirteen at the dinner table. . . .

The fun was quite intense today. I went bush-bouncing, better known as contour-chasing, only I went in a Camel. It's great sport to get going about 120 mph right around five feet above the ground and head straight for a hangar or a tree and stay at five feet until you get the "wind up" and then jump the object. . . .

Dave Ingalls, who also enjoyed this activity, added one note of caution. "It's great fun," he agreed, "unless the motor stops. Then you're 'up the creek.'"

London, 30 January 1918

Beloved,

I'm in an awful mess. I flew up to London yesterday, and landed out at Hendon.[1] It takes about an hour and a half to get into town from there. I came in, had lunch, and got out too late to start back. Of course, this morning there's a London fog so thick you can't see your hand in front of your face, and I can't start back. Nice luck, eh? I think I'll risk it and try to get up through it. It won't be anything but a funeral if my motor goes dud before I get out into the country.

I feel sick as the deuce today. I felt sick yesterday too. I wonder what's the matter with me. Why don't you ask a doc? Good idea, never thought of that. I guess it's this darn foggy air. I missed lunch, tea, etc., and arrived on a meatless day. You can hardly breathe outdoors today. All the street lamps are lit, and it's a circus to watch people bump into each other. Taxis have to be led about by a man with a cane. I can't write any more now, I feel too rotten. I think I'll cut this off and write to you when I get home tonight. . . .

1. *An RFC aerodrome eight miles northwest of London.*

Providing sufficient food and raw materials to fuel the war effort meant that civilians were asked to share the burden. On both sides of the Atlantic, citizens endured a rotating schedule of "meatless," "wheatless," and "heatless" days.

Beloved,

. . . I decided to fly back [to Gosport] in spite of the fog, but when I got off the train at Hendon I changed my mind. It was so thick that when I stood in the middle of the street I couldn't see either curb. I was half an hour going a few blocks because I couldn't tell when I came to a corner unless I was lucky enough to fall down every time I tripped on a curb. I stayed in town last night too, and today I got disgusted and came home on the train. About five miles out of the old hole it was clear, beautiful weather.

I forgot to tell you how it all happened. Shorty Smith and I were going to fly to London for practice, and also to get some checks cashed. Someone had been flying my Camel on its back, so the compass was all out of order. The agreement was that I would lead the way up to Farnborough aerodrome, as I knew the way.[1] When we got over the sheds I was to do some vertical turns, and Shorty was to lead and fly directly northeast, as his compass was good. Well, I found Farnborough, though the clouds were quite thick. Shorty took the lead there and the first thing I knew, he swerved way off his course, and started flying about west. Then he cut his motor and started to glide. I cut mine, thinking he was going to land. We looked around for a field and found one that looked pretty good, until a second view. I saw two rows of telegraph poles across it. The ground mist was very thick and in it I lost Shorty, who had landed in spite of the poles. I had no idea where we were (I forgot to say that I had looped my Camel and the compass worked after the loop, so I had a compass). I didn't know where I was, and worse, I couldn't find the field Shorty landed in, due to the mist. I decided to try and find London anyway, as I was hungry and needed money. So I flew northeast from there. I saw an aerodrome and landed; it was Brooklands Track.[2] They directed me to Hownslowe, and I started off again.[3] I must have gone over it without seeing it, because I flew about ten minutes, which meant about twenty-three or -four miles, with a thirty-mile tail wind. I knew I was wrong, but through the mist and clouds I saw some hangars and I landed to find it was Hendon.

I went to the American Express Company office to cash some checks and while there Shorty paraded in. The poor nut didn't know how to fly by compass. When it swerved over, he followed it, instead of turning away to bring it back. Then he just cut off his motor for fun, there wasn't anything the matter with it. He thought I wanted to land, so he did. He flew back the same night, but I couldn't because when I arrived at the field they hadn't filled my machine up or fixed a broken spark plug wire. Also, I had a sneaky feeling that there would be a[n air] raid and I wanted to see it.

I sent a message down [to Gosport] that I wouldn't try to fly back, but it wasn't delivered. About six o'clock they got word that a machine had crashed into the sea off the Isle of Wight, and were asked if this station were minus a machine. It was, and the machine was mine. Dave, Shorty, and Captain Brearly almost went crazy. They phoned to Hendon and asked when I had left. They were relieved to find I hadn't left. . . .

I had so many baths when I was in London that I'm light in the head again. I had three in two nights and a day. I think one has to be in training for baths to really be able to stand the strain. It's pretty violent, luxuriating for an hour in water that is really warm. . . .

1. *Farnborough aerodrome is situated in Hampshire, northwest of Guildford. Since 1906 it had been the home of the Royal Aircraft Establishment.*
2. *Brooklands, eighteen miles southwest of London in Surrey, was the site of the first automobile racetrack and the first aerodrome in England. An RFC school opened there in 1914.*
3. *Hownslowe aerodrome lay ten miles west of London.*

Like so many soldiers overseas, Kenneth MacLeish was suspicious, and a bit jealous, of those who remained behind. The added pain of leaving loved ones and worrying whether the bonds of affection would survive the strain of lengthy separation heightened his distress. Of particular concern to Kenneth was Harry Davison, a fellow member of the Yale Unit. In a half-serious, half-ironic note MacLeish bemoaned his fate.

Gosport, 1 February 1918

Dearest Old Pal,

. . . Goodbye, Priscilla. I feel you slipping away from me. It's been a hard fight and I played my last card long ago. I hate to see you leaving me flat this way, but that dirty Dude Davison is a most attractive man. I hate that man, but it would be most embarrassing for me to tell him why. Oh, I loathe the thought of him. This staying-at-

Kenneth MacLeish (*extreme right*) soloed for the first time while training at the Yale Unit's private base at Lake Worth, Florida. (*Adele Brown*)

After joining the navy at New London, Connecticut, in March 1917, the entire Yale Unit traveled south to Florida to begin serious training. In this group portrait Kenneth MacLeish appears on the far right in the second row, chatting with one of the navy enlisted men who helped the camp run smoothly. (*Adele Brown*)

Spark plug Lieutenant Eddie McDonnell trained the Yale Unit in Florida and New York. He is seen here in September 1917, wearing the Congressional Medal of Honor he was awarded for his actions at Vera Cruz, Mexico. (*National Archives*)

The Curtiss F-Boat served as a primary navy trainer throughout the war. MacLeish first soloed in an F-Boat in May 1917. With a wingspan of 45 feet and a length of 27 feet, later models of this craft could reach a maximum speed of approximately 70 mph. (*U.S. Navy*)

Chief organizer of the Yale Unit, F. Trubee Davison suffered a near-fatal flying accident in July 1917 that kept him from active service for the remainder of the war. (*Adele Brown*)

A classmate of MacLeish's at both Hotchkiss and Yale, All-American football star Di Gates later went on to command NAS Dunkirk in the summer of 1918. He is shown here the previous year at the Yale Unit's training site in Florida. (*Adele Brown*)

The Curtiss N-9, used as both a primary and an advanced seaplane trainer during World War One, was actually a modified JN-4B, better known as the Jenny. The Yale Unit learned to fly this machine while stationed at Huntington Bay, New York. (*U.S. Navy*)

Curtiss R-6 floatplane

Bob Lovett, seen here in the late summer of 1917, occupied a series of increasingly important posts during his service with naval aviation forces. (*Adele Brown*)

Priscilla Alden Murdock met Kenneth MacLeish while she was a student at Westover School in Connecticut and he was a freshman at Yale. (*Chloe Bowen*)

Shortly after receiving official notification of his promotion to lieutenant, Kenneth had this portrait made in Paris in the summer of 1918. (*Chloe Bowen*)

These three close friends, Priscilla Murdock (*left*), Alice Davison (*center*), and Adele Brown (*right*), each had a boyfriend in the Yale Unit. After the war Alice Davison married Di Gates and Adele Brown married Bob Lovett. (*Chloe Bowen*)

The Murdock home at Peacock Point, Long Island, was situated next door to the Davison estate. Kenneth MacLeish was a frequent visitor there during the summer of 1917. (*Chloe Bowen*)

After a short stint at the aviation training base at Tours, Yalie Bob Lovett reached Moutchic in southern France in September 1917. There he oversaw the fabrication and test flights of the navy's first FBA aircraft. (*Courtesy of the John Callan Collection, Naval Historical Foundation*)

Following his stops in London and Paris, Kenneth MacLeish traveled to the navy's training base at Moutchic where workers raced to erect hangars, shops, barracks, and other facilities. (*Courtesy of the John Callan Collection, Naval Historical Foundation*)

Kenneth MacLeish served at Moutchic in the fall of 1917. There he learned to pilot FBA flying boats. This view of the just-completed barracks was taken about the time of MacLeish's stay there. (*Lawrence Sheely*)

WAR DEPARTMENT No. 9501

BUREAU OF AIRCRAFT PRODUCTION

Pricilla A. Murdock

BUREAU OF AIRCRAFT PRODUCTION, IS AU-
THORIZED TO VISIT FOR THE PURPOSE OF

Official Business

SUCH PLANTS AS MAY BE INDICATED IN
LETTER OF INSTRUCTIONS TO HIM, WHICH
HE WILL BE PREPARED TO SHOW.

BY AUTHORITY OF THE DIRECTOR.

Major, SIGNAL CORPS.

Denied the chance to serve with the navy as a wireless operator, Priscilla Murdock instead worked for the Signal Corps inspecting radio components manufactured at New York–area factories. (*Chloe Bowen*)

With officers' quarters at the base still under construction, MacLeish spent his weeks at Moutchic billeted in a nearby hotel. Kenneth's seaside quarters offered neither bath nor heat. (*Courtesy of the John Callan Collection, Naval Historical Foundation*)

Lieutenant Godfrey DeC. Chevalier, seen here in a postwar photograph, commanded both the Dunkirk air station and the Eastleigh supply base during MacLeish's service there. A pioneer naval aviator, he was killed in a plane crash in November 1922. (*Official U.S. Navy photograph*)

Captain Hutch I. Cone, seen here in a 1912 portrait, commanded the navy's overseas aviation efforts from headquarters in London. He was severely injured in September 1918 when the ship carrying him to Ireland was sunk by an enemy submarine. (*National Archives*)

A notoriously dangerous plane for novices to fly, the Sopwith Camel finished the war as the Allies' most successful fighter. MacLeish loved this aircraft. He flew one on his last patrol. (*U.S. Navy*)

Hanriot-Dupont

The Donnet-Denhaut flying boat acquired from the French served as the workhorse patrol craft at NAS Dunkirk. The navy purchased fifty-eight of these machines, which were capable of top speeds of only 72 mph. (*Courtesy of the John Callan Collection, Naval Historical Foundation*)

During his stint at Dunkirk in April and May 1918 MacLeish flew the Hanriot-Dupont H.D.2 seaplane, an aircraft much favored by the Belgian and Italian forces. This example, much the worse for wear, was photographed at Eastleigh near the end of the war. (*Lawrence Sheely*)

Irving Sheely, from Albany, New York, was a member of the navy's First Aeronautical Detachment, which reached France soon after the outbreak of the war. He served as Kenneth MacLeish's observer during the summer of 1918 and later transferred to Eastleigh at MacLeish's request. (*Lawrence Sheely*)

This aerial view of Pauillac taken late in the war clearly indicates the enormous scope of the navy's aviation campaign. (*Official U.S. Navy Photograph*)

Duty at Clermont-Ferrand in the spring of 1918 entailed learning to master the Breguet Br.14 day bomber, a plane widely used in both the French and American forces. (*Lawrence Sheely*)

When MacLeish returned to Moutchic in the summer of 1918 he found the base much changed from his time there the previous autumn. The bustling flight school produced scores of competent pilots. (*U.S. Navy*)

Kenneth MacLeish spent most of August 1918 stationed at Pauillac in south-ern France, with orders to assemble the D.H. 4 aircraft destined for the Northern Bombing Group. This shot of the assembly and repair shops at Pauillac gives some idea of the quantity of equipment that began pouring into France at the end of the war. (*Official U.S. Navy Photograph*)

MacLeish's duty at Pauillac in August 1918 included a course of instruction in the Marlin machine gun and several trips to the Moutchic firing range. (*Courtesy of the John Callan Collection, Naval Historical Foundation*)

Following his service with Kenneth MacLeish at 218 Squadron, Irving Sheely joined the Northern Bombing Group near Dunkirk. He is seen here (*center*) in the late summer of 1918. (*Lawrence Sheely*)

MacLeish's primary responsibility at Eastleigh involved assembly of D.H. 4 day bombers for service with the Northern Bombing Group just across the English Channel. (*Lawrence Sheely*)

Bob Lovett, seen here inspecting a newly arrived Caproni bomber in the fall of 1918, repeatedly tried to obtain a commanding officer's slot for Kenneth MacLeish with the Northern Bombing Group. His efforts were unsuccessful, and Kenneth returned to the front as a combat pilot instead. (*Adele Brown*)

Enlisted personnel of the Northern Bombing Group quickly set to work digging bombproof dugouts when they took up residence at the Dunkirk-area flying fields. (*Lawrence Sheely*)

MacLeish (*center*) enjoyed his work at Eastleigh but longed to get back into the thick of things. He is shown here just a few days before returning to France in October 1918. (*Lawrence Sheely*)

Throughout the summer of 1918 MacLeish hoped to be assigned to a navy squadron flying D.H. 4 day bombers. Instead, the aircraft went to the marines, much to Kenneth's dismay. (*Official U.S. Navy Photograph, by Zimmer*)

Captain David Hanrahan (*center with mustache*) and officers of the Northern Bombing Group. Operating from bases near Dunkirk, Hanrahan's crews attacked German targets in Belgium in the final months of the war. (*Official U.S. Navy Photograph*)

After downing his fifth enemy aircraft, David "Crock" Ingalls (*left*) was assigned to the navy's base at Eastleigh, taking over Kenneth MacLeish's old job. (*Lawrence Sheely*)

home business, instead of fighting, is fine for one's family, and one's matrimonial ambitions, but it's h____ on the men over here who have loved ones at home. You ought not to tell me when he kisses you, it spoils the rest of the month for me and, if carried too far, may spoil an otherwise promising career. I hate him, and I'm mad, and I won't play war anymore unless I can play when I'm home too. I'm not alone in that view. Ken Smith, Freddy Beach, and an army bloke named Kimball, to say nothing of Al Sturtevant, have had their girls stolen by the little boys who stayed home. I feel I shall have to enlist in their ranks soon. . . .

I didn't think I could get so mad, but I nearly did when I read that letter. I don't mind you kissing him, or vice versa (very much, that is) but what drives me nearly crazy is the fact that he can and I can't.

Gosport, 2 February 1918

Beloved,
. . . I was very much surprised to hear that one of my letters [probably 14 December 1917] had been censored. I wonder what I could have said that could have given aid and comfort to the enemy. I'm as puzzled as you are. I know I might have mentioned the name of the school [Turnberry] we are going to. But that wouldn't take seven lines, and besides, I don't even know where the place is.

The weather here has been nice and obliging. It hasn't stopped raining for two days. We leave tomorrow or the next day, and I guess my Camel will have to stay in town until someone takes pity on it and flies it home . . . .

I think I'm going to be a spiritualist. Keep this under your hat, but did you know that Aunt Mary [Hillard] was a rabid one? When a woman of her education and mental ability takes it seriously, there must be something to it. She isn't inclined to kid herself. She has written me three letters and they are as comforting and wonderful as any letters ever written. I never knew her until I read those letters. . . .

Crock just breezed in singing "I want to be, etc., etc.," Did you ever hear him sing? I can't write any more unless he shuts up, which he won't do, so goodbye until tomorrow.

Continued foul weather prevented MacLeish from recovering his errant airplane. The fog, which halted most operations, also slowed his departure from Gosport. Originally scheduled to last just two or three weeks, Kenneth's stay at the coastal aerodrome stretched to nearly six weeks, and he was itching to move on. Instead, he commuted back and forth to London, waiting for the weather to clear.

London, 3 February 1918

Dearest Mother and Father,

Here I am back in London. I've had a hectic time lately. You see last Monday, or rather Tuesday, I flew from the station [Gosport] up here for lunch. It was good cross-country practice, and I wanted to get paid. . . . That night gave us a London fog for the next morning. . . . I got discouraged and went home by train. Today another boy and I flew up in a two-seater machine, and we could go nowhere else around London except where my machine was [Hendon]. We got about four miles from the ill-fated aerodrome, and at about 200 feet we couldn't follow a canal—the easiest thing in the world, next to a river. We got downhearted and flew home again. Tonight I came back to town on the train, and here I stay until the weather clears from the aerodrome.

Two letters have come from home, but they both were marked "Soldier's Mail," so they went to army headquarters in France, and were two months getting here. I wish you could have seen one envelope. Evidently the army people were fed up trying to find an ensign in the army. They had ensign underlined, and a line drawn with an arrow pointing at the Soldier's Mail, and along the line was scrawled, "What the _____?" So you see, army folk are as touchy about calling me a soldier as I am about being called one. . . .

Finally in early February the orders came through, and within a few days Kenneth was on his way to Scotland, ancestral home of the MacLeish clan. Taking the early-morning train from London, MacLeish, Ingalls, and Smith journeyed northward. As they crossed the border into Scotland young girls at the stations came forward offering cakes and other delicacies. Ingalls found the trip especially interesting. At every stop, he wrote, "we would get out and have the time of our lives listening to any Scotchman we could prevail upon to talk. Their brogue is divine. . . . I certainly have fallen for Scotland; it is a great place."

Turnberry, 7 February 1918

Dearest Pal [Priscilla Murdock],

I'm afraid you've been very much neglected lately, and I'm terribly sorry, but I've been in such a hurry. The last time I wrote you I was between the devil and the deep blue, with a Camel in London and a mad instructor at the station. I was commuting between the two, trying to find a little good weather. I finally got started and the weather, even at first, was questionable. When I got into the hills I realized what I was up against. The clouds were about 400 feet up and hung on the hilltops. I had to cross the hills to get home. It was sport while it lasted, and it lasted too darn long for my comfort. At 50 feet I couldn't see the ground, so I went up. The clouds were about 3,000 feet thick. I finally came out between two layers of clouds. It was very beautiful, and all that, but I hadn't the faintest idea where I was, or where I was going. I flew by a rotten compass, allowing for the wind, which changed directions on the way up. I was very lucky. I figured how long it would take me to fly the fifty miles I had to cover with the wind against me, and I hit it right almost to the mile. I came down through the clouds right on the coast, and only a short way from the aerodrome. Of course, it was all sheer luck. When I got there I found that Shorty and "Restless Reggie" [Ingalls] had already gone back to town [London], so I hopped the next train and joined them.

We left for this place yesterday morning and arrived after a pleasant little thirteen-hour train ride in a cold car. My turn to laugh came yesterday after months of kidding. I had been kidded ever since I can remember because my father is Scotch. I was told that the Scotch race were very selfish and stingy. Well, we went all day without food on the train. At the very first station in Scotland a couple of beautiful girls came up with trays of tea and cakes, and boxes of cigarettes. We were wonderfully taken care of and fed till our eyes bulged, all this for no charge. Shorty and Dave had nothing to say, but I had quite a bit. Later on we discovered that the people in little Glasgow contributed £11 million to the Tank Bank, against £7 million from London, the largest city. . . .

Wonderful news comes from Di's station. The men who were to be in our flights will be held as reserve. The flights will be made up of men recently shifted from the Lafayette Escadrille. Trubee will know who I mean if you tell him George M[osely], Stuffy S[pencer], and

Alan W[inslow], and others more prominent as aviators. They're a wonderful crowd and it's a compliment to our crowd that they joined us and not the army.

There's work to be done here. I can see where my end of the correspondence weakens for the next twelve days. We start in at about eight-thirty, get ten minutes off for a smoke at ten-thirty, quit at noon, lunch at half past, start again at one-thirty, get a few minutes off at three, and finally stop at four or four-thirty. But that isn't all. Then the work begins! We're given pamphlets (they're really libraries) to copy notes from. One gets to bed just in time to get up for breakfast. But not a second is wasted. It's all wonderful "dope," that we all must know, and it's taught in the quickest, most efficient way. There isn't a great deal of flying, and what there is is done in heavy, slow machines[1] for the most part, though I understand there are scouts here too. The course is over in two weeks at the outside, and twelve days is an average. From here we go to another station near here [Ayr] for aerial fighting and formation flying. That course is about the same length. Then we leave merry, rainy England and join Di.

1. *Possibly Royal Aircraft Factory B.E.2e machines or Sopwith 1½ Strutter two-place biplanes.*

The three Yalies boarded in an old hotel that made Dave Ingalls "homesick for Palm Beach." He admired the "beautiful golf links by the sea, with beautiful hills rolling away inland. A really heavenly place, evidently once a famous golfing resort." Another difference from their previous station at Gosport was the relative absence of experienced flyers. Instead, according to Ingalls, "there were only young, inexperienced cadets, slews of them, as this is practically a nonflying course." Rather than stunting across the sky, trainees spent their days "sitting on hard wooden benches in sorts of classrooms, studying twice as hard as I ever did in school."

Turnberry, 10 February 1918

My Beloved,

By working all last night I am now able to write a letter to you, but I'm so tired I fear it will be uninteresting, and it may be bluish too, because I haven't had any mail from since about the first. I guess your ship sank too. By the way, I saw several survivors of the *Tuscania* a day or so ago.[1] They were torpedoed a few miles from here on the night we arrived. From their stories, I think I prefer aviation in any sector to ocean cruising which includes torpedoing.

Who do you think came here yesterday? The twelve "Roughnecks" [enlisted men] who are going to be in our flights later on. Can you beat that? I never really appreciated what an American Roughneck can be, and I have every opportunity to so do now. If I had my way, I'd line them all up in front of a machine gun, kiss 'em goodbye, and let drive.

There are certain drills all men are required to go through here. Of course, the drills are slightly different from those in the army or navy, but they're not hard to learn. The formation of "fours" or squads is quite different. These boobs were in line when the order came to "form fours." They got all mixed up, and one of them in his typical way slouched off and audibly informed the community that he'd _____ if he'd do any fool drills for anybody. We three were so mad we were trembling, but we couldn't leave our ranks or yell at them, and the officer in charge was a prince of a man, and he let it by without comment. We three were going to ask that they make the twelve men drill. Also, they all have on "Sam Brown[e]" belts,[2] which are strictly non-reg in the navy, and they all say most emphatically that they'll wear what they _____ _____ please, and won't take any orders from anybody. Oh, what those men have coming to them. And thank goodness four of them are going to get it from me. I never took delight in reprimanding men before now, but if I have my way, I'll have them court-martialed and, if I possibly can, have a couple of them shot!

This station happens to be within sight of a place we [the MacLeish family] all spent the summer years ago.[3] I remember I was just a little kid and it was always my ambition to climb this particularly high mountain [Goat Fell]. I couldn't persuade Mother to let me because it was supposed to be dangerous. I finally let Satan go too far and I ran off on my own, with the summit as my objective; I made it, but I don't know how, and as I was thinking how wonderful it was to be so high above everyone a cloud came along and enveloped the whole thing. At first I was carried off my feet with ecstasy, to think that I was in the clouds. But soon the problem of getting down again, when I couldn't see a yard ahead of me, became all-absorbing. I nearly fell all the way down the mountain, but got home with most of my clothes on, bodily intact, for which I was most humbly grateful, which led to sobbing repentance and confession, and you know the rest, it always follows confession when you're young, no matter how sincere, and it always hurts! Now it gives me a weird sort of feeling to think of flying thousands of feet over the top of the very same mountain which I thought was so high.

This course should keep us buried in work, and then we'll move on, about the 20th, to another course in aerial fighting and formation flying which should take our attention until the end of the month. We will probably do our first actual fighting almost exactly one year after we began training.

1. The troopship Tuscania *was torpedoed on 5 February 1918 off the coast of Scotland, and forty-four lives were lost.*

2. A wide leather belt worn at the waist around an officer's long tunic, with an additional strap worn across the chest and over the right shoulder.

3. The entire family visited Scotland in 1910 to attend the World Missionary Conference in Edinburgh. The twenty-eight-hundred-foot Goat Fell is on the Isle of Arran.

The operation and maintenance of machine guns proved to be the real heart of the Turnberry course. Dave Ingalls found the guns "darn hard to shoot, not like playing a hose, and the gears which synchronize the propeller and bullets, and the sights for a deflection, etc., are pretty complicated." The Yale men had never attended a formal ground school and had missed much of the preliminary work. Instead, they crammed as much as they could, and then readied themselves for competitions on the firing range and, finally, shooting at different targets from the air.

Turnberry, 12 February 1918

Dearest Family,

. . . I have gotten in touch with Cousin Jane [MacLeish Yule] and will be able to visit them in a day or so when I move from here up to the School of Aerial Fighting [Ayr], which is only fifteen or twenty miles from them and well known to you. When pronounced it sounds like something that we need all the time that we're alive (air!), and it's southeast of Cousin Jane's, if that helps you any. I'm at a station now which is on the coast, still further southeast. It's a tiny little town consisting mostly of a hotel, which is quite large and comfortable, with a wonderful golf course in front of it.

I have been very fortunate so far in this flying game. I've never lost a real friend in it, until yesterday. A man in the army training here [Fred Stillman] collided in the air with another machine, and they both came down in flames.[1] I knew this boy well at Yale. He was a class ahead of me, but he was on both the water polo and the track teams the years I was, and I got to know him very well indeed. . . .

1. *Stillman, from Brookline, Massachusetts, joined the Army Air Service and was killed in a training accident at St. Albans, England.*

When not working or writing letters home, the Yale fliers passed the time speaking with the tremendous assortment of men passing through the school. Besides U.S. Army and Navy personnel, there were Englishmen, Irishmen, Canadians, and South Africans, even a few Australians. One diversion that elicited nothing but scorn from young Dave Ingalls was billiards. "Of course they play a rotten game on a big table which they call billiards. I think it was invented some thousand years ago and compares to real billiards as a bow and arrow does to a machine gun." If not billiards, then a game of bridge might also wile away the hours. "If one asked me what England's national game was," Ingalls reflected, "I'd say bridge. They play all the darned time, but as far as I can see it's not with the result that practice makes perfect."

If weather permitted, an excursion to a nearby village might unfold. On one such trip Shorty Smith obtained a box of matches, at that time worth their weight in gold. After supper everyone in the mess pulled out a cigarette and turned to Shorty for a light. Extracting one match from the box, he accidentally ignited the entire supply. Dave Ingalls noted, "There was really quite a universal sorrow. I'm surprised that no monument has been erected."

Turnberry, 13 February 1918

Beloved,

Today being the 13th, of course I had to have something happen, and it came in the form of the worst news I've ever gotten. Two of my closest friends have been killed flying. Also two more men that I knew very well. Stuffy Spencer was one of my best friends. He lived in Highland Park. He was going to transfer from the Lafayette Escadrille to our naval aviation last week, and the day before he was to officially transfer, he was killed near Paris. Also, a New York boy whom I knew very well at Hotchkiss and Yale, Lyman Cunningham, was killed here in England at the RFC school. Another Yale man named Fred Stillman, in Archie's class, was killed or nearly killed a few days ago. He collided in the air with another machine and they fell, locked together and both on fire. Fred, I think, will die. The other man was killed.[1]

I understand that we have to go back to _____ when we're through in England. That dear old wart on the face of creation. Lord, how I hate that hole. It seems that we have to get in some formation flying, and that's the best place to do it. Isn't that rotten news?

These new cadets have been telling us what wonderful pilots they are and telling us how to fly. They've never looped, or spun, or done vertical turns, but they're marvelous pilots! One said, "My Nieuport clumb (notice spelling, also pronunciation) better than any other bus I seen. It climbed (pronounced with 'i' short, as in limb) best than the lot. . . ."

I told you, did I not, that the naval attaché at Rome ["Rollie" Riggs], the man I crossed with, has written to headquarters and asked that I be transferred to duty in Italy? Now do you suppose he meant to be nice when he did that? Who wants to go to Italy, where coal is $146/ton, and where sugar, butter, milk, and eggs are kept in safes and handed on as heirlooms? No, no Italy for me if I can help it. This Europe place is a snare and a delusion. I heard all about "sunny France" when I was a boy, but I never saw the sun shine once in France, and I was there a month. I heard about merry England, but though it has it all over France, I've heard no bells or music as yet. I also heard about warm, sunny Italy, but not this time, boys. No, twice is enough. But it's a piece of coal to a doughnut that I end up there. By George, Old Rollie will have to quit being attaché and show me the sights—he got me into it, he'll either have to get me out, or make me comfortable. . . .

1. *Dumaresq "Stuffy" Spencer, a member of the Lafayette Flying Corps, was killed in action near Belfort on 22 January 1918. Lyman Cunningham joined the RFC in Canada, sailed for England in October 1917, and died on 13 January 1918 in a training accident on Salisbury Plain.*

As far as most American servicemen were concerned, the Italian front ranked rather low in the overall scheme of things. Those members of the Yale Unit who served at Italian bases had little positive to say. Kenneth MacLeish was not alone in his aversion to duty in the Mediterranean, despite the undeniable appeal of warm weather and good food. Even in adversity, however, an anonymous Yalie was moved to poetry, composing a little serenade describing one particular Italian aircraft, the Caproni bomber. Titled "O, Mia Nosediva," it went something like this:

> Aviatore he fly th' Caproni;
> Maldito! Machina is phony!
>   He go up for a hop,
>   Por Baccho! She flop!
> An' il bimbo he break da boni.
>
> Pilota say In God We Trusta,
> Because this damn thing she go busta!
>   Milan and La Roma?
>   There's no place like homa!
> Aviatore feel sad an' he cussed–a!

Turnberry, 16 February 1918

Beloved,

With a couple of good days we should be finished here at this gunnery school, and then we'll go to the School of Aerial Fighting near here for a course of not over ten days, and then we'll go back to France. . . .

We went to a town near here this afternoon and found a shop where we could buy some real chocolate. It surely tasted good. On the way to the train I saw a postcard that reminded me of Adele and Bob and I tried to get it to send it to Adele so she could send it to Bob. It read, "If silence is golden, you must be solid gold. . . ."

I heard that Hobey Baker got his first Hun the other day, and that Vernon Castle[1] was killed. Vernon excluded, I've lost four friends through accidents in the last two weeks. . . .

1. *An Englishman who, along with his wife, Irene, attained great fame in the United States as a ballroom exhibition dancer, Vernon Castle (1887–1918) joined the RFC in 1917, downed two enemy aircraft in France, and was then posted to Talieferro Field, Texas, as a flight instructor. He was killed in January 1918 in a midair collision with a cadet pilot.*

Turnberry, 16 February 1918

Dear Bruce [MacLeish],

I haven't much time at present, so this note won't be long, and I'll condense it as much as possible. First of all, without any condensation or abbreviation, let me thank you from the bottom of my heart for the Fatimas. You couldn't have pleased me more by declaring peace. If you knew how good a real cigarette tastes, you could appreciate my joy upon receiving same. Thanks a thousand times. The article by [Grover] Loening was fine.[1] You should see the bus he had reference to. I was just like a rube on my first trip to the city when I saw one. I got the roof of my mouth sunburned looking up at it. You have to change your ideas of proportions when you dabble in aeronautics these days.

I've made up my mind about one thing. I'll have an airplane at home after this war if I have to build it myself. The type I have in mind is the greatest bus for playing around in that I've ever seen. It's called an Avro, built by the A. V. Roe Co. It is used exclusively as a training machine, and I have yet to see its equal. It's the only machine that I know of that will do exactly what you want it to. It goes 80 mph, which is slow, but plenty fast for pleasure. I've seen a good pilot land it in a field so small that there wasn't enough room to put another machine in the same field. He did it by sideslipping. These buses loop, roll, spin, cartwheel, sideslip, stall, and climb as well as any bus with 100 hp I've ever seen, barring scouts, of course. It's a two-place machine and I'll bet I can teach you to fly one in five hours. It's as safe as a church. I saw a man plunge straight down from 400 feet and though he smashed the bus to bits, he only cut his hip a little. . . .

1. *Loening was a pioneer aircraft designer, especially of seaplanes. He developed the tiny M-2 "Kitten" for use aboard ship.*

Turnberry, 17 February 1918

Beloved,

. . . The more I think about going to Italy, the better I like it. And then again, when I take everything into consideration, it really doesn't make much difference. This flying game is all luck, and you have to be a fatalist to have any peace of mind. If I'm going to get crocked, that's that, and there's nothing under the sun to stop it, but the other side is more cheerful—if I'm not, well, there you are, right where you started. So it really doesn't make a particle of difference where I am. Only this, if I do get crocked, I want to get it while I'm really fighting, and not in a simple crash way off in the wilds of Italy.

I'm glad now that I'm having a rest from flying. Just before I came here, I'd forgotten what caution was. But since I've been up in this part of the world, I've had time to think it over, and to profit by the deaths of friends of mine. One needs a letup now and then to give him time to sort of cogitate. It doesn't detract from his flying, he does the same things, but he does them carefully, without putting too much strain on the machine. . . .

The frequent crashes and deaths at RFC flight schools were legendary. The British training system pushed men ahead at a rapid pace, and large numbers of accidents inevitably resulted. At Ayr many cadets first encountered machines they would fly at the front, Sopwith Camels and SE-5s. Princeton's Elliot White Springs recorded a long list of victims in Scotland, all in Camels, and all doing right-hand spins. Even planes as sturdy as the Royal Aircraft Factory's S.E.5 were vulnerable. On one ill-fated day George Vaughn, a native of Brooklyn, and later an ace in both the RAF and the U.S. Air Service, was circling Ayr at low altitude when his engine cut out. He sliced through a maze of phone wires, knocked the chimney pots off a farm house, and crashed into an orchard, losing his wings, tail, and landing gear in the process. Only the cockpit where Vaughn sat remained intact.

Ayr, 20 February 1918

Beloved,

I've just moved over here to this School of Aerial Fighting, and I'm waiting now until I'm assigned to a flight. I find that in the past four flying days there have been twenty-three crashes, and that I'll be very lucky if I get a chance to fly. If they keep this up they'll have the factories working day and night. . . .

I told you, I believe, that the enlisted men who are to make up our flights came to Turnberry while we were there. They certainly are impossible for the most part. There are two nice boys, but the rest are hopeless. They won't obey orders and they don't have any guts at all. Whenever I see a yellow man I have a wild desire to sail into him with both hands and feet. The only trouble is that I would be arrested if I did, in this case. One thing is certain, those men who will be in my flight will obey my orders, if I accidentally have to shoot them down with my own guns. It has happened many a time before and for the same reason. I know of two men who were shot down in flames by their own flight commanders.

Three Americans were killed in one day, and one the day before that at various aerodromes. This week I never saw such a discontented crowd as these army cadets. They came over in June [1917], after going through a six-week course in ground school in the U.S. They were sent to ground school here for eight weeks, covering the same work. Then they were tossed about from pillar to post, never paid, and discouraged at every turn. None have been commissioned yet, and only a few can even fly alone. They were promised [commissions as] first lieutenants, and now they can't get them. They were told they could get an honorable discharge, but they find that they can't. No crowd has ever been treated the way these men have. They came over full of enthusiasm and loyalty, but now they've lost it all. They received commissions as second lieutenants, but they won't take them, and I don't blame them much, because I've even seen some specimens of the first lieutenant variety strolling along the streets of London and Paris, and well—I don't blame them. What are they doing in the States anyhow? Are they just seeing who looks best or worst in first lieutenant or captain's uniforms and sending them over here? They used to do that in the navy, but they soon stopped it. . . .

I heard today that Di [at Dunkirk] took two men for a joyride. They didn't see another machine all the time, but when they got back, their machine was full of bullet holes. Pretty darn lucky, weren't they? . . .

Those "army cadets" whom Kenneth met were part of a larger group of more than 450 trainees and officers dispatched from the United States to Britain for flight instruction in the summer and fall of 1917. The first group of fifty-three reached Liverpool in early September, followed by several hundred more in October, November, and December. After ground school at Oxford, they moved on to preliminary flight training at Uphaven Flying Center on Salisbury Plain. From there it was on to Turnberry and Ayr and, for many, service with an RAF squadron in France.

Much of the early frustration experienced by the high-spirited cadets resulted from the United States' inability to dispatch trainees quickly in the spring and early summer of 1917 when places were available at British flight schools. By the time Americans began arriving in England later that fall, the RFC had embarked on a program to increase its front-line forces from 200 to 240 squadrons, and training facilities were stretched to the maximum. Hence a shortage of places and a surplus of discontent. Their ranks ultimately produced a score of aces, including George Vaughn, Field Kindley, Elliot White Springs, Reed Landis, Lloyd Hamilton, Laurence Callahan, and Frederick Luff.

Ayr, 22 February 1918

Beloved,

. . . Since the first of February there have been two full days of good weather. One whole day at Gosport and two half days at Turnberry. You ought to see my little diary; it starts out rain on every page almost from the first of January. I'm getting wet feet.

A letter came from Bob today. He is in the Paris office now as an aide to the chief of naval aviation [Captain Hutch I. Cone]. The chief has gone on a tour of inspection, and Bob is in entire charge of the whole business. Bob is working like a dog to get us promoted, and to get us some land machines, and to kick out this bunch of enlisted men. He says he can't do all three before the captain gets back, but he's on his way in all of them. That boy has a better head and more ability than any two men in this branch of the service, and I'm glad they're beginning to appreciate the fact. He'll be in Paris a couple of months and then go and take over his station.

The man we're rooming with was at Gosport with us. He's a sketch. He can find something funny in a funeral. He was telling us about his solo in a "Rumpty."[1] He came over the 'drome after flying around and saw six Rumpties, all crashed. When he came back, instead of finding more room, he saw another wreck. He decided he better get down before they put any more in, so he picked out a corner of the field which looked like a billiard table from where he was, only it had grass about six feet high. When he got down to what he thought was about five feet he closed his eyes and waited. As a matter of fact, it was nearer a hundred feet, and to his dismay, he became number eight on the list of crashes. He got out to view the mess, and a man ran up and said, "You'd better stop your engine." He looked over and saw it was still going. He told us this tale last night in a slow, drawling way, and we laughed until we almost cried. He's a Canadian; 82% of the RFC are colonials, and 50% are Canadians.

There are some American army mechanics being trained here.[2] You'd laugh yourself sick if you could be away from American slang as long as I have, and then hear this crowd. It was very windy the other day, and a pilot asked one of the mechanics to hold onto his wing tip while he taxied out onto the field. He taxied out like a fool, so fast, I mean! The poor mechanic was trailing through the air, absolutely all in. When they finally got out far enough, the mechanic stumbled over to the pilot, and when he could get his breath enough, spoke as follows: "Say, Boss, if you want a marathon runner, get Tom Long-boot, the Indian. I came over here to see the big fight, not work out on cross-country. If I want to join the harriers, I'll join see?" You can't appreciate this unless you are used to seeing English mechanics. They're always polite, say Sir, etc., and never fresh.

Another bit of slang amused me—a new pilot was practicing landings. Whenever he landed he forgot to open his throttle again and consequently the motor would stop, with the result that the mechanic had to run out and crank him up every time he landed. The C.O. got fed up on this and sent an American mech out to tell him to stop losing his motor all the time and only fly around the 'drome without landing if he couldn't help losing it. These were almost the exact words of the C.O., but this is how the message reached the pilot. "Hey, Boss, the chief wants you to cut the rough stuff and stay up if youse can't come down like a regular pilot." It does my heart good to hear them. . . .

1. *The Maurice Farman "Shorthorn" trainer, also known as the Rumpty, was a pusher-type aircraft barely capable of 60 mph.*

2. *Probably mechanics from the American 25th Aerosquadron, who were learning to service British aircraft while also relieving RAF personnel for duty with front-line units.*

Ayr, 22 February 1918

Dearest Family,

Time never passed so slowly as it does these days. Every hour seems to be a week long. I've only been here [Scotland] twelve days, yet it seems like I've been here twice as long as at my last station, and I was there about six weeks. There isn't a thing to do here when there's no flying.

I busied myself with a comprehensive report on the last station [Gosport]. From what I can see, the whole thing started this way. The English were in a hurry to get their pilots into action. Some evidently got away before they were fully trained. The result was a criticism from the very brilliant squadron commander in France. He was invited to return to England and employ his own methods of instruction. He returned as a captain, established his own school, became a lieutenant colonel, and is now a brigadier general in charge of the Southern Training Division. When he returned he found that the whole trouble was not with the material, but with the instructors. It was found that practically all the instructors were either home on rest, or were waiting their turn to be sent overseas. Under such conditions it is no wonder that the instructors took no interest in their jobs. How could they, when their hearts were elsewhere.

In my report, which will go first to headquarters and then to Washington, I made three suggestions which I always felt were much needed. First: All seaplane pilots should be trained on land machines first, because instruction on land machines is more efficient in respect to time, upkeep, expense, feel of the air and machine. Second: I suggested that the greatest care be exercised in choosing instructors, as everything seems to show that the pupil reflects the instructor's character in flying. Instructors should be chosen with the following points in mind—men who have a keen interest in their jobs, men who have the ability to impart knowledge easily and who have a great deal of patience, men who are good pilots themselves and who are daring enough to awe their pupils. Third: I suggested that the English method of training mechanics be employed. In an English aerodrome a man starts as an unskilled laborer. If he shows any aptitude in caring for motors or planes, he is promoted to either rigger or fitter. A distinct line is drawn between men who take care of the planes (riggers) and men who take care of the engines (fitters). Their duties do not in any way overlap. If a man shows himself very able and reliable, he is made a corporal, or perhaps a flight sergeant. I hope these suggestions are read and not torn up, because I've seen the need for such changes. I'm ashamed of the way I instructed at Norfolk, but my mind wasn't on the job. . . .

In fact, Kenneth's report was submitted to Bob Lovett and Captain Cone in Paris and then forwarded to Washington. From a postwar perspective Lovett recalled, "Ken's greatest contribution to the service was his outline of training for single-seaters in gunnery and acrobatics. I am convinced that a layman, reading Ken's description of the proper way to loop, would find no great difficulty in doing so."

Ayr, 23 February 1918

My Beloved,

There's been no flying here for eight days on account of this beautiful Scotch weather, but I'm in hopes that we'll have a good day before the war is over. . . .

I had a delightful afternoon the other day. I went to see a dentist because a filling had come out of one of my teeth. He found a nerve and then drilled on it until I was blue in the face. He was trying to scrape part of the old filling out, and his pick slipped in his fingers and broke the tooth in two, so that I'm minus a perfectly good tooth now. I was so weak I couldn't get out of the chair, and I felt cold all over. Is that how one feels when one is about to faint? After about an hour more drilling he told me I was through, and I heartily corroborated his statement.

I got some wonderful news today. Curt [Read], Bart [Read], George [Mosely], and Charlie [Fuller] are going to be our bombers [at Dunkirk]. They're real men, every one of them, and that gang of enlisted men will last about five minutes when we get together. The C.O. [Chevalier] of Di's station won't stand for them. I think that we three, the Lafayette bunch, and some others will do the convoying. I certainly hope so. I'd rather do three men's work than have that bunch to relieve me, and I think we all feel the same way about it. . . .

Well, the game is started. I've always felt sort of worried until now, but after this I'm mad, I want to fight. I don't care what kind of machine I'll fly or who flies with me, I'm out for blood. I suppose you've heard all about Al Sturtevant. I haven't any particulars, but the general idea is that ten or twelve Hun single-seater pontoon scouts lay for that bunch down there [Felixstowe] every day. They tackled Al and another machine. Al was shot down in flames, but the other machine got back. The Hun's name was Christianson. He's one of their star pilots. He shot down an RNAS ace in a "Baby" Nieuport last year. He may be a crack and all that, but he's got twenty-eight more of us to deal with before Huntington is through with him. We're all sore now that there's going to be hell to pay. I don't miss Al the same way I miss those four others. They were all wonderful friends, but Al and I were more. We worked together, we were planning to fight together. Al's death is an inspiration to me. . . .

Al Sturtevant had been stationed at Felixstowe since early December 1917, and by February he was flying convoy and antisubmarine patrols over the North Sea. On the morning of 15 February Sturtevant, along with Flight Lieutenant Purdy and two other crewmen, set off aboard an H–12 flying boat to escort a convoy of merchant ships headed for neutral Holland. Attacked by an enemy patrol of single-seat scouts led by Freihar Kapitän Christianson, the awkward flying boat attempted to escape by heading toward the European mainland, but it went down in flames somewhere near Ostend. Christianson, a prewar officer in the merchant marine, survived the conflict with twenty-one victories. During World War Two he served as military governor of Holland.

Ayr, 24 February

Beloved,

 . . . I'm so sorry, I feel so foolish, Budge, but just pardon me for today. I simply don't dare be serious! I never knew what a dear friend Al was, until he was killed. His death was the biggest shock I have ever had, and I guess it opened my eyes in more ways than one. I lay awake last night thinking about it. It must have been a frightful death! I dread being shot down in flames more than anything else in this world! It's too awful! As I was thinking, I was suddenly impressed with the fact that Al wasn't exactly gone. I realized that he is still the same dear old pal, that he still holds the same warm spot in my heart. And then I began to wonder. I wondered if, after all, my ideas of the great realities of life weren't a bit twisted. I thought that the greatest things in life were the visible, tangible realities, but I came to the conclusion last night that I must be wrong. The best things about Al, the friendship, the influence, and all that, are still realities to me—but they're unseen. I must be wrong, the truly great realities must be the unseen realities. . . .

Though death at distant stations and apprehension about the days to come intruded on the scene at Ayr, the daily routine proceeded uninterrupted. Whenever possible aviators hiked to nearby villages or grabbed a train to Glasgow where they could take in a variety show, attend the movies, and spend the night in a real hotel. Of course, even such simple pleasures exacted a certain price, in this case catching the 5 A.M. return train to Ayr.

At the field the round of mishaps continued. Dave Ingalls described one such accident in a letter to his father. "One poor nut started off with his motor missing badly. He kept on, however, and did a circle about the field, refusing to land while he had the chance." Just as the cadet swooped overhead, his engine quit completely and he crashed right on top of a hangar, embedding the "bow" in the roof. Ingalls further related how the unabashed flyer then posed for photographs.

Whatever the conditions or circumstances at the aerodrome, the young aviators had one common concern—mail, especially the shortage and irregularity of it.

                                        Ayr, 27 February 1918
Beloved,

    . . . The weekly packet came in today with American mail for
Shorty and Crock and myself, but there wasn't any from you. That
means I won't have another chance until next Wednesday, March
5th. . . .

    Our roommate was called overseas tonight. He's going over on a
new bus no one knows about.[1] It was tried out in France and brought
back again somewhat altered. It will be interesting to find out how
they get along. This boy is Canadian and a fine pilot, but the best pilots
always get "crocked" first. . . .

    1. *Possibly an early version of the Sopwith 7F.1 Snipe, designed to replace the Camel.*
Production began in early 1918, and the first combat aircraft went to France in March.

With each passing day, the course in aerial fighting drew toward
completion. Ayr was normally the last stop before heading to a front-
line aerodrome, and several of Kenneth's friends and companions were
posted to squadrons in France in preparation for the expected German
push. A further reminder of the dangers that lurked just beyond the end
of training, if one were needed, was a letter MacLeish received belatedly
on 28 February from his Yale friend Al Sturtevant, who had been killed
two weeks earlier. It seemed a voice from beyond the grave.

                                        Ayr, 1 March 1918
Beloved,

    . . . I got the most awful shock yesterday that I ever received. I
found a letter from Al in my box. I didn't dare open it because I was
afraid it was written before he was killed. It was written February 14th
and wasn't mailed. Someone posted it when they were looking
through his belongings. It made me awfully sad, of course.

                        [eight lines censored]

    Al wrote on Thursday and was killed the following Saturday. Here
are some excerpts from his letter that give me queer feelings about the
throat:

    "John [Vorys] and I are on the war flight now and have made
several patrols. With luck we ought to do some damage to Old Man
Hun if we stay here long enough. . . . I got my first leave this

Saturday [day he was killed] and will be in town all day Monday and Tuesday. How about a small soiree in London about that time? You ought to be just about getting through and on your way to France by then. In any case, let me know a few days ahead of time when you are going to be passing through town, and if possible, I'll get forty-eight hours' leave and come up to see you off. . . . Well, if I don't see you in London, old man, take care of yourself at the station. If the papers are any judge, there is certainly going to be hell to pay in France and Belgium very soon, and you will come in for the worst of it. Don't get yourself 'crocked' if you can help it, because a wooden kimono would not be becoming to your style of beauty. Yours, Al.". . .

Kenneth MacLeish tended to be outspoken when it came to issues close to his heart: slackers at home, "Hard Guys," army men, marines, Frenchwomen. Sometimes his opinionated and caustic remarks ran afoul of prescribed military guidelines, and he often seemed to be marching just ahead of the censor. On more than one occasion letters were returned and notations entered in his personal file.

Ayr, 3 March 1918

Beloved,

I'm sore. I just finished writing you a two-page letter, and now it's in the fireplace. I got scared because there's an army man here who knows my chief in London who says that the letter I wrote Trubee has been returned to H.Q.—I'm on the black list—and if I break any more censor's rules I'll be sent to the concentration camp in France. You see, I told you all about how one of our men (one of the "Hard Guys") crashed today, and got badly hurt, but I've got a vertical draft now, and I don't dare. From now on I'm scared to say anything at all. I had no idea the censorship was so strict, but I guess it's absolutely necessary. Anyway, if I'm on the black list, I must be pretty close to the edge by now. I've written all kinds of stuff that this chap says is hard on the censor's eyes. Tell Trubee I'll have the report sent through by the navy. . . .

Ayr, 4 March 1918

Beloved,

I certainly had an exciting time today. I'll use my jurisprudence about telling you, and see if you can make any sense of it. A big bunch of machines were attacked by another big bunch. I was in the bunch trying to break through a defense, and we had the best old sham fight you've ever seen. I hope never to be mixed up with so many machines again. They were on top, below, in front, behind, and on either side of us. The air was just black. We were convoying and our group got through without being attacked. I got into four separate fights, one with the colonel [Rees] here. He has a Victoria Cross with a bar and a Military Cross. Of course, he put it all over me after we got started, but when we began the first picture I took of him with my camera gun was a dead hit, and I got four more of him later. I almost got into a scrap with what was evidently a novice, because he spun almost all the way to the ground. Maybe he meant to. We had two more hedge-hopping patrols. On one of these Shorty was behind and above me. The next thing I knew I saw a gray streak to my right, felt an awful crash, and I was in a sideslip. He had run into me about 1,000 feet up in the air. Talk about a sensation. He smashed one of my top planes, and put one control on the fritz, and I smashed one of his tail controls, but we both got down without much trouble. He's as blind as a bat!

The "Hard Guys" were on a couple of patrols with us, don't ask me anything about them, because you're apt to get a rude reply. We three have decided that we can't see flying with them anymore. That's all I dare tell you about it, however, as I don't want to be "concentrated." I guess I'll have to go back to a full diary, as such days as this one are so intensely interesting that it seems a shame not to be able to tell you about it. . . .

After a month in close contact with the "Hard Guys," MacLeish was barely rational on the subject. At this point in his career he simply could not appreciate their contributions, or understand the obstacles they encountered. He also failed to acknowledge that they had been among the first naval personnel to reach Europe in June 1917.

Glasgow, 8 March 1918

My Beloved,

Crock, Shorty, and I came up here to wait until the "Hard Guys" finish their course. It's too depressing to stay there, as they kill off too many men to suit me.[1] We should be leaving England within the next week. Wait till we show up at our station with this troop. If there's not a war then, I don't know as there ever has been one. Don't you think it was a sort of dirty trick on us [the First Yale Unit] to split us up this way and then, in order to bring up the numbers, to shoot in material like the "Hard Guys" instead of our own men again?

I went up to visit my Scotch cousins for two days and had a perfectly wonderful rest. I was pretty tired when I got there, all of which leads me up to a very funny thing. I hope you won't be angry, because I can promise you that it ended and will go no further. My cousins went walking, and I sat by the fire and daydreamed. I finally fell asleep, holding your picture in my hands. When they came in and woke me up an explanation was necessary. They have promised not to tell anyone (about our engagement) and they also went simply mad about the picture. They made me s-w-e-a-r that I would bring you up to see them someday. They plied me with questions of every conceivable nature, and, as the ice was already broken, I was not in any way loath to volunteer information. . . .

Talk about the irony of fate. Admiral Sims is pretty "bucked" about infringement on the censorship rules, and he sent an order to the "senior officer present" to establish a system of censoring mail written by men in the USNAF. Who do you think the S.O.P. is? Why, it's your devoted servant, yours truly, sincerely, and as ever. Now that I have the job I don't know what to do with it, and it can't be much, due to my own position in the mess. . . .

1. *Several of the "Hard Guys" were killed at Ayr, including Harry G. Velie on 8 March 1918 and Frederick Hough on 13 March 1918, both Chicago natives.*

Kenneth's visit with his Scottish cousins offered a rare, tranquil interlude in his busy training regimen. With the course nearly finished, all thoughts turned expectantly toward the return trip to London and then across the Channel to Dunkirk.

Ayr, 10 March 1918

Beloved,

Everything seems to point towards our leaving tomorrow. There won't be twelve "Hard Guys" with us, however. One crashed and broke both his legs, the other killed himself, so there will be only ten. Both of them spun in from about 1,000 feet.

A whole bunch of army men arrived the other day when I was away. Most of them come from Chicago. One is engaged to a girl I knew very well who lives in Kennilworth. He [Reed Landis] is the son of the well-known Judge [Kenesaw Mountain] Landis of the federal court.[1] The kid knows his father is a great man, I wish you could hear him talk.

One of the Chicago delegation was killed the other day. He graduated from Sheff [Yale's Sheffield Scientific School] about George Catlin's time. He was a pretty good athlete, too. If you see George ask him if he knew Andy Ortmeyer.[2] I think that Ortmeyer used to race automobiles, though I'm not sure. . . .

1. *From Ottawa, Illinois, Landis trained with the British, served with the RAF where he downed nine aircraft and an observation balloon, and finished the war commanding the U.S. 25th Aerosquadron.*

2. *A 1906 Yale graduate, Andrew Carl Ortmeyer trained in Tennessee and Illinois, served as an instructor at British schools, including Turnberry and Ayr, and died in a March 1918 training accident.*

Ayr, 10 March 1918

Dearest Family,

. . . I think we shall leave here tomorrow and go to Paris via London. I don't know whether they will keep us in the latter city or not. I think some changes of plan are to be expected soon, as two of our men are out of the game. One broke both legs and the other was killed.

I understand that [General John] Pershing has cut off aviators' extra pay because flying is not more dangerous than other branches of the service. It's probably quite safe if one knows how to fly, but unfortunately not all of us know how to fly. I don't quite understand why they take the average casualties from the list of the entire personnel, including mechanics and clerks. There is about one pilot for every six or eight mechanics and clerks. I should think if they wanted to know the average casualties to aviators they would take all pilots, instead of averaging every Tom, Dick, and Harry in the army.

I heard a wild fairy tale the other day that the Huntington bunch was the next in line to be promoted. That means that yours devotedly will wear a bit more gold and be inclined to look askance at the general public, but not be a bit better off for all that. I'll let you know if I get a boost. Goodbye for the present. I'm going to see the Bobby Burns cottage.

Rumors concerning promotion were notoriously hard to verify, but this one turned out to be true. Though MacLeish failed to receive confirmation for many weeks, he and most other members of the First Yale Unit were promoted to lieutenant (jg) on 23 March 1918.

London, 12 March 1918

Best Beloved,

. . . We leave to join Di on Thursday. This being Tuesday, I think the future looks very bright now. My prophecy that plans would be changed is nearly a reality.

I'm pretty blue. John V[orys] appeared on the scene today, on his way back to the States. What the? Who the? Why the? How? Some people have luck thrust upon them. He says he's going to cut us all out and marry you, Adele, Alice, and Betty—all of you. And why do you suppose? He's sore because he can't stay over here. John, what have you done with your mind?

More rotten news. Curt Read was killed at Di's station [Dunkirk]. He crashed into the seawall. Really, Budge, I try not to let this sort of thing affect me, but it's not natural. I'm very fond of my real friends, and I guess I take Curt's and Al's and Stuffy's deaths a bit too badly, but I simply can't be coldhearted enough to make it otherwise. . . .

London, 13 March 1918

Beloved,

My cold is slightly better today, after a hot bath, etc., etc., which included almost everything the chemists have for sale. . . .

It seems almost sacrilegious to try to be cheerful today, with Curt "Gone West" and Al only a short time ago. But I guess it's best to look at the finer side of it. They gave their lives in the noblest effort possible to maintain the ideals that they so splendidly stood for.

I get my last written orders tomorrow morning until it's all over "over there." May the next bunch of written orders, when translated into our language, reveal the following: The States, a marriage, and forever Priscilla and a wonderful life. . . .

With its large community of Americans, and the tremendous number of transient army and navy officers, London provided many opportunities for socializing and catching up with old friends. During his brief stopover in the English capital before crossing to France, Kenneth "crashed" a dinner for American fraternity men, where he was able to decipher a lot of the "secret stuff."

London, 14 March 1918

Beloved,

I finally persuaded "Restless Reggie" [Ingalls] to stay over in London another day, so we won't leave until tomorrow afternoon. I have my orders, however, and we are practically on our way. I have made out my will, etc., and am ready for what may come my way. I'll still maintain that plans will probably change, and that our job will be far from bad. I doubt very much whether the "Hard Guys" will ever be with us because I got a letter from Di saying that their fate is entirely in my hands, as I am the senior officer present. I think that for the following two reasons I will queer them. First of all, men whom they will convoy are the dearest friends I have, and I'd rather die a thousand times than see anything happen to them. In the second place, the "Hard Guys" can't fly, and it would be suicide to send them out.

So you wonder what the new dope about Bob is? I swear, I can't see the point about being so childishly mysterious. There's no mystery about it. It may be either of two things. First, he might have meant that he is going to be the "first aide" to the commander of naval aviation, he is that already and a darn fine one. Secondly, he might have meant that he was going on active fighting patrols with RNAS. He has already done that too. That is, he has been on some night bombing trips. A third possibility is that he may get charge of a fighting station. He probably will, but when I saw him last, he wasn't too bucked about it. So that's the big dope that is very mysterious. . . .

Bob Lovett, the chief aide to Captain Hutch Cone, spent the winter shuttling between Paris headquarters and Allied bombing squadrons, inspecting aircraft and operations. During his time in Paris he roomed with Eddie McDonnell, sharing a little apartment in the Latin Quarter, "among the long-haired men and short-haired women." In early March he traveled to an RFC field near Dunkirk. About this turn of events he informed Adele Brown, "I am off on a great stunt. The only fly in the ointment is the fact that I cannot share it with you." A few days later he announced that he had just returned from the front but was anxious to get back for a "big stunt" expected shortly.

While Lovett prepared for action in Flanders, MacLeish crossed over to Paris en route to Dunkirk. He had been preparing for this moment since March 1917. He fully realized that the average career of a combat pilot lasted only a few weeks. In a letter to an unidentified friend,

Kenneth used a few of his last quiet hours to contemplate the future and the meaning of the crusade he had embarked upon.

Paris, 19 March 1918

Henry, you old wonder!

I just received your letter telling of Stuffy's death and telling me to be careful. Of course, I'll be careful, Henry, but you all at home must realize this! We all feel it so strongly, and it's such a consolation that it seems a pity you can't share it. We are all men with more or less red blood, and thank God we have ideals which are really worthwhile.

. . . To me the finest miracle in life is to be able in the last few moments on this earth to revolutionize one's entire existence, to forget a life of failure and weakness, and to die a hero. The Gates of Honor are opened to us, those lucky ones of us who are over here. . . . You know, Henry, these aren't normal times. If Stuffy had died before the war, I should have grieved, but we are at war—circumstances are topsy-turvy—I'm not sorry. I'm proud as I can be that Stuffy was once a dear friend of mine. I'm proud to have known him. You can't be proud of a man and sorry for him at the same time; therefore, be proud of him. That's my philosophy and it works too.

I'm going to the front tomorrow. I don't think anything will happen to me. If it should be my lot to make the supreme sacrifice, you'll know that I did it gladly, and that I bought life's most marvelous reward, Honor, at a dirt-cheap price. . . .

Just before departing Paris in late March, Kenneth enjoyed a brief reunion with Mr. Henry Davison, the J. P. Morgan partner and virtual godfather of the First Yale Unit. As head of the American Red Cross, he was touring facilities in Europe. Both MacLeish and David Ingalls used this opportunity to catch up on the news from home. Davison's appointments that day also included lunch with General Pershing at Chaumont, American Expeditionary Forces headquarters.

Paris, 20 March 1918

Beloved,

What a full day. For the first time since I left England I have had enough to eat, and I had enough, more than enough, twice today.

Who did I see? Why, Mr. [Henry P.] Davison, of course. He was here this noon on the way to the front. He will be back here next Tuesday, and if Di comes back, I think I'll come with him. (We will "come back" from our station.) I trust you know where that is; if you don't, ask Mr. Davison when you see him.

Wally Winter was brought down, and Tommy Hitchcock, after getting three Huns in six weeks, is now a prisoner. He was shot down out of control, but made an easy spiral and a good landing, so he can't be hurt much. . . .[1]

1. *Wallace C. Winter was shot down behind German lines on 8 March 1918. Thomas Hitchcock was reported missing, then captured, a few days later. Both were serving with French escadrilles at the time.*

Finally the time had come for the American aviators to leave Paris and head for the front. Tension within the Allied camp was palpable, for signs of a massive German buildup were everywhere. On the evening of 19 March General Sir Hubert Gough, commander of the British Fifth Army defending the Somme sector, predicted, "I expect a bombardment will begin tomorrow night, last six to eight hours, and then will come the German infantry on Thursday [March] 21st." His prediction was correct almost to the hour.

3

"Old Loegenboom and Mournful Mary":
On Active Duty at NAS Dunkirk

March 1918–May 1918

Accompanied by Ensigns Dave Ingalls and Shorty Smith, Kenneth MacLeish reached the Dunkirk naval air station after a lengthy train ride. That very same day Major General Erich Ludendorff unleashed his powerful spring offensive, the "Kaiserschlact," against British forces in Flanders. Before dawn on 21 March the long-awaited blow fell along the old Somme front between Arras and Laon. Utilizing the "Hutier" tactics that had proved so successful in Russia and Italy, intensively trained divisions of shock troops, aided by a short, sharp artillery and gas barrage, overran Allied strongpoints and broke into open country. As in 1914, floods of refugees crowded the roads.

Within two weeks the Germans seized Bapaume, Noyon, and Montdidier, advancing as much as forty miles along a seventy-mile front. Amiens was threatened. General Sir Hubert Gough's British Fifth Army was all but destroyed in the process and every available replacement, including service troops and cavalry, was thrown into the gap. With only a confused picture of events transpiring to the south, the newly arrived Americans were uneasy. As Dave Ingalls informed his father in late March, "The German advance and British retreat is greatly disturbing everyone. . . . We know very little of what is going on. I wish I could look a week ahead or so." By early April, however, stubborn resistance, logistical difficulties, and heavy casualties brought the German assault to a halt.

Barely a week later Ludendorff tried again, hurling his forces against the British First (Horne) and Second (Plumer) armies along the Lys

River, less than thirty miles from the American station at Dunkirk. Again the Germans scored impressive initial successes, Armentières fell, and fears were raised that the Channel ports and installations might have to be abandoned. General Douglas Haig, the British commander in chief, was forced to issue his famous "backs to the wall" order, forbidding further retreat.

Desperate resistance again slowed the German advance, though a surprise attack south of Ypres on 25 April seized the heights of Mont Kemmel, a key defensive point in the Allied line. Fierce counterattacks by French and British infantry, aided by air units, failed to dislodge the enemy troops. Elsewhere, however, Germany's strength in Flanders was spent, and Ludendorff halted this phase of the offensive on 30 April. Sustaining 350,000 casualties, British forces had been badly battered and forced to abandon much hard-won ground, but they had not broken.

Allied aerodromes along the Channel coast were among the most active and exposed during the battles of March and April, and the American seaplane base at Dunkirk was no exception. Located just a half hour's flying time from enemy submarine pens and naval installations at Bruges, Ostend, and Zeebrugge, and perched astride the Flanders battlefields, the Dunkirk facilities were subjected to nightly bombing raids and heavy shelling from across the lines. Many of the buildings that had survived earlier attacks now succumbed to the hammer blows of artillery and aerial bombardment. Even the German navy got into the act, sending out destroyers on nighttime raids to shell the Allied-held coast.

Despite the uproar, MacLeish and his companions were thrilled to be at the front. The ride to the seaplane base nestled among acres of wrecked buildings was awe-inspiring. Accommodations, however, were surprisingly good, an "old French mansion," Ingalls called it, with excellent food, a piano, plenty of stoves to keep warm, even a phonograph (but no decent records). Better still was the chance to be reunited with old friends like Di Gates, Bob Lovett, and Eddie McDonnell. Gates had reached Dunkirk back in November 1917 and in the intervening period served as chief pilot, with responsibility for assembling, testing, arming, and repairing aircraft, and commanding the men in the flight division. With relatively few pilots available and plenty of foul weather, actual patrol activities were limited. Instead the former Yale football star played tag with incoming shells. In February he was supplanted as chief pilot by Lieutenant William Haviland, a veteran of the Lafayette Flying Corps. Gates was demoted to assistant chief pilot and intelligence officer, taking on the new duties of tracking enemy submarines, collecting data, and planning patrols.

Bob Lovett's time in Dunkirk was spent in rather more dramatic fashion. After a stint at the Felixstowe seaplane base in December 1917, he took bombing and gunnery courses at British schools, and then passed several weeks with the RNAS Intelligence Department. From there he returned to Paris in January, where he was appointed assistant to the chief of naval aviation in Europe, Captain Hutch I. Cone. All this time Lovett labored over a plan to eliminate the German submarine threat, not by random open-water patrolling but through round-the-clock bombing of enemy bases and facilities at Bruges, Ostend, and Zeebrugge along the Belgian coast. To investigate the feasibility of establishing American naval bombardment units and examine various types of operational equipment, Lovett was dispatched to Dunkirk in early March just before the German assault. He was assigned to RNAS #7 at nearby Coudekerque, then equipped with Handley Page bombers. Almost immediately he went out on raids, including a spectacular nighttime assault against Bruges on 23 March that he called "the greatest experience in my life." Lovett was thrilled and frightened by the searchlights, which "stabbed and darted at us," and the "perfect barrage of anti-aircraft fire and flaming onions we had to go through as we ran the gauntlet to Bruges." From an altitude of 5,000 feet he watched the effect of several tons of bombs, observing how the "earth seemed to split." Other raids, equally perilous, followed into mid-April.

A third member of the Yale "crew" already gathered at Dunkirk was Lieutenant Eddie McDonnell, their navy instructor from Palm Beach and Huntington Bay. He accompanied Lovett to Dunkirk and also participated in numerous sorties against enemy targets. He made his first Handley Page raid on 20 March, and several more thereafter. He also visited other British aerodromes in the vicinity, watching operations, inspecting equipment, and interviewing officers with an eye toward eventually establishing American bases in the area. After submitting his report to Captain Cone, he returned to the United States in late April with orders to expedite the shipment of men and matériel for the proposed bombing campaign.

At first Kenneth was unable to join his comrades in attacks against the enemy. There simply weren't enough aircraft to go around. Instead, he spent his first few days at the navy seaplane station as base ordnance officer, inventorying supplies of weapons and equipment on hand. Eve-

nings were spent dodging artillery fire from "Loegenboom," a heavy
German gun positioned nearby, and trying to catch a few minutes' sleep
uninterrupted by the warning sirens ("Mournful Marys") that seemed to
wail all night long. Everyone was affected by the shelling. Bob Lovett,
for one, experienced "a rather strange feeling to be writing [to Adele
Brown] while we are being shelled by a 15-inch gun." Dave Ingalls
objected to continuously rushing from a warm couch out into the cold
night air and back into a hot and stuffy dugout.

As the scope of Germany's spring offensive against Allied forces
broadened, England mobilized every available aviation unit to cover her
retreating troops, obtain crucial intelligence, and attack enemy concen-
trations. Casualties mounted alarmingly, and U.S. Navy pilots were
soon drawn into the struggle. Lieutenant Godfrey Chevalier, the C.O. at
Dunkirk, offered his men to the beleaguered British forces stationed at
nearby Bergues aerodrome, an offer immediately accepted. By the end of
March MacLeish, Ingalls, Shorty Smith, and several others were assigned to RNAS #13 (soon to be renumbered RAF #213) flying Sopwith Camels. Di Gates accompanied them to the same aerodrome with
RNAS #17 (217) flying D.H. 4 day bombers. After a year of training, the
young aviators from Yale were about to begin their combat careers.

The American flyers found their new comrades an admirable and
congenial lot. Di Gates reported that "we all have temporary jobs with
British squadrons and are enjoying it immensely." Bob Lovett called
them the "bravest lot" he had ever seen, and Kenneth MacLeish enthusiastically concurred. The English flyers, including the many Canadians
and Irishmen who filled the squadrons, were also partial to youthful
pranks, and evening raids on neighboring messes were as common in the
RAF as in the U.S. Navy. But despite the hijinks, the pilots' work was
deadly serious. Within days Kenneth and his companions were out on
war patrols in one of the hottest sectors on the front, not always with
auspicious results. A near-attack on a friendly airplane marred Ensign
MacLeish's first patrol on 2 April. A few days later an early-morning
flight at high altitude left him with painfully frozen fingers. On 11 April
he joined in an attack on Zeebrugge, attracting heavy anti-aircraft fire,
and vowing never again "to be the last machine in a daylight, low
bombing stunt." Throughout the month that followed enemy artillery
maintained its incessant barrage, while Gotha bombers continued the
aerial assault. With a mixture of pride and relief a man like Lovett could

explain at the end of his stint with British forces, "I have at last been through it. I feel a different man altogether."

On 19 April the Americans returned to their station at Dunkirk to resume antisubmarine patrols. MacLeish, for one, was not pleased to be leaving the British. As Di Gates observed in a letter home to Trubee Davison, "Ken, Dave, and Shorty are going to be ordered back [to Dunkirk] very shortly. They will certainly hate like poison to go back, and I don't blame them one bit." To compound his woes, no sooner had MacLeish been assigned a new single-seater pontoon scout than a midnight bombing raid severely damaged it, further delaying his return to combat. Instead, the impatient officer spent the time conducting more ordnance inventories and overhauling machine guns. One evening another German bombing raid rocked him out of bed, destroying the building beside his bivouac.

By 1 May Ensign MacLeish was back on seaplane patrol, scouting for enemy submarines and searching for downed aircraft. Neither mission offered the risks and thrills of sorties behind enemy lines. When C.O. Chevalier asked for volunteers to fly day bombers, part of the burgeoning effort to develop the Northern Bombing Group strategy, MacLeish jumped at the chance. Several others went with him, including Ingalls, who admitted, "I'm feeling good now, as a lot of us are leaving for further training on land machines. Two-seaters, rumor has it, but after these flying canal boats, anything with wheels makes me feel like Ken does when he gets a letter from Priscilla." Chief pilot Gates was less excited about the imminent departure of several of his most experienced pilots, lamenting, "Ken, Dave, and some more of our good pilots are busy packing to leave us." Gates was sure that with "the amount of training they already have, they certainly do not need any more."

Di Gates's objections notwithstanding, two weeks later MacLeish was called back to headquarters in Paris and posted to the army's day bombardment school at Clermont-Ferrand. Stationed more than two hundred miles south of Paris, he was temporarily far from the fighting, but still very close to the war.

Dunkirk, 22 March 1918

Beloved,

Well, I'm here, and it's a gaaraand and galorious place. I saw Archie [MacLeish] day before yesterday, and I went into Paris and got dizzy

with him. He did it. The war has corrupted him. He talks to gen-
darmes and smiles at conductors. Oh, he's awful!

Di is very well. He is the officer here who deals with information.
He's the most flagrant example of unintelligence I've ever seen. He
goes growling around—sees nothing, hears nothing, knows nothing.
But everybody is happy. Di is just so sick of bombs and "Busy
Berthas"[1] that he has lost some of his old, true interest in life.

We got bombed last night, not badly, but enough to make it
interesting. Bob [Lovett] was here for dinner. He and Mr. [Eddie]
McD[onnell] are over at the RNAS station near here. Bob and I went
out and watched the barrages go up.[2] It was very pretty. The night
before some Hun destroyers shot up the town a bit, aided by a
bombing raid. Today I had my first ride on these buses.[3] They're
good, too, and I had a scrap with a Frenchman in a land scout, and
though he put it all over me, I'm not too discouraged.

While I was up I looked toward the sky and right above me was a
Hun photographer taking pictures of the town. Then the Archie[4]
began to burst—Wowee! By the law of gravity, what goes up must
come down, and I happened to be just where it was coming down, and
not so very far away from where it was going up that I was over-
comfortable, so with not much presence of mind, and no deliberation,
I came down fast. I only got here a short time ago, most of the others
have been here for months, and I have the unique distinction of having
been closer to a Hun than anyone else—I was too close. Of course, he
was above me, but not enough. . . .

1. *Heavy German artillery aimed at Dunkirk; named after Krupp's famed "Big
Bertha" super-heavy siege gun used to batter Liège forts in 1914.*

2. *Wall of shells, flares, and machine gun fire directed against enemy aircraft.*

3. *Hanriot-Dupont H.D.2 pontoon scouts; more commonly used by Belgian and Italian
forces.*

4. *Anti-aircraft fire.*

The Allied complex of bases and facilities clustered around Dunkirk
played a vital part in the war against Germany's submarine and zeppelin
threats. During the winter of 1917–18 C.O. Chevalier, with the assistance of chief pilot Di Gates and many others, labored to make the naval
air station at Dunkirk operational. They struggled to procure, assemble,
and maintain equipment, erect buildings, organize patrols, and dig
bombproof quarters. The Americans were greatly hampered by short-

ages of men and supplies, horrid weather, and continual bombardment from German ground, air, and naval forces. Not until late winter was flying conducted on a regular basis, while seaplane patrols were delayed further still.

Dunkirk, 23 March 1918

Beloved,

Fast and furiously it comes. Tonight the dirt bums are using the big boomer, not much damage, but oh what a noise!

I had another ride in these buses today which was less eventful, thank goodness. I'm getting lots of confidence in them now, which helps.

We play baseball with an indoor baseball down on the beach. It's lots of fun as the whole town turns out and roots for each side. They are the most genuinely neutral baseball fans I've ever seen. They cheer every time the ball is hit, every time it isn't hit, every time it's caught, and every time it isn't caught. When anyone falls down we have to stop playing until the audience stops the riot. They think it's wonderful. Our little game was a fizzle this afternoon because almost every inning the sirens would blow as a signal that one of the big shells had been fired. Then, in a minute and a half—well, then the game went on.

Mr. McD. and Bob came over to see us this afternoon, but didn't stay very long. Old Eddie says that night bombing is all right for "them as likes it," but that he prefers going walking down home on Sunday afternoons.

I am ordnance officer here at the station. Do you know what that is? I don't. I have charge of guns, ammunition, bombs, sights, and a million other things that I know very little about, but it's fascinating work and I'll catch on sooner or later. I don't like playing with this high-explosive stuff, but you may be sure that I handle with care. I almost died today carrying eight bomb detonators in my hands, in a springless truck, over the world's worst road. Every squeal of the springs seemed to say "goodbye, Kenney."

Mr. Davison and Bob seem to think that Adele [Brown] and Alice [Davison] are coming over this spring. I hope not, I really am serious. I admire their spirit, of course, and yours too, but they don't know what they're getting into. It's not bad if one hurries through on a visit, but not for a long stretch. Bob and Di talked it over, and here's our conclusion. One soon, very naturally, begins to countenance things which they would never, never countenance at home. They absorb the very contagious attitude over here of "I don't care" nature. They lose a certain sweetness and naturalness that, once lost, can never be recovered. We, who must come over, have already become this way, more or less, even against our wills. . . .

There is only one room here where we can write, and it's already noisy, so I can't concentrate. It's hard to do that anyway with the Huns overhead. I haven't been given a machine of my own yet, but hope to have one in a few days' time. Then things will commence to look even brighter. Lord, what a relief it is to actually get to the front, or near it, after so many months of training and waiting. We don't live near the station, thank the Lord, as the station is very much on the map as far as the Huns are concerned. Each one of those big shells weighs 1,900 pounds, nearly a ton, the gun is a 15-inch, and the shells are nearly five feet high. Give me a bombing raid any day. . . .

Following their rebuff by the navy several members of the Girls' Wireless Unit discussed the possibility of traveling to Europe instead, perhaps to serve with the Red Cross or a similar organization. Evelyn Preston, a close friend of Adele Brown's already stationed in Paris, strongly encouraged such a move. In the end, however, the would-be radio operators remained at home for the duration of the war and secured alternative employment from the U.S. Army Signal Corps in the New York area as "Inspectors of Airplanes and Airplane Engines, Signal Service at Large."

Dunkirk, 24 March 1918

Dearest Family,

. . .We get bombed every night, but that isn't bad. The worst thing is that big gun up the line. . . . Last night they shelled us from five-thirty until five this morning, every forty-three minutes, with one lapse around midnight. That really is a bit hard on one's nerves because when the shell explodes it nearly shakes one out of bed. All the shells landed within a half mile of the house, but none were very close, as we are either out of range or very hard to reach.

. . . Those bums! They're at it again tonight with their big gun. I just heard the siren, but didn't think it was that. I thought it was just another bombing raid. I've changed my mind because just now I nearly bounced out of my chair. Well, cheer up, nothing more for forty-three minutes. The siren just blew four times. That means a land bombardment. It will blow once now every time they see a flash in the sky, which signifies the departure of a shell some twenty miles away.

A wild rumor says they shelled Paris from the lines—that's nearly sixty miles. That's too much for me; twenty is quite enough to overwork my imagination, but the Boches have perhaps been rude enough to disregard my imagination. I have no machine yet, so I won't go on patrols for a little while. But this ordnance job will keep me busy for some time to come. . . .

Historians of World War One have frequently noted that a front-line soldier's primary duty was to sit in the trenches and patiently endure the incessant shelling. The same held true for aviators and enlisted personnel at Dunkirk, which was well within reach of the enemy's long-range artillery. During Ludendorff's spring offensive the pace of shelling intensified. The Germans also utilized specially modified naval guns to bombard Paris. Fired at tremendous elevation, these guns were able to reach the French capital from distances of sixty to seventy-five miles.

Dunkirk, 25 March 1918

Beloved,

A wonderful letter from you, dated March 2d and addressed straight to me, arrived this morning. You mentioned facts which must be in letters prior to March 2d but which I haven't received yet. You see, we're practically cut off from Paris now because of this Hun offensive, so I don't think I'll get any mail until things get settled. The Huns may be making a tremendous push, but it is terribly expensive, and they can't possibly hold it all very long, to my mind. The dirty bums shelled us again last night, too. That makes only one night in the last four that I've had more than one hour's sleep. And all day long I have to work like a dog in my new job.

We read with horror in today's paper that Frank L[ynch] was probably fatally injured.[1] Poor old Higgy. I knew him well. He was a marvelous end, and one of the finest men that ever lived. Finny Cooper also died of pneumonia in New Jersey.[2] He was, without exception, the nicest fellow and had the sweetest disposition in the world.

I'm so dead tired, beloved, that I simply cannot be interesting. This new Boche drive is sort of on my nerves, too. This news from

Bapaume is pretty tough, isn't it? Thank the Lord there's a high wind tonight. We'll need some sleep around here. . . .

1. Yale Unit member Frank Lynch was seriously injured at a training field in Texas and spent a week in the hospital. He recovered fully and served in Europe later that year.
2. James Fenimore Cooper, Jr. (Yale '13), a member of a field artillery unit, died of pneumonia while training at Fort Dix, New Jersey.

Initial German successes along the old Somme front between Arras and La Fère were rapid and dramatic. The Allies evacuated Péronne, Ham, and Chauny on 24 March. Bapaume and Nesle fell the following day.

Dunkirk, 26 March 1918

Beloved,
Nothing much of interest to report today, skipper. The Huns are still shelling us. This makes the fifth day and night. I didn't know there were so many shells in the world, or so many guns, or so much noise, or so many days. I know what they're trying to hit, too, but I can't tell you. If they ever do, you'll read about it in the papers.

I've been working three days on the ordnance report. I finally finished today, much to everyone's delight, as I worried them all to death with foolish questions and dirty jobs. The man that had this job before me is now in England, and it's just as well for him. Lord, what a mess here!

It's the most gorgeous night I've ever seen. The English are evidently bombing the daylights out of the Huns because you can see the Hun star shells and flaming onions [anti-aircraft fire] bursting over the lines. The moon is fuller, and brighter, and more wonderful than I have ever seen it before. I wonder if it will look down on you tonight and give you some of the messages I told it to give you. . . .

Dunkirk, 27 March 1918

Beloved,
Now what do you think has happened? I wrote a letter in which I happened to mention the name of the machine I was flying, and it was sent to H.Q. with a request that immediate action be taken. To begin with, the machine I mentioned has, on two occasions that I know of, been shown in the mooovies. Huns have been seen flying these machines. But when I mentioned the name of it, giving no dope on its

performance, instead of taking a pen and scratching out that hateful, horrible word, the whole letter was sent to H.Q. Words absolutely fail me. I certainly would like to lay my hands on some of these birds with soft office jobs who are trying to make life more like————for those who do the fighting. Why, great green frogs in the bulrushes. The Huns know more about the machines than I ever thought of knowing. I wouldn't be surprised if a Hun gave it the name I so vulgarly mentioned. . . .

It's off! George [Mosely] and Bob held a council of war and decided that if I didn't shave it off, they'd pull it off. They're all jealous because it's a beauty. Of course, I didn't shave it off because I was scared of them, no. You asked me to, and I was just waiting for a suitable opportunity.

George just came by. We may all transfer to the English if the need is pressing. Eddie McD. went home after one awful raid. . . .

In fact, Lieutenant McDonnell, already a Congressional Medal of Honor winner for his exploits in Mexico in 1914, participated in several raids aboard both Handley Page and D.H. 9 bombers. Some of his exploits were hair-raising. On the evening of 20 March 1918 he served as rear gunner on a Handley Page. When one of the bombs refused to separate from its rack as the plane lumbered over the target, McDonnell shoved it loose by hand. Three days later in a daylight attack against the Bruges docks his plane encountered severe anti-aircraft fire and was also attacked by a flock of enemy fighters. On the evening of 26 March he participated in still another nighttime raid, this one against the heavily defended German railroad junction at Valenciennes.

Dunkirk, 28 March 1918

My Beloved,

Things are perking up wonderfully. At last I'm going to get some action, and it will be on machines I flew in England [Camels] with the same people [Ingalls, Smith]. All plans are therefore changed. If I weren't so scared of these bloody censors, I'd tell you who Crock, Shorty, and I are going to fly with, but I can't. Di will probably let the Davisons know, or else Dave will.

This is the most wonderful thing that ever happened to me, as the people I came to fly with are the best in the world, and the machines are absolutely A-1. I will be way down the line where things are

happening these days, right in the middle of the greatest battle the
world has ever known. Won't that be worth—doubly worth—all the
weary months I spent waiting for my chance. . . .

Kenneth MacLeish's new comrades at 13 Squadron, RNAS, formed
one of the most illustrious aviation units on the western front. Among
their roster of past and present fliers was Canadian ace Ray Collishaw,
who scored sixty victories during the war.

Dunkirk, 29 March 1918

Beloved Pal,

Every step takes me nearer. I'm only eight miles away [from the
front lines] now, perhaps a bit more, I don't know exactly where, but I
feel it's about a hundred yards. The work will be perfectly fascinating
as there will be plenty of fighting, and several little trips which I can't
describe, but which will add spice to life.

The RNAS is a wonderful organization, and the men in it are
perfectly wonderful too. There's no crowd I'd rather fight with at the
moment. Cord M[eyer] was here for a couple of weeks [February
1918] during which time they certainly introduced him to some
healthy excitement, as far as I can make out.[1]

The weather is dud today, in fact, it has been for a couple of days,
consequently I've had some sleep the last few nights, with the exception of last night when I was so excited about getting to the front on
good buses that I couldn't sleep.

Watch out for Eddie McD. when he gets home. He's a great boy.
He went bombing one night [26 March] and got into a searchlight
[over Lille]. He was 7,000 feet up and began to fire at the searchlight.
The Huns got the wind up and put it out. Eddie swears he shot it out
from 7,000 feet.

He also had a scrap with a Hun, and he was shooting low. His
tracers went way under the Hun, but he claims he put the wind up the
Hun. You ought to hear the RNAS pilots kid him. He took it all in.
Don't tell him I said so, but he did. If you thought he was nervous at
Huntington, you should see him after going on a raid. He's full
out—he was so tickled that he couldn't stand still. . . .

1. *Yale man Cord Meyer from New York City was a lieutenant in the U.S. Air
Service and later flew with the 103d Aerosquadron. Injured in a crash on 8 August 1918,
he spent the rest of the war in the hospital.*

With his inspection of front-line operations completed, McDonnell returned temporarily to Paris headquarters, where he prepared a report for Captain Hutch Cone outlining his experiences and recommendations, including advice that the navy immediately begin acquiring British and Italian bombers, rather than wait for aircraft to be produced in the United States.

Dunkirk, 30 March 1918

Beloved,

Tomorrow is Easter Sunday, and I shall be thinking of you all day, trying to imagine you at a wonderful Easter Service. How I wish we could go to one together. I shall probably be keeping Easter Sunday by going on my virgin patrol over the Hun lines. My service will be far from in keeping, but it will be inspiring nonetheless. Crock and I are in the same flight which is perfectly wonderful for both of us, as I have absolute confidence in his flying, and he feels somewhat the same way about mine, the reason being that he and I have been brought up together, aeronautically speaking, and we've done nothing but fight each other in the air for months, consequently I know exactly what tactics he uses, and just what he will do in every possible position, so that I can plan my tactics accordingly. He knows mine from A to Z, and he also knows just what I will do if a Hun gets a dangerous advantage over me. We're both "full-out" for it, and we only pray that we get the chances we want. We will fly exactly the same machines [Sopwith Camels] we flew in England for the present. We may get a new and better type of motor if we show the right stuff.

Rumor hath it that Di is shifting with us, to another squadron [#17 RNAS] on the same aerodrome. It is a bombing squadron. If it's true, there won't be any holding Di. He was so mad when he couldn't come with us that he was absolutely sick. He refused to eat and locked himself in his room. . . .

By the end of March several of the American naval aviators had moved to nearby British flying fields. Kenneth MacLeish, Dave Ingalls, Shorty Smith, and William Havilland all joined 13 Squadron, RNAS, at Bergues, flying Sopwith Camels. Di Gates was initially refused permission to transfer, but C.O. Chevalier soon reversed himself, and Gates was assigned to the Royal Navy's day bombardment squadron #17 flying D.H. 4 bombers at the same field. Sharing the base was #2 RNAS, a photographic reconnaissance unit, also equipped with D.H. 4 bombers. Bob Lovett continued his service on Handley Pages with #7 RNAS at Coudekerque aerodrome about five miles away. Following the merger of RNAS and RFC aviation forces on 1 April, the Royal Navy's former Dover-Dunkirk Command was reorganized as the Fifth Group, RAF. The three squadrons at Bergues were then redesignated the 61st Wing.

Dunkirk, 1 April 1918

Beloved,

It's April Fool's Day. To begin with, I thought I was going on patrol, I thought so until the patrol left, then I remembered the date. Instead, they sent me over to a depot to get a new bus. The mechanic gave me the wrong dope on starting it and I got off the ground, headed for a sandbank, beyond which lay cold and blue water. I thought the motor was working splendidly until the fool thing conked out altogether, then I remembered the date.

Di went on a patrol today, and although there were only two machines in the flight, when eleven Huns spied them they all stuck their tails up and dove like blazes for home. Did I tell you that Di is at the same aerodrome as us, flying bombers? He went out as observer this morning, and he's out tonight too. Bob came over to see us this afternoon, he's only five or six miles off. He went on an awful raid last night, and has the wind up so badly today that he can't stand still. It's ticklish work all right, and old Bob can't kick about not getting any action. He ought to be ready to go home in a few weeks; I would be!

Last night the RNAS and the RFC ceased to exist, and became merged into the Royal Air Force. If there are any particulars you want to know, simply ask me and I can furnish all the details. We raided #2 mess, a crowd of photographers[1], and after smashing every chair, window, picture, and glass, and after having absorbed all their liquor and ruined their quarters, we all moved over to #17, where operations were repeated. Only I think they were worse, as they knocked a red-hot stove over, and when it was set up again someone crawled on the roof and dropped a smoke bomb down the chimney, which blew the stove all over the room and blinded everyone, to say nothing of ruining all clothes. The objectionable characters [13 Squadron] were removed after that, and on the way back there was a business of pushing everyone into a small canal by the road. Two men disappeared from view. The party finally broke up when #2, making a

determined effort to withstand us, unlimbered a couple of fire extin-
guishers in our faces and began to shoot an automatic pistol. About
that time I felt so sleepy that I covered the entire distance between #2
and #13 in no time at all. Just to prove to you that the party wasn't as
bad as it sounds, the three worst offenders got three Huns this afternoon; they each got one. I'm not on duty tomorrow, but I think I'll
take a couple of practice flips to get my hand in again. I may work in a
low patrol too, I don't know.

We took a lorry and went up to town between here and the lines
yesterday. There's an American hospital there with real live American
nurses. They're quite a bunch, but I think they're moving back, or
shipping back. . . .

1. *2 Squadron, RNAS, later #202 RAF, was an observation unit flying photographic
reconnaissance. Several American enlisted men served with this group during the April
battles.*

The morning after his late-night revelry, Kenneth MacLeish embarked on his first war flight, a low fleet patrol that lasted from ten until
eleven-thirty A.M. He had been thinking and talking about this moment
for a long time, and when it finally occurred it only partially met his
expectations. Overeagerness almost led to a tragic mistake.

Dunkirk, 2 April 1918

Beloved

. . . I went on my first patrol today, and I was full out! I took it
more or less for granted that any bus I saw over the lines would be a
Hun! We spied some Hun seaplanes[1] off in the distance and proceeded
to climb and get into the sun. When we had our position we nosed
down and dove at them. I had mine all picked out, and became so
absorbed in my sights that I forgot to look at the leader. When I
looked, he had come out of his dive and was turning away. This sort of
rocked me, as I was all alone. I decided not to open up, but to get back
into formation. The old Huns were diving like blazes for shelter. I flew
directly over one with my eye on him all the time, and keeping both
height and the sun. I was just praying that he would open on me, as I
had him cold, but nothing happened. Thank the Lord I didn't fire!
They turned out to be Allied machines! Do you blame me for feeling
cheap? I couldn't see any recognition signals on his planes or rudder on

account of the haze, but I should have known the "bus," as I've flown them myself.

Talk about cold! It certainly can get that way upstairs. We were quite high this morning, higher than I've ever been before. It was perfectly beautiful too. The clouds were those big fluffy bunches that make one want to climb out of his bus and jump into them and roll around. They seem so soft and yet so buoyant. You sometimes feel when you dive into them that you ought to feel a check in your speed, and are quite disappointed when nothing happens. We were about three miles above the tops of the clouds in the sky of purest blue and a brilliant spring sun. Way below and through the clouds we could see the trenches stretching away southward. There was evidently some artillery action going on, from the flecks of white smoke. . . .

> 1. *Allied machines mistaken for enemy pontoon scouts operating out of Zeebrugge or Ostend.*

Poor weather and administrative duties kept MacLeish grounded for the next few days, though he did manage a short morning test flight on 3 April. He used a portion of his spare time wondering what was holding up promotions for the aviators overseas. He also attempted to send a simple birthday cable to Priscilla back in New York, but the censors would have none of it, much to Kenneth's disgust.

Dunkirk, 5 April 1918

Beloved Pal,

Cheer-ho, you priceless thing. I couldn't write to you yesterday because I was officer of the day and therefore had little spare time. . . . It is a dud day today so there's no news to report. Dave got a letter from the Dude [Harry Davison] which informs us that he and Irish [R. Livingston Ireland][1] are going to get lieutenant (jg) commissions. The Dude, of course, is due for one, but where does Irish come in for one. He was a second-class seaman when I was an ensign. Dave and I are naturally furious, as it seems as though the only place to get any reward in the service is at home, and that we poor devils who do all the dirty work are not considered a necessary element in the thing. Most of the staff and birds at home feel that the war can be won from an office, and that the men doing the fighting are merely there for their health. . . .

I'm doing my best to get a birthday cable through to you, but things are agin me. You'll understand some of the obstacles by reading the enclosed letter. That is the second letter of reprimand in two days. I caught perfect _____ for low stunting over our own base day before yesterday. All I did was loop a couple of times, roll a little, spin, and then dive. They objected because I wasn't over 2,000 feet. Perfectly absurd! . . .

1. *After training with the Yale Unit, Cleveland-born R. Livingston Ireland served at Hampton Roads and then Morehead City, North Carolina.*

U S NAVAL FORCES OPERATING IN EUROPEAN WATERS

MEMORANDUM FOR ENSIGN KENNETH MACLEISH, USNRF

There has been brought to my attention a cablegram which you wish to send to the United States. Some months ago a letter was received from the commander of American Naval Forces in European Waters [Sims] stating that officers should avoid sending cablegrams to the United States except in cases of emergency. The reason for this is that the cables are working under tremendous press of messages and it is our duty to avoid crowding them with personal messages of negligible importance. It is therefore requested that you convey the message which you desired to have cabled by letter.

Dunkirk, 5 April 1918

Dear Bruce, Elizabeth, Jean, and Hugh [MacLeish],

"Cheer ho!" the whole gang of you. I'm so happy I can't see straight. I'm actually on fighting patrols and I actually fly over Hun land. You should have seen me on my first patrol. I'd never been so high in my life. You know when you get up real high, about four miles, the air is so rarefied that if you move around much or exert yourself, you begin to pant and feel as if you had just run the hundred-yard dash. And cold!!! Thank the Lord they don't make that kind of cold near the ground. We went way behind Hun lines. You could see the line stretching away in the distance, marked on either side by flecks of smoke from the artillery, and, back aways, the captive balloons, mere specks so far down. I had a good look at two of the Huns' biggest bases. It gave me an odd feeling that it was up to me to destroy those cities lying apparently so peacefully, way down there below the clouds. At first I couldn't see why, but changed my mind when I heard a ping, and a screech, and saw a puff of smoke below. It was "Archie" and he wasn't very friendly, though he wasn't near enough to worry about. . . .

If there was one thing American flyers at Dunkirk could count on, it was the weather. While the calendar clearly said "spring," the sun failed to appear with any frequency. Rain, fog, mist, and bone-chilling cold were the norm instead, and oftentimes the elements proved more of an obstacle than the nearby Germans. A special patrol scheduled for 7 April turned back because of bad weather. Instead, some of the pilots at 213 Squadron were pressed into service test flying D.H. 4 bombers.

Dunkirk, 7 April 1918

Dearest Family,

    Just a word or two which will shatter all your illusions about this flying game. It may be great sport some of the time, but when it isn't sport it's positively torture. Yesterday, for instance, we were ordered up into the rain. The clouds were low and the visibility almost impossible. All we did was get wet, cold, and mad, also frightfully "Archied" as we were low and beautifully silhouetted against the clouds. Today was worse torture than any I have ever read about. In the first place we went 4,000 feet higher than I've ever been before in my life. I had on a pair of silk gloves next to my hands, a pair of rubber gloves over that, and then a pair of fur-lined, fur-covered flying gloves. To my mind that combination is the warmest possible, yet I froze two fingers absolutely solid, and my thumb and one other finger were frostbitten. The altitude gave me the worst headache I've ever had. Of course, there was practically no pressure up there, because it is halved at only 7,000 or 8,000 feet. It affected me strangely. At first it was nauseating, then I felt weak and dizzy. Finally, after about half an hour, I got used to it, and the only effect was a splitting headache and a funny noise in my ears. The veins around my ears expanded enormously at every heartbeat, and cut off my hearing entirely, so that when my heart throbbed I couldn't even hear the terrific roar of my motor or the tat-tat-tat of my machine guns which were firing about eight or ten inches in front of my face. I was in this condition for about an hour, under some really enterprising "Archie" fire. But, by George, I wouldn't give it up for all the love, money, and marbles on earth.

If you want to do me a favor, get me some very heavily knitted silk gloves. They are the warmest things on earth. Ishbel's helmet is in use every moment; when I'm not wearing it, someone else is. It went through two flights today alone, for instance, and kept three aviators warm where it seems impossible that anything could.

The extreme cold aloft proved especially troublesome for pilots and observers aboard reconnaissance aircraft. Despite the introduction of electrically heated flying suits, long hours at extreme altitude took their toll. Irving Sheely, an enlisted navy observer serving with 202 Squadron at Bergues, participated in the operations against Bruges, Ostend, and Zeebrugge. He later wrote to his mother, "It was so cold up there . . . I froze my nose and lips and both cheeks so bad[ly] that they all turned brown and peeled off. . . . I have grown a très jolie mustache to prevent irritating my lip which was the worst place frozen."

Dunkirk, 7 April 1918

Beloved,

Well strike me perishing pink with purple dots! You'll have to excuse this letter if you can't read it, or if it's short, because I froze three fingers and the thumb on my useful mitt. . . .

I'm mad! The patrol ahead of us saw five Albatros two-seaters[1], and the patrol after us saw at different times eleven mixed single- and two-seaters, but we saw nary a one. Cheer up. One of these days I may see too many. Shorty nearly ran into one but didn't know it was a Hun until told so, and then he claimed his guns were jammed, or rather cold; you know they get so cold that the oil freezes, or congeals, and prevents anything but single shots until they become warm again. Di took me up in his new bus [D.H. 4] today. I thought I knew what a fast machine was, but that one is too fast for words.

By the way, Shorty has announced his engagement. His girl is in Buffalo. How, please, can that be done? Did he cheat? . . .

1. *German observation craft produced by Albatros Werke GmbH, either the older C X model, introduced in mid-1917, or the newer C XII.*

Despite Kenneth's expressed amazement, the actual facts were simple enough. Edward "Shorty" Smith had trained at Buffalo, New York, from April to November 1917, and maintained an active correspondence with his sweetheart thereafter. When Shorty finally revealed the big news in early April, Di Gates observed, "Oh, Kid! He has just announced his engagement and is so much in love that he can't see or talk straight. He gets no enjoyment out of flying anymore, and should be home instead of over here." In fact, Smith, who suffered recurrent bouts of airsickness, was declared unfit for flying in early May and was temporarily assigned as ground officer in charge of repairs at the Dunkirk station.

Dunkirk, 9 April 1918

Beloved,

. . . It was dud yesterday, and my fingers are still so rotten that I couldn't fly. The natural result was that a few of us took a joyride down the coast to the next big town [Calais], and after buying everything but a haircut we had a marvelous dinner. China plates, plenty of knives, forks, spoons, even napkins. Fresh fish, omelette, steak, all kinds of fresh green vegetables, and fruit. Can you beat that? That's the first time I've had a steak in months, and also green vegetables. We saw old Charlie Chaplin [in a silent movie], which was "bon" for the troops. . . .

If my fingers weren't so sore I'd go on and give you some of your own medicine, but I'm afraid I can't. Shorty froze his nose, and you should see him now. Mumps aren't anything like it. If you think I'm kidding about the cold, here are two facts which will prove the temperature. The alcohol mixture in my compass was frozen solid. Also, the oil gauge on the instrument board was frozen solid. Ask someone how cold it has to be to freeze castor oil.

Dunkirk, 10 April 1918

Dear Henry [an unidentified friend],

. . . Poor old George M[osely] had a spill a few days ago. He was flying a bus that I was going to paint "Henry, Henry" on. He got off and couldn't climb fast enough, which meant that he crashed into a wireless apparatus in a ship's rigging, turned upside down, and fell on deck. He was badly shaken up and has strips of adhesive tape all over his face, but he didn't break anything and his injuries aren't severe. He doesn't worry anyhow because he just announced his engagement to Queenie, but please explain to me how it can be done with Queenie five thousand miles away from here. . . .

For some time British headquarters had been planning a low-level daylight raid against Zeebrugge, using specially equipped Sopwith

Camels carrying small bombs. The proposed aerial assault was timed to complement a major effort by the Royal Navy to destroy Germany's submarine bases along the Belgian coast.

An aerial attack from a height of 400 or 500 feet required special flying conditions—specifically, heavy clouds to provide cover against early detection. Otherwise the airplanes and their pilots would be exposed to crippling anti-aircraft fire. This raid, which began just after lunchtime, was MacLeish's first major sortie across the lines, and could very easily have been his last, for the Zeebrugge-Ostend-Bruges triangle was one of the best-defended areas along the western front. Moreover, bombing from low altitude in broad daylight was one of the riskiest possible maneuvers. Not only did planes run a gauntlet of high explosives and heavy machine guns, they were also easy prey for any infantryman with a rifle and a good eye. The squadron commander later reported, "Heavy anti-aircraft fire was experienced by all pilots." Unable to locate his target on the Zeebrugge mole, MacLeish dropped his single 50-pound bomb on the hangars at the Ostend seaplane base instead.

Dunkirk, 11 April 1918

Dear Bruce, Elizabeth, Jean, and Hugh,

I don't know of anything else to write about except myself, so you must tolerate a bit of egotism. This little stunt we had today will suffice to give you all a thrill, as I had one starting with the ankles and gradually going all over my body.

They rigged our scouts with bomb-carrying devices for little bombs. The idea was a bombing raid in broad daylight. For a good time give me one of those things anytime. Wow! I don't think I'll ever get over it. The clouds were only 1,000 feet up, and we were to get near to our objective, climb into the clouds, and when we thought we were directly over, to dive down to about 300 or 400 feet and let go our "pills." The first man over had a wonderful time—they didn't even shoot at him. The second had a little hot weather, the third some real hot weather, the fourth had a _____ of a time, the fifth had to turn back and try it again, the sixth wasn't much more successful. Then I came! In my wildest dreams of all hell turned loose, I never pictured anything like that. There must have been a thousand machine guns working on a twenty-four-hour day schedule. The tracer bullets were doing loops and split turns around my neck. I got dizzy watching them. I put my fingers on both triggers and had my two guns going full blast while I dove. It was no use. I saw in a second that I never in the world could get there. The rapid fire pom-poms were putting up a barrage in front of me, and it was getting closer and closer as I dove. There were so many bursts of smoke that I lost sight of the target. I thought of home and Mother and zoomed back into the clouds and waited for it to quiet down. When I came back out again I was completely lost—I couldn't even see land. I flew by compass until I came to the coast, and, thinking I was east of my objective, began working my way west along the coast, "Archied" to blazes every foot of the way, first on one ear, and then on the other, and once in a while on my back. I came to a town I'd never seen before and thought I was in Holland. I kept on and finally came to a town I knew, but it was twenty miles west of my objective. I didn't like the idea of going back, so as this town was an excellent objective, I at once decided to drop my pill there instead. I looked around for my target, found it, and went into the clouds. After flying for a second or two, to my horror, I popped out of the clouds into a patch of perfectly blue sky, only 1,200 feet up and directly over the hottest "Archie" battery the Huns have. I thought I was sure gone, but I guess the Huns were as surprised as I was, and about as scared, because I dove on them, both guns doing their ——est. I dove right for the Archie battery first, and you should have seen them drop their work and find that they had a date miles away and were late already. Lord! Did they run! Then I leveled off, dropped my pill, and absorbed myself in the business of getting back to the clouds, without flying straight for a second. Do you know, they never even fired a single shot at me, not one.

When I got back I expected to find the bus had been riddled with bullet holes, but to my surprise there wasn't one. I was disappointed and tickled to death at the same time—this combination causes one to itch violently. I learn something every day. Today I learned never to be the last machine in a daylight, low bombing stunt. I may know enough to keep out of trouble one of these days. One never knows, does one?

Even with the sights and sounds of his recent adventure painfully fresh in his mind, Kenneth quickly turned his attention to a very different area of concern, his relationship with Priscilla. Though he fully expected to announce their engagement when the time proved appropriate, he feared that one or two of his Yale companions might yet steal her away. In early April he begged Trubee Davison back in the United States, "Will you tell that dude brother [Harry] of yours that I will absolutely kill him for the dirty trick he played on me at Christmastime, the lowdown snake! When I'm three thousand miles away. . . ." Barely a week later Di Gates related a similar story, noting that Kenneth had stopped by that very afternoon with a long tale of woe. MacLeish had just received "thirty-odd pages from Miss Priscilla," who also seemed to be attracting the attentions of another Yalie, John Vorys, recently returned from duty in Europe. MacLeish believed that Vorys was attempting to carry out his earlier threat to "steal" Priscilla. As Gates observed, "Our Ken has quite a miserable time. He is also very much in favor of Harry coming immediately to France." Even a month later, when all these misunderstandings had apparently been cleared up, Kenneth remained uneasy. Di Gates remarked, "Ken's daily prayer seems to be that 'Harry be sent soon to France.' " While German fighters and "Archie" batteries might threaten Kenneth's life, these shenanigans back home were *serious!*

Dunkirk, 12 April 1918

Dearest Pal,

I thought I would be immune for at least a day after my little stunt yesterday, but I changed my mind when I was roughly hauled out of bed at the crack of dawn and pushed into a machine before I was well awake. It's lucky we didn't see anything because, on account of the nervous strain of yesterday, and the fact that old Loegenboom was working full blast all night, and the shells were landing rather near us, I didn't get what you'd call a full night's rest.

These early-morning patrols on good days are the most marvelous things in the world. You rise up above the ground mists and come into the sunlight long before it reaches the earth under you. You look down and it seems like night, and yet the morning is shining on you in all its glory. The sunrise is exquisite. You see the ground mist rise and form into layers of clouds, and then a breeze springs up and whips the strata into all sorts of fantastic shapes, and gathers great puffy masses. Some fine morning you and I will go up together, and if it doesn't thrill you, you have no romance. Of course, it's cold, but you soon forget that in the splendor of your surroundings.

I think I'll have a day off tomorrow. A cracked bloke tried to see how badly he could smash my bus without hurting himself—he succeeded admirably—the only thing he didn't smash to pieces was the gun sight. I suppose they'll soon set to work and build a new machine around the gun sight. It was the simplest procedure in the world. He was landing apparently very well. All of a sudden up went his tail and he shot on his motor, Lord knows what happened, then there was a crash–bang, and I was brokenhearted.

Di rushed in with some mail for Shorty and then tore off again saying he had a stunt on. Then we saw every machine in his squadron get off as though the war depended on it. One bloke had to land suddenly with his bombs still on. I stopped up my ears and ducked, but he got away with it. I must run over later and ask Di what was up. . . .

RAF records indicate that Di Gates's "mysterious" mission was an attack by seven aircraft from 217 Squadron against the mole and German seaplane base at Zeebrugge. In addition to heavy anti-aircraft fire, this daylight raid conducted in late afternoon attracted swarms of enemy Albatros D V scouts from German marine *Jagdstaffel* 1 and 2. Like MacLeish's mission of 10 April, the raid preceded a planned Royal Navy attack against Ostend and Zeebrugge. Poor weather conditions, however, forced the assault scheduled for the night of 12 April to be postponed a second time.

Dunkirk, 13 April 1918

Beloved,

. . . What do you think of this for a dirty trick? I was scheduled for a low patrol yesterday, it wasn't to be high, and it wasn't to be long. I naturally didn't bundle up much. I put on flying boots, your sweater which, by the way, after seeing remarkable service, is beginning to show signs of wear. It has a bullet hole through it (but nobody was in it when the bullet came to call). I also had a scarf, but no coat, and not very heavy gloves. Everything went fine until we spotted some Huns above. I forgot that I wasn't dressed warmly. The flight commander forgot that he promised not to go high, and the Huns forgot to wait for us. Result—patrol goes to 12,000 feet; MacLeish gets such a cold he'll never be the same, and freezes the same three fingers again. Now that they're frozen again, the nail on one is starting to come off. Pretty mess!

Bob Lovett came over to Di's squadron this afternoon, and Dave and I went over to tea. Bob says he hasn't received a single letter from Adele since he's been up here. He almost fainted with surprise when I, instead of weeping on his shoulder, casually remarked, "You

damn fool, it's your own bloody fault!" Dave, Bob, and Di send love.
Their kisses are censored, as I send all kisses to you!

Shortly after Bob Lovett visited Gates, Ingalls, and MacLeish at their
aerodrome, he returned to Paris to "put through information I gained
while with RNAS." Out of that experience came a lengthy report, duly
submitted to Captain Cone, chief of naval aviation in Europe, and
speedily forwarded to Washington, along with Eddie McDonnell's earlier analysis. Their observations and recommendations provided the
basis upon which the Northern Bombing Group program was approved.
In clear and occasionally dramatic language, Lovett described his missions over enemy lines, the nature of anti-aircraft defenses, the capabili-
ties of various aircraft, and possible sites for placement of American
squadrons. He also made several policy recommendations, stressing the
necessity of bombing one objective continuously "until it has been ren-
dered untenable." Lovett cautioned against intermittent bombing, and
urged that any navy squadrons employed in the antisubmarine campaign
not be called upon to "do any promiscuous bombing" except at times of
great crisis. Finally, he highlighted the need for carefully prepared pilots,
well trained in night flying, perhaps at a new school to be established in
the United States.

Dunkirk, 14 April 1918

Beloved,
    Do you remember the low bombing stunt [10 April 1918] I told you
about a couple of days ago? Well, yesterday morning the following
signal came through: "Photos show that _____ at _____ were
badly damaged by direct hit from bombs." Well, I was the only one
who had dropped any bombs on that objective, so it looked as though
I was scheduled to be mentioned in dispatches and a decoration. I
knew it was too good to be true. When the photos were enlarged it
was found that the Huns were merely repairing the hangar, after it had
been hit two or three weeks ago. There was a newly made bomb hole
near there, which was evidently mine. . . .
    I'm down at our [NAS Dunkirk] mess just now seeing the boys,
hence the inconsistency of the note. There's a little French girl in here.
She's about ten years old. She's an outcast due to the war, probably an
orphan. She is without exception the most adorable little kid in all the
world; just as polite as can be. She's teaching us all how to speak
French. She is serious and businesslike about it. We don't dare laugh,

and if we make a mistake she jumps all over us. She doesn't know any English except swearwords, so you can imagine the circumstances the poor little kid has been forced to face. . . .

Despite the battle raging around them, personnel at Dunkirk experienced frequent periods of calm and idleness. Except for brief spurts of maximum effort, only a portion of each day was spent flying or servicing aircraft. Officers and enlisted men devised a wide range of activities to fill their free time. Sleeping and writing letters were immensely popular, as was playing cards or billiards, listening to phonograph records, or joyriding behind the lines. Baseball games played on the wide, sandy beach attracted large crowds from town and neighboring aerodromes.

Dunkirk, 15 April 1918

Beloved,

We had a great baseball game today. We got up a team here and played another squadron up the line. They had eight Canadians and one American on their team. I don't think there are any Englishmen in the squadron. They were all good ballplayers. I speak in the patronizing tone of the victor when mentioning his vanquished opponents. We beat them about 16–1. Di was the umpire. I thought he knew enough to cheat for us, but he got the teams mixed up or something, because he was determined to have them win, but we foxed him. I only made one decent hit, but I got on base by hook or by crook four times out of five, and ran all afternoon, it seems to me. After the game was over I flopped down on my bunk to rest till teatime, which was in seven minutes, and the next thing I knew it was half-past dinnertime—three hours later.

The weather has been dud for several days, so we haven't had any work. I look forward to these dud weather streaks because then all the machines are put in shape, and likewise with the Huns, so that on the first good day, after a bad spell, you have scraps galore.

I got word from Paris which states that Archie is on his way to the front. He's going to have a warm time, allow me to state. The battle is nothing to kid about. All I can do is sit above it and look on. . . .

After attending artillery school at Saumur, Archibald MacLeish traveled with his unit, the 146th Field Artillery, to the front, where he participated in the opening phases of the Second Battle of the Marne.

213 Squadron, 61st Wing, RAF, 16 April 1918

My Beloved,

Do you remember how old "Poosh" [Reginald Coombe] tried to find out which way the wind was blowing when he was flying by wetting his finger and holding it up to see which side got cold first? Well, a chap here tried a better way than that. There's a Dutch windmill near the 'drome (one of the houses on a pivot with a big bunch of fans on it). When it works (and it works now and then) it faces the wind, so you can see which way the wind is blowing by looking at it. But you want to make sure that the wheels are going around. It stopped last week when we had a strong south wind, and hasn't moved since, although the wind is north and just as strong. This chap took a look, saw it facing south, and without noticing whether the wheel was turning, he landed. He wasn't hurt much, but it was a clever idea, wasn't it? He was flying my bus. That makes it twice as clever. That's the second bus in a week.

There's a lot of speculation and excitement about an order [Haig's "backs to the wall" command] which just came out. You should hear the old guns roaring up and down the line. That makes the speculation and excitement twice as bad. . . .

I'm fed up with Di. The day after we had that low bombing stunt, Di and some others in his squadron went out [12 April 1918] and did the same thing, only they were at 15,000 feet. They got one direct hit on the target, and not a single bit of "Archie." Has he any right to crow about that? . . .

Every dud day we have to work an hour and a half in the vegetable garden. You should see me planting potatoes. It's a sight you'd never forget. The real work goes on for about five minutes, and then there's a mud fight. This morning mud didn't suit some Christy Mathewson very well, so he took to throwing the little potatoes. I think I got most of one out of my ear, but every once in a while I find more. . . .

As part of the overall American campaign to bolster the Italian war effort while also obtaining training on giant Caproni bombers, a number of army and navy aviators were detailed to Mediterranean schools and bases in 1918. For a while MacLeish believed he might also be ordered south to a staff position in Rome. In mid-April, however, he learned that the slot had been given to another officer, Lieutenant William B. Havilland, a veteran of the Lafayette Flying Corps and the man who replaced

Di Gates as chief pilot at Dunkirk. The Yale men apparently resented this "outsider" for displacing one of their heroes, and despite Havilland's service with 213 Squadron, Kenneth never mentioned him in his correspondence, except in rather disparaging terms. Havilland later went on to command the U.S. naval air station at Porto Corsini.

213 Squadron, 18 April 1918

Beloved,

. . .There's no chance of my going to Italy now. A man who flew with the French for two years, and who was here with me at the squadron, has become a "two-ringer" and has gone to Italy to take the job they were considering for me. You see, he asked to go home, but instead they gave him this job which is supposed to be a rest cure. All work in Italy is, for that matter, and if you are there six months—they only allow four months' active service—as the work is too soft there. For instance, up here we run into scraps about every day, and every week nearly we have these suicidal low bombing stunts in daytime. We had another one yesterday, but when we swung in over the coast, we ran into hail and rain, and the thing was washed out. One of the boys didn't see the washout Very signal [flare] and kept on going. He was gone two hours and a half, and when he found his way back, he was all shot to blazes. He also got a couple of slight bullet wounds on the hand, but nothing very serious. Shorty, as usual, got lost, and came very near to dropping his bombs on a French aerodrome. The fog was so thick at 200 feet that a machine was out of sight. You should have seen a huge bombing machine that carries umpteen tons of bombs land on our aerodrome. He was completely lost.

So Alice and Adele are coming over. Of course I'll be tickled to tears to see them, but I do pity Bob and Di, don't you? Here's what they will be up against. Alice and Adele probably think that rules here aren't any stricter than they were in Huntington and that Bob and Di and Crock can get off whenever they please. If they don't come to see them all the time the girls will probably get mad about it. As a matter of fact, Bob is in Paris right now, but can't even get off for lunch at noon. There's no such thing as leave. We used to be able to get forty-eight hours once in a while, but now that the big push is on, we don't get forty-eight minutes. . . .

Despite the fact that Alice Davison, Adele Brown, and Priscilla Murdock all had boyfriends in the Yale Unit, and that the letters that passed back and forth across the Atlantic were uniformly filled with laments of loneliness, the men universally opposed any visit by the young women. The flyers seemed to feel that their sweethearts would distract them from the higher calling of fighting the war, and that somehow the girls' innocence and femininity would be compromised by exposure to the realities of combat in Europe.

Dunkirk, 19 April 1918

Beloved,

Business has been very bad today. We were all sent back to the base [NAS Dunkirk]. The RNAS could use us, but the RAF are too good for us. I guess Di is way down in the mouth, and Crock and I are worse. Shorty is indifferent. Crock and I had our last flips in land scouts, and believe me, they were good ones. I never had so much fun in my life. We each tried to do everything we knew or ever heard of. Things looked like a circus gone completely mad until I got lost. I came to on my back with a Very pistol hanging under my chin. I lost the Very pistol, but nothing else. What made me laugh was that everybody thought I meant to fly on my back, and they all congratulated me when I got down. I must have been upside down for about five minutes.

I have a brand-new bus [H.D.2 pontoon scout] all of my own down here, so I'm not mad. It's the latest type there is, and looks pretty good, only of course this job won't be any fun because we'll never see any Huns, and we won't have any daylight bombing stunts. I guess I can do without a little of it for a while, however.

Yesterday we all nearly dropped dead on the spot. We were playing baseball when one of the boys looked up and saw two Huns right over the aerodrome. Real Huns only 7,000 feet up and twelve miles behind the lines. Everybody tore for a bus and went up after them. They all came back, except one chap, and said they hadn't seen anything. Later we got a telephone message from the missing link. He picked up a scrap over the lines, and was shot down with an explosive bullet in his engine, but he brought the Hun down with him, so what are the odds?

I must close now, it's late. I'll write more tomorrow when I'm settled. The Huns are over again tonight and we were shelled this evening. . . .

Kenneth MacLeish's return to the Dunkirk seaplane station did nothing to improve his spirits. He saw impediments and enemies everywhere. The Belgians proved a convenient scapegoat. Despite the fact that concern for the fate of "poor little Belgium" had triggered British intervention in the war, many soldiers quickly came to resent anyone and anything responsible for their dreadful predicament. Such resentment soon focused on the Belgians, and numerous rumors of their supposed perfidy circulated through the English (and apparently American navy) ranks. Some believed that local civilians provided distant German artillery with bombardment coordinates. Belgian farmers supposedly signaled with horses or by plowing signals and signposts into the fields. Farm wives were accused of hanging laundry in prearranged patterns and millers of turning windmills in a certain direction. Nor were such rumors confined to the Flanders front. Similar stories circulated in French territory and in Alsace. Taken together, they bespoke the great cynicism and weariness experienced by the men at the front, to whom the war seemed destined to last a hellish eternity.

Dunkirk, 22 April 1918

Beloved,

Darn! Just when I get my bus all fixed up, it gets shot to blazes. Enclosed you will find pieces of the shrapnel that did the trick. A large piece entered the fuselage behind the motor, burst inside, and cut my main gasoline line in two, cut two pressure pipes—one piece entered the gas tank and almost tore the bottom out of it. There were only two other holes, but oh boy! One hole was two feet behind my seat, and the other entered the trailing edge of the top plane [upper wing] right over the seat. Do you know what I think? I think the people who built that bus started with the gas tank, and built the rest of the machine around it. We had to take everything off that bus to get the tank out.

Tell me the German spy system isn't O.K. The day before this station was completely ready, after a long spell of bad weather, the Huns dropped a bomb on it. I can't give the damage done, but believe me! We're all out for scalps now. Fortunately, no one was hurt.

Wasn't it funny? The day after we left the RAF they had three crashes at our aerodrome. One was fatal, but he was in 202 Squadron. Two were bad crashes, and both were from our [213] squadron. I expected to hear about one because I'd seen him fly, but the other was a good pilot. Bob came over from Paris in a "tin six" Packard to look us over. Who accused Bob of riding the gravy? Well, he deserves it, bless his little heart.

Alan Winslow passes as an American hero now; he shot down a Hun. That's because he's with the French. The boy I roomed with at gunnery school in Scotland was the first man to fly at the front in an American uniform; he has six Huns already, in a little over a month—have you ever heard of Lloyd Hamilton? No? Well, he's with the English![1]

A funny thing has just been reported. We were going to have an offensive patrol, in conjunction with the French, a day or so ago. It didn't come off. The Huns had a patrol of Albatros land machines out all day long, in the area we had planned to patrol, and yet people say, "Poor Belgians, they suffer so." I wish some of these people could come over here and trust their lives to the words of a Belgian—there wouldn't be any left in a little while. I can't understand where this sob stuff about poor Belgians comes in, any more than I can understand why the Belgians are fighting against the Huns.

An English patrol saw a Belgian airplane come out of a German aerodrome a few weeks ago, so they shot him down. Another patrol saw a Belgian airplane with a flock of Hun Albatros, so they shot him down too. The funny thing is the Belgians didn't lose "a single plane" that day. They all returned safely to their aerodromes. What are you going to do in a case like that?

There's no use now. The boys want to play cards. And as there is only one room, and one table, I guess I'll have to call this off. . . .

1. *While serving with the 94th Aerosquadron on 14 April 1918, Winslow and Douglas Campbell became the first members of an "American" unit to down enemy aircraft. They scored victories within minutes of each other. Vermont-born Lloyd Hamilton shot down four German aircraft while flying with the RAF and five more with American forces before he was killed in August 1918.*

While conditions at Dunkirk in no way approached the terror and misery of life in the trenches, it was nonetheless a rather unpleasant duty station. Constant aerial and artillery bombardment forced the men to spend much of their time in underground bunkers. Sleep became a rare commodity. Even when occasional periods of fair weather permitted active flying, shortages of machines, equipment, and trained pilots severely limited operations at the seaplane base. Not surprisingly, morale suffered. MacLeish and the other officers who had just returned from duty with British squadrons experienced the further letdown of passing from a period of great activity and high tension to a time of inactivity and frustration. He was probably not alone in believing that the dynamic Eddie McDonnell might restore some enthusiasm. But McDonnell was already back in the United States, and Dunkirk C.O. Chevalier was in fact doing the best possible job under very trying circumstances.

Dunkirk, 24 April 1918

Beloved,

. . . I worked all day yesterday and today on my bus, but it isn't ready yet. I'm off duty tomorrow so I think I can get it ready. In that case we ought to be bombed again tomorrow night. You see, when all the machines are ready for work, the Huns drop bombs on them. Of course the Huns don't know when they're ready, no! And the Belgians wouldn't tell them anyway. But by chance, the Huns, as I say, always call and drop a card or two when everything on the station is "jake."

We had an awful "crab fest" last night. Every one of the junior officers crabbed for all he was worth about everything he could think of, and all feel better today. It's good for us once in a while. But the evening wasn't in vain because we all came to two definite conclusions, that if two things remain unchanged, the station would simply go on as it is going now—but if either one of the two, or both, were changed, everything would be jake and everybody would be happy, and get back some of the old pep. My personal opinion is that I faintly hear one Eddie McD. being paged. I have every confidence in him.

My mechanic is a card. He comes from Texas and drawls. He had his head stuck way in behind the motor when a noisy mechanic came along yelling for him. When he saw that this boy's head was out of sight, he yelled louder. He was a little, tiny shrimp, but he made a lot of noise. After a while the head was slowly withdrawn, and slowly he turned around to see who it was, and just looked him over from head to foot. Then he drawled, "Don't shout at me that way. You're too damn small." I thought I'd die. It must have been the way he said it.

These are busy days and I don't get much time to write. There's no such thing as sitting around the way they do at a regular squadron. Every officer here holds some kind of job, and they all get in each other's way, and make five times the amount of work. In most squadrons, for instance, the ordnance officer is a ground officer, so is the supply officer, so is the repair officer. That is all the work they have, so they have plenty of time. Here, all officers, with one exception, are flying officers. Every bit of work has to go through the proper channels, and believe me, there are thousands of them. But it will all change when something important turns up to make the men see that flying is the most important thing at the station, not the least important. . . .

By late April the force of Germany's attack along the Lys River had waned, and it appeared that the British lines would hold. Conditions remained unsettled, however, and no one was sure when or where the enemy might renew the offensive. With the main axis of the attack only thirty miles to the south, contingency plans were developed for evacuating the Channel ports in the event of a German breakthrough. George Mosely reported that "our men and officers who do not fly will probably leave in destroyers. The rest of us will take as many rounds as we can carry in our machine guns and empty them into the close German formations as they advance. . . . They are getting gas masks and steel helmets for us—funny things for aviators." As part of the planning process ordnance officer MacLeish was ordered to inventory matériel on hand so that transport might be arranged if necessary.

Dunkirk, 27 April 1918

Beloved,

I've been so busy that I haven't even had time to sleep, let alone write, for the last three days, and consequently I'm tired by now. I had to make out an exact list of all the ordnance matériel on the station, how much it weighed, and the number of cubic feet required to transport it. If you don't think it's a job, you ought to crawl down into our ammunition dump in the pitch dark and try to count and estimate the size and weight of some five thousand cases of every size and weight in the world. Some of the cases only weigh a couple of pounds and others five hundred and up. . . .

Talk about a wonderful crowd of men! You should allow yourself to be turned loose in this crowd up here. (But you should let me stand guard.) No, really, they are wonders. Di went to one squadron, and three Canadians said that if he was called back to this base they were coming with him because they liked him so much, and now they're trying to transfer to our forces. One Englishman and two Canadians are trying to transfer to us from the squadron that Shorty, Crock, and I went to, and the latest dope is that some of the men from the squadron Bob went to are moving heaven and earth in an attempt to join the U.S. naval aviation force.

Ever since we've been recalled, we have averaged two guests a night for dinner between our two messes. The place is just infested every night. Our skipper [Chevalier] is known as the best man in the navy. The most attractive features of the station, however, are first, the wonderful food, and second, the fact that we have a baseball game down on the beach nearly every evening. The whole town turns out to watch it.

The fliers' accommodations included a villa right on the seashore, complete with kitchen and dining room on the first floor. George Mosely observed, "The food is great, real American meals. . . . We have oatmeal, nice white bread, and sugar."

Dunkirk, 28 April 1918

Beloved,

At present I'm having a very soft job, and consequently I have plenty of time to myself. Some men are being examined for commissions and all I have to do is sit here and do nothing. I'm not crazy about this court stuff, and now I hear there's to be a court-martial. We have a mess boy who was evidently born with a desire to swipe stuff. His record certainly points to that. We have all lost money, cuff links, etc., but regularly a package of cigarettes a day. We caught this fellow red-handed yesterday and now he's due for some trouble. You should hear him deny it. You can tell by the trend of his conversation that he has devoted a large part of his tender years to pleading his case before judges.

All the mess boys got a roaring crap game started the other day, and there wasn't any work done by anybody till it was over. We sneaked up to the alley door and opened it just far enough so that we could hear what was going on, and before five minutes had elapsed we were all lying on the floor with laughter. One big, burly seaman was so excited that tears were rolling down his cheeks, and he was alternately begging, cursing, and threatening the dice. There wasn't a thing he wasn't going to do to those bones if they didn't roll the right number.

Do you remember the Blue Jacket that I told you about who was driving a heavy bombing machine? Well, recently he wrote home that he had three hairbreadth escapes from the Huns without a scratch. He is now driving a fast fighting machine, so he says to the folks at home. He's a sketch. If he was half as healthy as his imagination he'd knock Jess Willard[1] from New York to Patchogue with one blow.

What do you think about the Ostend-Zeebrugge show? Is there anything that can beat it? They came as close to making an effective blockade in the canal as anyone ever did. Believe me, I take my hat off to those boys. I've been over the mole at 500 feet, and I swear on my honor I haven't the nerve to get any closer to it. They were foxed at Ostend by a change of wind and tide, but it was a splendid show. . . .

1. World heavyweight boxing champ.

On the evening of 22 April 1918 a Royal Navy flotilla of seventy-four vessels, including monitors, destroyers, blockships, smoke launches, ex-ferries, submarines, and the old cruiser HMS *Vindictive,* attacked the German naval bases at Zeebrugge and Ostend. At Zeebrugge two blockships were sunk in the canals and a submarine packed with explosives exploded against the mole, separating this artificial seawall from the mainland. Hand-to-hand fighting for possession of the seawall erupted when *Vindictive* lay alongside and disgorged hundreds of specially trained marines. In all, British forces suffered 176 killed and 462 wounded, and lost 49 prisoners. At Ostend the blockships became lost, ran aground, and exploded.

Despite its daring and the valor of the attackers, the Zeebrugge-Ostend raid was only partially successful, and the channels through which the submarines passed were not completely or permanently blocked. In a second assault on 10/11 May, a hand-picked crew scuttled HMS *Vindictive* in the Ostend canal, with the sailors taken off the abandoned vessel by rescue launches.

Dunkirk, 29 April 1918

Beloved,

I've had it more or less easy this afternoon, as the weather is a dud, and the brainless boys are scarce today, which means no guns to clean. We went out to 213 Squadron and had a baseball game. We beat them 15–1, but after our month's stay with them, they're used to anything from the Amex.

You should see the stunt some of the English boys have, I mean the "Buck-a-Navy" boys. The beach here is wide, level, and hard at low tide and runs for miles and miles. These boys have rigged a sail on a four-wheeled cart, and they sail up and down the beach. They just creep along into the wind, but you should see them go with it. There's about a 30-mile breeze tonight and they must go 30–40 mph.

Crock pulled a brilliant stunt the other day. They were on patrol after a Hun which was reported. Just as they hove into sight, Crock pulled up into the clouds and lost the rest of his flight. One boy landed in the flooded area, way inland. Some flight commander! Of course they lost their chance of getting the Hun.

I guess my mail ship went down this week. I find that now that I'm busy every day, I can stand not getting any mail without getting an awful grouch the way I used to in Scotland. I guess I'm a spoiled boy; you've been good to me. Just for that I'm going to name my bus after you. I've got the cap device copied on each side in red, white, blue, and gold. I've half a mind to write "Happy Days" on top of the eagle, or "Eat Less Bread," but I don't want too much writing on the insignia [design: American shield with crossed anchors, surmounted by eagle, with words "Priceless Priscilla" under shield]. . . .

Dunkirk, 30 April 1918

Beloved Pal,

. . . Still another cause for malady is the fact that I have both a headache and a stomachache. Can you beat that for one evening? Perhaps it's the food, perhaps it's the weather. Both are damnable, and again, perhaps it's just that I'm sick of the whole thing. So much could be done at this station, yet so little is really done. Flying isn't considered essential enough. There's too much NAVY about the place. It's a regular ship!

Old "Priceless Priscilla" certainly looks like an airplane, now the question is, will it fly? The answer is, if it doesn't, I hope a bomb hits it. I certainly have spent lots of time on it, especially on the guns. I want them to work perfectly, even if nothing else does. But I'm sure it will fly, just as sure as I am that this rain and wind will never let up. I wonder if it's possible to have good weather for three straight days in Europe. They'd fall dead if they ever saw a week of it. But there's no danger of anyone dying from that cause.

Well, I think I'll put my aches to bed. And I think if I don't get some mail tomorrow that I'll go look for some, or else sit down and write to myself and sign your name to it. . . .

As officer of the day Ensign MacLeish was also assigned responsibility for censoring the enlisted seamen's mail, an ironic position for a man who frequently ran afoul of the censor himself.

Dunkirk, 3 May 1918

Beloved,

Please excuse the somewhat camouflaged notepaper, but the camouflage is just Dunkirk dirt, and as I can't get home tonight, it will have to do. Somebody wished the job of duty officer on me, and I have to stick around the base all night, and go on early patrol on top of that!

I wish you were here by my side to read the gobs' mail with me. I've nearly passed out two or three times—talk about a scream , some of these letters are the same. You read about the English show up at Zeebrugge and Ostend? Well, two or three of our men were there, according to their stories, and I wish you could hear what they went through. They were home in bed all the time, as a matter of fact, but one of them let his imagination take him up "there" and also allowed him to capture nearly 130 Huns single-handed. . . .

Despite the risks he sometimes took, Kenneth MacLeish was a skilled (and lucky) pilot. While many aviation cadets destroyed their machines or suffered grievous injuries, he emerged from the long training process relatively unscathed. But the combined effects of continuous shelling, nervous strain, and a lack of sleep eventually dulled his reflexes, leading to the first serious crash of his career. In this case, he was able to walk away.

Dunkirk, 5 May 1918

Bestest Beloved,

Two days ago I was officer of the day, and we had an early patrol. I was called at four A.M., had to see that all hands were called, all machines out and armed, see to all the duties I had as O.D., and also go on the patrol. Yesterday I packed all night, that is until twelve-thirty, preparatory to moving over to the other mess (the captain's mess) and was called again at four A.M. and had to go on another early patrol. This last night I was working on my ordnance reports until eleven-thirty, and was called again at four A.M. this morning. I started on the patrol and it was called off on account of poor visibility. I tried to land, but was so all in, I give you my word, I didn't care whether I got down or not. The result is that I crashed for the first time in my life. I saved the machine pretty well by jumping out of the seat and turning it just in time so that the crash wasn't bad. When we went out the wind was in a certain direction. I was too worn out to notice whether it had changed when I came back. It had completely reversed, and you can't land these things tail to the wind, let alone when you have a narrow slip fifty yards wide to land in, and you're headed for a stone wall or dock. I was very lucky in not turning upside down to begin with, and more so that I didn't crash straight into the wall. I broke my pontoons and one wing, but they will both be fixed tomorrow. My mechanic and I tore down, cleaned, and set up my motor in four hours and a half this afternoon. How's that for two tired, young Americans.

Old "Mournful Mary" is going full blast. There are about six new Mournful Marys, some little and some big. She blew twice, and all the others did likewise, but I haven't heard the shell, so I guess it's a false alarm. How many shells do you suppose have fallen on Dunkirk since the war began? Just a few over five thousand. The night I arrived Hun destroyers put in five hundred alone, and since I've been here "Loegenboom" has deposited about twenty-five 15-inch shells, all of them within two miles of camp, and most of them within half a mile. Lord knows how many bombs. The Huns aren't satisfied with one trip a night. Sometimes they make three or four.

We had two crashes yesterday morning, but no one was hurt. One had his fatal beauty removed, that is, it won't be fatal anymore, I wouldn't even call it beauty. But you can't kiss a steel-bound wind-shield when your kisser is going 100 mph and the windshield is standing still.

Did you see the write-up that Eddie McD. got in the New York *Herald* of May 3d. He was the "intrepid lieutenant" who had flown in Italy. Bill Thaw, Seth Low, Cord Meyer and the Amex ace Baer came to see us yesterday.[1] They're up the lines a few miles in this Mont Kemmel show. Hobey Baker got lost yesterday morning, but he showed up in the afternoon and came over to tea. That makes the fifth time I've heard he was missing, and we call him the "missing link."

Well, beloved, they are so sore at the excuse I gave for crashing that they're going to call me at four A.M. just for fun, so I guess I'll get some sleep now. . . .

1. *After transferring from French to American aviation, Brooklyn-born Seth Low served with the 103d, 96th, and 26th Aerosquadrons, and later commanded the 185th, a night pursuit unit. Paul Baer from Fort Wayne, Indiana, finished the war with nine victories.*

In the waning days of the Lys Offensive, German troops unleashed a surprise attack on 25 April 1918 that seized the British strongpoint of Mont Kemmel, about six miles south of Ypres. When fierce Allied counterattacks failed to dislodge the enemy, General Sir Herbert Plumer, the British commander in that sector, withdrew his forces behind the Yser canal. Ludendorff's troops were unable to exploit this victory, however, and he halted the battle a few days later. Among the aviation units swept up in the fighting was the 103d Aerosquadron commanded by Major William "Bill" Thaw, an American formation composed of veteran pilots who had previously served with French escadrilles.

Dunkirk, 6 May 1918

Dearest Ones,

Well, may I never see another day like this one! If I do I'll fall over dead. To begin with, two big machines went out on patrol alone. [1] One got into a spin and crashed, killing the front observer [Edward A. Smith] and seriously injuring the pilot [Herbert Lasher]. The rear observer [Thomas C. Holliday] saw what was coming, threw his guns overboard and braced himself for the shock. When he came to he had a broken leg, but that was all. In that condition he sent in three messages by pigeons, rescued the pilot, and dove for the front observer, but though he could touch him, he couldn't clear him from the wreckage, and his body went down when the front half of the bus sank. That's quite a stunt for a man with a broken leg, and badly shaken up, isn't it? He's made of the right stuff.

The other machine came to the rescue, and with five men on board started to sink. Two other machines and two scouts went out, followed by another big machine. It reached the wreck and took all the load it could. One of the scouts arrived, saw what the situation was, brought two motorboats over, and just skinned into the harbor as his motor completely wrecked. Two of the three rescuing big machines collapsed before they got in. Only one of the seven machines came back without a mishap. Dave Ingalls was one of the scouts, and he left about ten this morning. At five this afternoon nothing had been heard of him. At seven still nothing. You can imagine how I felt, if you know what close friends Dave and I are.

My motor was completely down at noon. I put on some overalls, and my mechanic and I had it up and running by seven o'clock. Two big machines went out at seven, but came back with no news. While they were out nine Huns came over. I could only guess what happened to Dave. I loaded up my guns, and set out to either find him or get even with somebody. Just then a telephone message came through. Where do you suppose thè kid was? Way down to Le Havre. He just hit the coast in time. A few more miles and he would have been out in the Atlantic. I wish you could have seen the expression on the sailors' faces, from worn-out despair to a four-foot grin, all at once.

There was a terrific artillery duel up at the front tonight. I never heard such a scrap. The sky was just aflame with flashes. . . .

1. *Donnet-Denhaut flying boats, powered by 200-hp Hispano-Suiza engines, with a 750-pound bomb load.*

While friends at Dunkirk worried over his safety, Dave Ingalls was actually making the best of a bad situation. Lost in the mist and running low on fuel, he landed near a French schooner, which towed him to shore about a hundred miles south of Dunkirk. What with checking his plane and refueling, he was able to return only as far as Dieppe, where he spent the night. The French commander there introduced the wayward airman to the American consul, who invited Ingalls to lunch the following day. That luncheon inspired a further invitation to attend a dance held at the consul's home. As Ingalls later remarked, the consul "has two daughters who, although they have never been in America, talk and act quite naturally. And so, weather permitting, I'll return tomorrow after a very pleasant time."

Dunkirk, 12 May 1918

Beloved,

I know I'm sort of mean not to write for the last few days, but I've been too darn busy even to think. There's a heap of news to tell you. . . . Two nights ago the Huns raided us and dropped a perfectly tremendous bomb on a house back of ours. It used to be a three-story brick building, but now it's a pile of debris only about five feet high.

I've heard of people walking in their sleep, but never running, have you? Well, I did. I heard the bomb whistling through the air sort of subconsciously, and I don't remember much about the explosion, but I do remember clearly that when I was wide awake I was running across the room full tilt. The reason why I woke up then was because I ran smack into the wall. I turned around and made one dive for the bed. I was under the covers before the debris began to fall on the roof. None of it came through, but by golly there's something crooked about that building because there never were half as many bricks in it as fell on the roof over my head.

The other night Hobey Baker, Cord Meyer, and Seth Low came to dinner and the "little skipper" [Chevalier] and I drove them out to their 'drome in the Cadillac about twelve o'clock. On the way home we saw them put up the barrage over town so we thought we'd watch it from the country. The Huns shut off their engines and glided down over the town, dropped their pills, and opened up. They came over us so low that we could see them plainly. At the same time the big HPs [Handley Pages] were pushing off to bomb Germany. The HPs and the Gothas were passing each other in the air and didn't know it.[1] I had a joyride in an HP the other day. It was wonderful sport. They're so comfy I almost fell asleep.

The "skipper" called for volunteers to fly land machines, day bombers of the same type [D.H. 4s] that Di flew, and for the same sort of work. I volunteered because we'll never see any action on these seaplanes. And I expect to leave for training in southern France within the next few days. I'll write all the dope when I know what it is. . . .

1. *Handley Page heavy bombers were actively involved in the aerial assaults against Bruges-Ostend-Zeebrugge. The 0/400 model carried nearly a ton of bombs. German Gotha G V and G Va bombers carried out similar attacks against the Allied aerodromes and naval facilities at Dunkirk.*

On 30 April 1918 the secretary of the navy approved a plan recommended by the General Board and developed by officers like Cone, Lovett, and McDonnell to create a unit, later designated the Northern Bombing Group, to carry out concentrated raids against the Bruges-Zeebrugge-Ostend submarine complex. Several squadrons of both day and night bombers would be employed, flown by U.S. Navy and Marine Corps pilots. Volunteers for these positions were quickly recruited at bases in Europe and the United States. MacLeish was not the only Dunkirk pilot to step forward. So too did Dave Ingalls and George Mosely. Anything, they reasoned, was better than seaplane patrol.

Dunkirk, 14 May 1918

Beloved,

I have the deck as officer of the day again today, and I'm betting that they drop some bombs and things on me. In fact, I'm sure they will because the French are putting up kite balloons, and they never do that unless they expect a raid. I hope they don't "corpse" my machine, however, because I've worked so hard on it that it's a real child now, and what is a whole lot more, its official name is "Priceless Priscilla" instead of #236, and it is conceded by all to be the best machine on the station. It certainly is the best-looking. I'm having my ordnance gang stand by and I have a Lewis machine gun[1] in my room ready to work out on the first young man to work out on me.

Nothing of interest to report except that I'm so tired I can hardly hold my pen. And what's more, I'm scheduled for the early patrol, which means getting up at three o'clock. It's now about eleven and I don't see any sense in going to bed at all.

ᶳ ᶳ ᶳ

I knew we'd get it. We haven't been bombed for nearly a week now, and just what I expected has happened, and it is still going on. They are coming over by the thousand. I went out and tried to shoot the machine gun, but it won't shoot straight up, and I only fired about twenty rounds, and out of those I got three stoppages. I was trying to clear the last one when the shrapnel began to whistle and ping into the water beside me, so I called it off and ran for the dugout. They haven't tried to get us yet. They seem to be after the HPs and some of the squadrons out between here and Bergues, and they are also taking a shot at Bergues, to say nothing of Calais, which I think is the real center of the attack. The barrage has been up over Calais incessantly for the last hour.

Well, here it is one A.M. with the raid still on and a patrol at five, which means getting up at three. Shall I, or shall I not? I haven't the heart to call these poor devils at three! Some of them are asleep down in the dugouts. Another Hun is sneaking in now. I guess they'll have a pretty wet time there, because the balloons are up, and there is a thin layer of clouds only about 8,000 or 10,000 feet up. I've only heard three bombs so far. But more will be here directly. "Mournful Mary" is getting hoarse, she's been at it so much tonight, and all the little Mournfuls are getting tired too, poor dears. . . .

Oh, I forgot. Sam Walker came up from Le Croisic, he drove a Ford ambulance all the way up here. He says Ken Smith got a sub and was decorated with the croix de guerre.[2] They're all fed up and want to come up here. I guess it's sort of natural to kick about this place, but I wouldn't trade stations with anyone on earth. . . .

1. *Invented by American Colonel Isaac Lewis, the Lewis machine gun was a drum-fed weapon used in many aircraft.*
2. *Yale Unit veterans Samuel Walker and Ken Smith were stationed at the navy's Le Croisic antisubmarine base near St.-Nazaire. On 23 April 1918 Smith attacked a German submarine, probably destroying it, earning the croix de guerre, the Legion of Honour, and the Navy Cross.*

Dunkirk, 15 May 1918

Priceless Priscilla,

Quite a full day, as I told you in last night's letter, of which half was written before and half was written after the air raid. My bedtime was half past one. I got up at three and had a look at the weather. It was fine, but I didn't have the heart to call the men. I got unmercifully jumped for it. I don't care.

Did I tell you that I tried to fire the machine gun? I spotted one Hun very low. They caught him in the searchlights, and I had a go at him. The gun only fired about twenty shots before she jammed so badly that I couldn't dodge the shrapnel and fix it at the same time. I probably told you all this last night, but I was so sleepy then that I didn't know what I was saying, and so sleepy now that I've forgotten what I said.

I did two two-hour patrols today. On the last one I was flying way behind, and to the right of the formation. I don't know why I did that. It may have been because I had a hunch, or more likely because I had a severe case of spring fever, and just felt kittenish enough to stay out of the formation and pick a scrap. I was scouting around when I saw a suspicious-looking thin, blue streak on the water. I was about 3,000 feet up so I dove to take a look. As I dove it changed from blue to white and up came the periscope. I turned as quickly as I could and cut my motor so he wouldn't see or hear me, but I guess he saw me because he dove right away. I tore off after the formation and overtook them in about a mile. I dove on the lead bombing machine, cut across his nose,

and fired a Very light, which is the signal to attract attention, but the
pilot was green and didn't know what I wanted. I fired more Very
lights and also my guns, but he wouldn't follow me. I crossed in front
of him about ten times, nearly hitting him every time. He went on,
more or less annoyed with me, but in the opposite direction. I decided
to leave the patrol and go on home and get another bombing bus, as
we were only a few miles offshore at the time. I got in, but found my
engine overheated and couldn't go out again. Voilà! The chance to be a
hero gone caflooey!

Nothing very definite in the line of information to report, but I fully
expect that we will leave within a week. The schedule is growing for
us. There's a great big project afoot [the Northern Bombing Group]
for the USNAF and we'll be in on the ground floor for some cushy
jobs soon, unless they live up to their past reputation, or rather their
past program of systematically rooking all of us except Bob. They've
got it in for us for some reason or other down at H.Q.

We're due for the most glorious air raid tonight, so I guess I'll close
now and get some sleep before it starts. I could sleep right beside a
newly fallen bomb tonight. Eight different towns and three different
aerodromes were bombed last night. There must have been thirty
machines in on the job. But they just played around last night, tonight
will be the real thing. Wait till the 20th—full moon! "Good night,
Dunkirk! Au revoir!"

Not surprisingly, Kenneth's prediction of still another nocturnal visit
by German aircraft came true. Di Gates was one of many directly in the
line of fire. "We had our second very close shave from a bomb last
night," he recorded. "We heard one come hissing down through the air
and bang right across the street from our house, breaking several of our
windows and completely demolishing a wooden house about two hundred yards away."

Dunkirk, 21 May 1918

My Beloved,

You're a bright girl, and you know a great deal, so you will answer
the following questions and mail a reply to the office for a reward.

1st—Name one thing that has gone right for me in the last four
days?

2d—Tell me how a man can go on three five A.M. and one three A.M. patrol, also doing nine other two-hour patrols in four days and be fit?

3rd—What's the use?

4th—How do you know?

Two days ago one of the "Hard Guys" [John Ganster] flew into a building and was killed. Yesterday another "Hard Guy" left the patrol deliberately, way up off the Belge coast, and hasn't been heard of since. Today a third "Hard Guy" [Djalma Marshburn] was flying along straight when all of a sudden he went into a spin, and all we've found so far are two pontoons.

Of the twelve original Hard Guys, five have been killed, one is missing, and one is in Brest hospital with a frightful disease. There are four left on the station. I don't know where the other is. He may have been killed when I was with the English. I've changed my point of view about them. They aren't responsible. They aren't the right temperament. The man who selected them and sent them to England is indirectly responsible for the murder of six men! You can no more make an aviator out of a mucker than you can make a parlor snake out of a thug.

I've patrolled every inch of the Channel from below Dover to Ostend and I swear that the missing man either landed in some port, and hasn't had the intelligence to let us know, or else he made a bad landing and sank.

I drew some pay the other day, and I now have 4,246 francs, 754 more and I'll have enough to buy your ring, and then I'll always be able to feel that I earned every cent of the money I paid for it. That's one thing that I want to come out of my own pocket.

. . . By the way, the Dude [Harry Davison], as usual, beat me to it. I was having a little pair of gold wings made for you, with my name, number, and station engraved on them. They will be finished next Friday, but I can send them to Ishbel just as well, she's crazy for a pair. . . .

Poor old Di hasn't smiled for four days. When he gets gloomy, believe me, there's cause for gloom. These moonlit nights are about as welcome as a skunk at a lawn party. The Huns come over in droves. I wish it would rain forever. "Priceless Priscilla" was about as naughty today as anything could be, yet I'm glad because I can sleep in tomorrow morning. She caught on fire and nearly burned up. The mechanic had his head and shoulders inside the fuselage cleaning up and filling up for my fifth patrol when an electric light bulb exploded and the waste, soaked in gas, caught fire. The mechanic was badly burned about the head and arms because he couldn't get out quickly. . . .

Shortly after the accident that damaged "Priceless Priscilla," MacLeish and several other Dunkirk veterans received orders to proceed to Paris and then on to the army day bombardment school at Clermont-Ferrand. They all seemed very glad to abandon the wrecked Channel port, even if it meant leaving the scene of action for a while. Indeed, they looked forward to completing their bombardment training as quickly as possible and then rejoining Bob Lovett, Eddie McDonnell, and many others of the Yale "crew" in a campaign to destroy the submarine menace once and for all.

4

"Itching to Fight":
Clermont-Ferrand, Dunkirk,
Pauillac, Eastleigh

May 1918–October 1918

KENNETH MACLEISH SPENT the summer of 1918 in almost constant motion, shuttling from duty to duty and station to station. During this busy four-month period he received additional training with the Army Air Service and returned to the front for a series of daylight bombing missions. At other times he performed office duty in Paris or served as a test and inspection officer at the navy's assembly and repair bases at Pauillac, France, and Eastleigh, England.

MacLeish departed the Dunkirk flying station in late May, bound for the American Expeditionary Forces Day Bombardment School at Clermont-Ferrand, two hundred miles south of Paris. There he learned to fly two-seater bombing machines and accustom himself to U.S. Army methods and manners. A partisan navy man, MacLeish was not impressed and frequently chafed at the treatment he received from less experienced officers. Adding to his misery, he suffered a bout of the flu in late June that sent him to the hospital. Of course, he blamed that on the army too.

There were a few consolations, however. Kenneth was again able to visit his brother Archie, who was stationed nearby; he excelled in bombing and gunnery courses; and he also received word of his long-delayed promotion to lieutenant (jg). MacLeish's partner at Clermont-Ferrand was Irving Sheely, an enlisted observer from Albany, New York, who had reached France back in June 1917 as part of Lieutenant Kenneth Whiting's First Aviation Detachment. Both Sheely and MacLeish served at Dunkirk in the spring of 1918, though they did not begin flying together until being assigned to the army bombing school.

Despite his complaints, MacLeish's work at Clermont-Ferrand did not go unnoticed, at least as far as the navy contingent was concerned. Freddy Beach, another of the Yale Unit officers assigned to the day bombardment school, recalled that Kenneth had "succeeded in arousing so much enthusiasm and keeping all hands so good-humored that we made fast progress, and incidentally broke most of the school records." Beach was particularly impressed by the performance of the enlisted men "who were brought along as observers," which was "as good as, if not better than, that of the officers." MacLeish deserved special praise for his "tact and industry," and his ability to "maintain friendly relations with the school, despite the fact that at times there was argument and some feelings over questions of leave, etc."

Out of the sick bay at the end of June, MacLeish quickly finished his training and returned to Dunkirk. With no navy day bombers yet operating, both he and observer Sheely joined Britain's 218 Squadron flying D.H. bombers. Little had changed in his absence, for no sooner did MacLeish return to the Channel coast than the cycle of air raids and shellings began all over again. Despite the din, he enjoyed some respite in the antics of his new pet, a small, cantankerous puppy named George.

Lieutenant MacLeish's first flight over the lines came on 16 July 1918 with a daylight attack against the mole at Zeebrugge designed to wreck the port facilities there and to curtail the continued German submarine threat. Hampered by heavy anti-aircraft fire, several menacing enemy scouts, contrary winds, and a balky motor, he barely limped back to base. Other raids followed soon after, but in late July MacLeish again departed British service, this time for temporary duty at USNAS headquarters in Paris. His responsibilities there were light, and he quickly resumed his preferred leisure activities—enjoying dinner with "Aunt Emma" Guthrie of CPS & Co., sightseeing with fellow Yale aviator George Mosely, and lunching with Eddie Rickenbacker, the air service ace.

After only a week of desk duty Captain Hutch Cone dispatched MacLeish southward to Pauillac, the navy's burgeoning assembly and repair base on the Bay of Biscay. Anxious to return to combat, he found the work frustrating and bureaucratic. A wide variety of local entertainment provided some diversion—boxing matches, amateur shows, movies, and exhibition baseball games between a navy squad and a traveling team of professionals led by Grover Cleveland Alexander and Johnny Evers.

In mid-August, sporting another half stripe on his sleeve and the rank of full lieutenant, MacLeish became chief pilot at the Pauillac facility, assigned to assemble and test aircraft delivered from the United States and destined for front-line navy units, including the first of the Liberty-engined, American-built D.H. 4 bombers.

Just as he was settling into his new job, Lieutenant MacLeish was recalled to Paris headquarters, where he again entered wholeheartedly into the task of sightseeing and relaxing. Accompanied by friends he went rowing, swimming, and picnicking along the Marne River, toured Montmartre, and attended the Grand-Guignol Theater, which he found both amusing and scandalous.

In early September MacLeish crossed over to England to assume still another set of duties at the navy's Eastleigh assembly and repair base, the staging point for the planned Northern Bombing Group. As final inspection and test officer he exercised ultimate responsibility over aircraft headed to the combat squadrons. Though offered command of a night bombardment squadron, MacLeish declined, preferring to fly day bombers instead.

While Kenneth cheered the Doughboys' triumphs at St. Mihiel and the Meuse-Argonne, he desperately wished to return to action. The success of his close friend David Ingalls, by now the navy's first "ace," only strengthened his resolve. Instead, MacLeish endured a second severe attack of the flu. He did not fully recover for two weeks.

Finally, in early October Kenneth MacLeish received the word he had been waiting for; he was going back to France, first as a ferry pilot, and then to a front-line squadron. Thrilled with the prospect, he rededicated himself to the cause that had so consumed him for eighteen months.

Paris, 30 May 1918

My Most Sorely Needed Beloved,

Talk about homesick. Today is Decoration Day, and all the nurses from two Amex hospitals were here, to say nothing of about four regiments of artillery and two military bands.

The day I hit town I was walking down the street and who do you suppose I bumped into? I've never come so near to fainting! Archie! I thought he was at the front. He and Louis Middlebrook.[1] Tonight Bob DeVecci[2] came in. Everyone on earth is here, except you. . . .

1. *Louis Middlebrook, a native of Bridgeport, Connecticut, was a classmate of Archibald MacLeish's and served overseas with the field artillery.*
2. *Robert DeVecci, a Yale friend of Kenneth's, was a captain in the Sanitary Corps, assigned to an overseas hospital.*

Accompanied by Yalies David Ingalls, George Mosely, and Freddy Beach and several enlisted observers, MacLeish reached Clermont-Ferrand in late May. Mosely, for one, found the site lovely, situated in a valley surrounded by low, green mountains, "much like the mountains of Vermont." He was particularly impressed by the peacefulness of the place, "quite a relief from the continued bombardment to which we were more or less subject at Dunkirk."

The base itself had originally been a test field for Breguet bombers constructed by the Michelin Co. Later it was taken over by the Americans, who added hangars and a large number of white plaster buildings "with dainty pink roofs," including barracks, offices, mess rooms, and "last, but not least, a YMCA."

Clermont-Ferrand, 30 May 1918

Dearest Family,

I'm trying to learn how to do day bombing now. There's only one thing left open now that they haven't made me try, and that is night bombing, and I wouldn't be the least surprised if they tried that on me next. I'll always be going to school. . . .

The navy men loved the scenery but had a few things to say about the army. As Mosely observed, "We were spoiled at Dunkirk, I guess, for we miss our boys who used to take care of us, and we also miss the soft white beds and wonderful food."

Clermont-Ferrand, 31 May 1918

Beloved,

I wish you could see me now. I'm in the army for the time being, so I'm only "somewhere in France." But as soon as I get back to the good old navy again, I'll give you the dope. I never realized what I was in before I came down here. I kind of thought I was riding the gravy, now I know I was. It certainly rubs me the wrong way to come from a position of authority and responsibility after two months at the front, and after having seen more service and more of the war than any man in this place, including the C.O., and then be quartered off with our enlisted men in the same kind of quarters that they give their mechanics. For a bed I have a strip of canvas between two two-by-fours, no blankets, no mattress, no place to hang my clothes, and in the same room with seventeen men!

When I think of the marvelous meals and the courtesy and kindness that we showed the army men up at Dunkirk, it makes my head ache. We did everything under the sun for them, and I haven't seen even one bit of courtesy down here, except by some men that I knew before, and by the C.O., who is a perfect wonder, but whom I have only had the pleasure of seeing once. But I suppose it's all in the game, and I might as well grin and bear it, as it can't last long. But, by golly, I won't forget it.

I just heard today of the death of one of the very finest friends I ever had. I think I admired that boy more in the short three years that I knew him than any other friend I ever had, and I have felt his loss more keenly even than that of Curt and Al, and you know what I mean when I say that. He was killed at Newport News by a pupil. The pupil wasn't even scratched. His name was Leslie McNaughton.[1] He went to Hill and was in my class at Yale. Perhaps you knew him.

As you have guessed by now, all navy plans have changed, or most of them. Seaplanes are no more, or won't be soon. I'm down here on daylight stuff from an altitude. . . .

1. *Leslie McNaughton from Fort Edward, New York, served with naval aviation at Mastic, New York, M.I.T., Pensacola, and Hampton Roads, where he died in a training accident on 13 March 1918.*

The news of McNaughton's death did nothing to improve MacLeish's spirits, and he remained in high dudgeon concerning the army and its policies. His promotion to lieutenant (jg) helped relieve some of the gloom, however, as did the word that he might soon be promoted to command of a day bombardment squadron. He had not yet been informed that the navy planned to assign Marine Corps pilots to the day bombers. Finally, with his promotion and back pay, Kenneth hoped to purchase an engagement ring for Priscilla.

Clermont-Ferrand, 2 June 1918

Beloved,

Just suppose you had come over here and gone through some real warfare, and had gone through trials and deprivations of every sort, with the hope that at the end honor would be given where honor is due. Then you get a letter telling you that a certain bad egg whom you despised was parading around home with a wound stripe. Then you found out that the aforementioned bad egg had come over to Italy, had soloed, and then complained of a bad leg, and stated that he wanted to be sent home! He was taken to the hospital, and a very slight trouble was discovered in his leg which was quickly and easily cured, but still he insisted on being kicked out of flying, and finally admitted that he hadn't the nerve to fly! How would you feel if that same man finally got his wish, went home, put a wounded stripe on, and told a dirty lie. In so doing he cheapened the honor you were purchasing or seeking by risking your life! How would you feel towards him? That's how I feel about———, and that's what happened to him at Foggia, Italy.[1] He never saw the front and he has cheapened and disgraced the honor of wearing a wounded stripe to such a degree that I wouldn't wear one now if I were wounded a thousand times. . . .

By the way, you were right, I'm a lieutenant (jg) now. I got a telegram to that effect yesterday. So are Crock [Ingalls] and Freddy B[each], who are here with me now. Something very, very wonderful may come my way in a few months. I hate to tell you what it is because if I don't come through and I don't get it the laugh will be on me. Anyway, I'm not sure that I want it, because in the first place it would mean no more flying, and in the second place I don't have the ability. From the standpoint of honor, though, it's perfectly tremendous, and worth working like a slave for. I can't decide though, whether I want it enough to give up flying. I've just had a large enough mouthful of the real stuff to make me perfectly miserable without it. Oh, I guess I better not tell you what it is, because I probably won't get it anyway. . . .

I soloed yesterday after about half an hour of dual control on these things, so you see, they aren't so hard to fly after all. The only trouble is that they are so very different from a little scout.

This is a wonderful school if you are in the army, but little or no courtesy is shown navy men. Another point is that some of us pilots have had better training on land machines than the instructors, we have had the same training on land machines the instructors have, and our observers have had better training than the instructors, so the only thing we are getting here is a little teamwork with our observers, and a lot of abuse. I never fully appreciated what a fine institution the U.S. Navy really is, it's marvelous.

It's still warm and springlike here, and I'm still dopey and spring-feverish, but it can't last over a month at the most. I think that by the time I get to Paris again, I'll have enough money to buy the ring, as my commission as a lieutenant (jg) dates from March 23d, and I'm due for all that back pay.

This new drive isn't too hopeful, is it? Don't forget that what you read in the papers isn't always what really happens, so don't go thinking that the war will be over soon. . . .

1. *Foggia was the Army Air Service's primary training base in southeastern Italy. Major Fiorello LaGuardia was in charge of the officers stationed there.*

Clermont-Ferrand, 2 June 1918

Dearest Family,

WELL, what do you think about that? Your youngest son is now a lieutenant (jg). Who said the navy isn't O.K.? You don't rise so fast as you do in the army, of course, but a raise in the navy is much more valuable for that reason.

I hate to get your hopes up, but something very, very wonderful may happen to me soon. You see, there are going to be two squadrons of navy day bombers up where I've been [Dunkirk], and a regulation has come into effect prohibiting regular navy officers from holding down squadron commanders' jobs unless they have had experience. The only two regulars who have the experience are in headquarters, that is, and who have had the necessary experience. There are only two of us, Dave and myself, who have had experience, so it looks as though one of us would get a job as squadron C.O. "Di" will undoubtedly get the other. That may or may not mean a raise—I don't know. But at any rate, it's a great honor. The only thing is that a squadron C.O. can't fly anymore, and I refuse to give that up, so in one way I hope that I don't get it. I want to fight. That's what I came over here for. . . .

They are getting the submarine question very well in hand now. The only fear is that the Huns will spring something new. Wasn't that Ostend-Zeebrugge show[1] a wonder, the one that the English navy pulled? We saw the whole thing and it was a revelation. . . .

Well, I must close. This is a wonderful and much-needed rest for me—it will be as soon as I get suitable quarters, that is. This place is where Caesar defeated Vercingetorix. It's perfectly beautiful, and it's spring, and you'd never guess there was a war on.

1. *Most likely the British assault of 23 April 1918. The Royal Navy made a second attack on 10 May 1918 in an effort to close off these dangerous German submarine bases.*

Clermont-Ferrand, 3 June 1918

Beloved,

. . . I don't know what will happen to us when we get through here, but I think that if we get a couple of weeks to spare, we'll all put in for ten days' leave, get "Di," and go down to Nice or Biarritz and just absolutely, thoroughly enjoy life. I haven't had a good swim for ages, and I haven't had any leave since September 14, 1917, so I guess I rate some leave.

Maybe I don't feel pretty good with this extra half stripe. I know one thing for sure. If the army-navy aviation are consolidated, all of us will get out of aviation, because it will be exactly the same affair that the RAF is, where the army, if it doesn't get an advance, at least remains the same, and the navy gets horribly rooked. For instance, an ensign would be a second lieutenant. Now you know as well as I do that an ensign in the navy has had just as much, if not more, experience than a first lieutenant in the army. They make all cadets ensigns in the navy and first lieutenants in the army. The only thing will be that the uniform will be like the navy uniform. That's what happened in the RAF, and take it from me, if I can help it, it will never come my way. I'll get out altogether, go home, and then get drafted. . . .

At the same time MacLeish was worrying about a possible amalgamation of the army and naval air forces, Bob Lovett in Paris was working hard to implement his ideas for the Northern Bombing Group. In mid-June he wrote to Adele Brown back in New York, who surely relayed the news immediately to Priscilla, "I have gotten all the old [Yale] crowd together. Good old Ken will be in one of my night squadrons and I shall make him a flight commander as soon as he finishes his course."

Clermont-Ferrand, 7 June 1918

Hello Fiancée,

. . . The news from H.Q. about delivery of planes is most encouraging. I have real hopes that all of this stuff is just army gossip. Eddie

McD[onnell], to say nothing of Bob and Di and Chevy, will be prominent figures in the outfit [the Northern Bombing Group]. We're all in on the ground floor, full up to the eyebrows with high purpose. If we're on the job we surely have a golden opportunity, and here's right where your devoted fiancé gets on the job. But oh! How I'd hate to have to stop flying! I'd never do it, it really couldn't be done.

I wish you could have seen some of the scores that the navy put over today. In bombing, one man made a direct hit and was only six feet off on the other from 3,600 feet. No one has ever made two direct hits straight, and this is the closest anyone has ever come to it. Excuse me, I have to smirk a little.

Only a few days into the course, the navy men were busy indeed, learning to pilot their Breguet Br.14 day bombers. George Mosely described them as "very large French bombing planes." At first the navy pilots went aloft with instructors, "as the machines are very different in many ways from the little sensitive machines most of us have been driving. You have to be very hard on the controls of these machines, and even then they answer very slowly. They seem to be very heavy and very lazy in the air."

Irving Sheely, Kenneth's observer, described the process as high-altitude light bombing, flying in a formation of from five to eleven machines at an altitude of 20,000 feet. The intent was to penetrate "far into German territory, dropping bombs on their factories, railroad centers, ammunition depots, etc." Of the Breguets, Sheely told his family in early June, "Believe me I'm glad, because I hate those old seaplanes. Also, it's darned tiresome flying over water all the time. Also, I don't fancy a watery grave like four of our number have already gone to."

Clermont-Ferrand, 9 June 1918

My Bestest Beloved,

I'm over spending Sunday with Arch in his billet. He certainly picked the best one that I've ever seen, as the people are perfectly wonderful and very, very hospitable. It's one of those glorious spring days, with a brilliant sun, and the fields all shades of wonderful soft green. It's too perfect for words. So marvelous, in fact, that I can't force myself to realize there's a war on at all.

Tonight we are going over to [Royat?] to have dinner and hear the music. I know I shall be perfectly frantic because when I hear beautiful music I invariably think of you, and the associations are too much for me. I realize then with overwhelming force how terribly I miss you, and then, more than ever before, the beautiful memories I have of you become lifelike. When I get home, the very first thing we must do, after we're married, is to go to the opera and sit through a wonderful performance together.

I guess I got a demerit, or was bad or something yesterday. They told me to go up and fly the target machine while the other machine maneuvered for position and took pictures of me. I started off and just got off the ground when my motor began to sputter and cough. The air was bumpier than I've ever seen it before, and with just 50 feet of altitude, and JUST flying speed, I had to work that treacherous bus all the way around the field to be able to land again. I banked up vertically once and couldn't get out of it for a very long time. My old observer was all ready to throw his camera and gun overboard, and I figured we were cooked. I quickly got down after blowing a spark plug out of the cylinder entirely, and all they did was put in a new spark plug and send me out again. I was so mad that I didn't care after that, and I broke every flying rule, and got the instructor simply furious by consistently outmaneuvering him, in such a way that his observer couldn't take any pictures of me, although he had a much faster machine than mine. He doesn't know anything about fighting, evidently, because I had him cold every single minute that we were up there. Even my observer with an ordinary camera got better pictures than his observer, who had a special camera with gun sights. I flew too far away from the field, I cut across it, and then flew over a little town to see if I could get any pictures of it, all of which are broken rules. So I suppose I'll have to go sit in the corner or let the C.O. spank my hands with a ruler, or get a demerit, or something perfectly horrible like that.

Did I tell you that I saw Quentin Roosevelt[1] in Paris? He flew the same machine we're to have [D.H. 4], on a test flight, and liked it very much. . . .

1. *The son of ex-president Theodore Roosevelt, Quentin Roosevelt served with the air service's 95th Aerosquadron. He was killed in action on 14 July 1918.*

Clermont-Ferrand, 9 June 1918

Dearest Family,

. . . The country down here is, without exception, the most beautiful I have ever seen. I admit with some malice that this is the first time

I have seen the weather behave for two weeks straight since October. Every day is a perfect day, and every night is glorious. Aviation usually takes one away from mountains and to monotonous plains, but in this case scenery rather than efficiency was sought and the result is that the countryside is beautiful beyond words, but the places to land are as scarce as hen's teeth, with the result that every time there is a forced landing the machine is totally wrecked and the government loses $17,000 and an aviator or two. . . .

Clermont-Ferrand, 10 June 1918

Precious,

. . . Am I a senior lieutenant? I don't see how that is possible because I've only been a junior lieutenant for five days. But as long as you were sport enough to tell me this, and in view of the fact that it corroborates my dope on this wonderful thing that is going to happen to me, I may as well loosen up with my information. But first promise that you won't be disappointed if it doesn't come off, because I don't see how I can rate it.

Di is the first one of the Huntington outfit to get a station [Dunkirk] on the front. He was the one I left a short time ago. The dope is that I'm to have the first squadron of land machines and be directly under Eddie McD[onnell], who will have the first wing. That means that I'll have this bunch that I'm with now.

My observer [Irving Sheely] is a real HE-observer! He invented a modification for a bomb sight whereby you can't miss the target. It's perfectly marvelous.[1]

Enclosed you will find a picture of "Priceless Priscy"[2] that Eddie DeCernea[3] just sent me. He says it's all smashed up now, which nearly brings tears to my eyes. I loved that dear old bus, because I painted it with my own hands, and I worked on it quite a bit too. The name is painted on the front so you can't see it. But perhaps you don't think that it looked wonderfully with a pure white tail and a rich, dark blue stripe all the way around it with that crest painted on, the shield in red, white, and blue as it should be, and the anchors gold.[4] One of the guns shows up well, and the long telescopic sight, right in front of my face. The seat in that bus was just as comfortable as a big Morris chair, with that little bump to streamline my head. You can see how very narrow the slip was in which we had to land by looking under the lower wing at the ships which were tied up to the other side of the slip. My

mechanic is the "gob" with the cross under him. He is a gem, too. I'm
going to put in for him when we get back. . . .

*1. Sheely told his family, "I have been working on a little invention which I hope will
pan out pretty good. If I am successful it will play——with the Dutchmen."*

2. MacLeish's Hanriot-Dupont H.D.2 pontoon scout at Dunkirk.

*3. Born in Philadelphia, Edward DeCernea trained with the Second Yale Unit at
Buffalo, New York, and later served at Moutchic, Dunkirk, and London and with the
Northern Bombing Group.*

*4. Fliers frequently decorated their aircraft. While at Dunkirk George Mosely reported,
"We all have some insignia or sign painted on the machine." He emblazoned his own
Hanriot-Dupont with a broad blue band and red hearts on both sides of the fuselage.*

Clermont-Ferrand, 12 June 1918

Beloved,

. . . Crock and I have a wonderful idea, so if you'll just tell Mr.
Davison about it, we'll fix it all up. After we've been over here for a
short time, or rather, at the front for four or five months, we'll put in
for home leave, get a couple of little "Camels," and come over to tour
the States, doing stunt flying and having exhibition flights for the Red
Cross. A real aerial scrap, or rather, a good imitation of one is perfectly fascinating to watch, and ought to make money for the Red
Cross. What do you think? So you'll see about it, won't you? And
there are two Canadians up in 213 Squadron, 61st Wing, who will tour
Canada for the same purpose, and then we'll all fly to New York and
have a gang flight over the center of the city, land in Central Park, and
proceed to have ourselves an enjoyable time.

My observer is THERE. He made three direct hits in three passages
from 1,200 meters, the best done before was two out of three, and that
was made by another navy observer. The school record, before the
navy arrived, was one out of three. All the observers are having a
songfest in the next room, which is very disconcerting because one of
them has a voice that is naturally higher than Charlie Hathaway's, but
not as well trained. It's the same sort of voice and it drives me wild. Do
you remember that night? What a fool I was. Why didn't you slap me
and make me behave myself? . . .

Clermont-Ferrand, 14 June 1918

Beloved,

My old HE-observer and Crock's observer have figured out a new
sight which requires a tremendous amount of calculation, and also

deals with lenses and prisms, and I told them I would do all the mathematical calculations for them, but I have forgotten how! If I do the dirty work on this sight I will get some of the credit, but I don't think I can, as all my notes on lenses and prisms are at home in my desk.

They tell me we'll be finished here in ten days of good weather. I got a letter from one of the Englishmen in 213 Squadron and he says the weather is simply horrible, because every day is a beautiful day. I'm sort of sorry I have to be training all this spring, but at the same time, spring is by all odds the worst possible time to go up to the front for the first time because there is so much work, and because machines fall like leaves in autumn then.

Budge, I'm too discouraged for words. Do you realize that they charge 60% duty on a ring, and 20% on the stone, and that jewelry has gone up almost 90% in price. If I have to get the ring in New York it will take away half the romance of the thing. There is a possibility I can avoid the duty by sending it in the embassy pouch. . . .

The boys are arguing now as to whether there will be one of us left by next Christmas with these new Fokker triplanes[1] the Huns are using. In that light, isn't all this foolish? But it can't be considered in that light as we can [illegible] on the Fokkers in our buses. . . .

1. *The Fokker DR-1 triplane, designed by Reinhold Platz, gained its first victory in August 1917, and production models became widely available after November. Approximately 170 were in service by May 1918.*

Kenneth's efforts to buy an engagement ring for Priscilla and then have it shipped home across the sub-infested Atlantic lasted nearly two months and took on all the characteristics of an international spy thriller.

Clermont-Ferrand, 16 June 1918

My Bestest Beloved,

I haven't written to you for two days, but it's been because I've been too excited to sit still long enough. I've been very, very busy trying to arrange the purchase of your ring. I have telephoned Paris every ten minutes and spent "umpteen" million francs, but it has been just glorious. Enclosed is an exact drawing of the two best outfits that could be found. They are both drawn to scale. I have decided to get the top one because the stone is perfectly beautiful. I don't know how you will like the setting, but this is the information I have gathered. . . .

Miss Guthrie, the lady at Carson, Pirie, Scott and Co., and a sort of Paris aunt to me, has suggested this. She says it would be very risky sending the ring over just now. She also suggests (though it made me smile a little) that an exact duplicate could be made which only an expert would ever be able to tell was not real, and that could be sent over, and it wouldn't be much of a loss if it were sunk. How does that appeal to you?

There is no telling what may happen in the future. It is perfectly possible I may be sent home to see if I can help improve the system of instruction, it is perfectly hopeless now. John [Vorys] and Nugent Fallon[1] went home—perhaps I may be sent—who knows?

1. *Nugent Fallon, a member of the Harvard group of naval aviators trained by Henry Cecil and William Atwater at Newport News, Virginia, met MacLeish at the Hampton Roads station in the early fall of 1917.*

Though MacLeish and his companions were sent to Clermont-Ferrand to learn day bombing as part of the buildup for the navy's planned Northern Bombing Group, the decision had already been made in the United States to create several Marine Corps squadrons and assign that duty to them, with the naval aviators carrying out night bombardment missions instead. Three marine day squadrons and a headquarters company totaling 107 officers and 654 enlisted men reached France in late July, and then proceeded to Dunkirk and Calais to join the Northern Bombing Group. A fourth squadron arrived in October.

The news was greeted with dismay by the navy pilots. Freddy Beach recorded, "We found everything in a mix-up due to the insistence of the Marine Corps that the land flying of the navy should be done by them." He lamented, "We saw our dreams of a crack naval squadron that we had striven so hard to obtain and perfect sort of vanishing into thin air." The decision to assign marine pilots to day missions effectively ended Mac-Leish's chances of commanding a day bombardment squadron.

Clermont-Ferrand, 18 June 1918

Beloved,

The whole thing—that wonderful dream—is gradually crumbling away under our very eyes. Another man from the squadron is being sent away, he has lost his nerve. The marines insist they are the only ones capable of flying land machines. Isn't it a shame that just because the marines have that reputation of being first on land or sea, they are small and childish enough to prevent the navy from fighting side by side in the same cause with them because they know darn well the navy pilots are better than theirs are, and they would show them up. Isn't it pathetic? I always had the fondest respect for the marines, and I could never understand before why they were so cordially hated by the army and the navy. If it weren't for the fact that they have the efficiency due to a central command, and can thereby account for themselves very well, they would certainly be washed out.

I got a very interesting letter from Trubee yesterday. Isn't it funny that you should know more about me and my rank than I do? I haven't heard a word about it yet. I also got a letter from Di. He's out with an English squadron [#214]. I wouldn't be surprised if Crock and a fine boy named Eddie Judd[1] and I went with the English too, but that seems like another wonderful dream to me.

We just heard today that forty Hun machines bombed D[unkirk] for three nights straight and dropped seven hundred bombs. They absolutely wiped out the HPs [Handley Pages], killed my old flight commander [Painter] just as he was getting into bed, and killed several men over at 217 Squadron where Di was. Though I didn't hate the Boche when I came, I absolutely hate them now, and have several serious scores to even up. . . .

1. *David Edward Judd, a Boston native, attended Harvard, then drove an ambulance in the American Field Service, served with the Lafayette Flying Corps, and finally joined naval aviation in February 1918. His later assignments included Moutchic, Dunkirk, and the Northern Bombing Group.*

Clermont-Ferrand, 19 June 1918

My Bestest Beloved,

. . . Di, as I think I told you, is riding the gravy for about the first time in his life—he's out with the English. I've never been so jealous in my life. If I can't fight pretty soon, I'll lose all my nerve. I never had enough to make a dog chase a cat anyway. What will happen if I lose what little I have? . . .

Kenneth's aviation career was interrupted in late June by a bout with the flu, part of the opening phase of the great Spanish influenza pandemic that struck millions worldwide. Ever loyal, MacLeish blamed it all on the army.

Clermont-Ferrand, 22 June 1918

Beloved,

Well, this is quite a letdown. The last letter I wrote you was finished about ten or ten-thirty last Wednesday night. When I went to bed about eleven I noticed I had a little tendency to cough, but it wasn't bad. The next morning at five o'clock I was the sickest man you ever saw. They sent me out to the hospital as quickly as possible, and for the last three days I haven't seen any fun in anything, not even in being alive. There may be some combination which can make you feel worse than grippe, bronchitis, and influenza all at once, but if there are any, I don't want to try them out.

I have been in a sort of sleepy stupor for the past three days and nights, just waking for meals, medicines, and calldowns by the nurses. All the doctors and nurses are from the University of Pennsylvania, and believe me, your dope on Red Cross nurses is all wrong.

Our nurse puts thermometers in our mouths and then curses us out for fair! Of course, we can't answer back, and by the time she has taken them out, she has said something nice, so nothing is left open to discussion.

This is the first time I've been sick since I've been in the navy, and it's all due to the fact that I'm attached to the army. They kicked us out of our barracks to make room for some of their enlisted men. It's just as well, because there's an epidemic of grippe in our room. Lord, how I hate the army.

Well, beloved, I better lie down before I fall down. . . .

Base Hospital, 24 June 1918

Beloved,

. . . I thought I was going to get out of the hospital tomorrow, but now after all this, I'm flat on my back again, so I guess there's no chance of getting out again for a couple of days. . . .

While recovering in the hospital Kenneth learned of one of the most bizarre aviation incidents of the war. A plane piloted by army Lieutenant Samuel Mandell, with observer Lieutenant Gardiner Fiske aboard, was aloft on a training flight, with Fiske standing up on the rear seat firing a camera gun at an attacking scout. During some rough maneuvering the gun broke loose from its fastenings and the mortified observer was pitched out of the cockpit at a height of 3,000 feet, traveling at 100 mph. What followed was nothing short of miraculous.

Clermont-Ferrand, 27 June 1918

Beloved,

We now have one of our naval aviators writing a letter. He is here depicted sitting up on top of a double decker trying to make a conversation with a girl he left behind him, and is getting a cramp in the attempt. How's that for misleading you? When I called it the attempt, you thought I was trying to avoid telling you where the cramp really is, don't you? Well, it wasn't, that's where it is.

I wish there had been a movie man here today. One fellow was flying along in rather bumpy air when such a tremendous bump hit him that his observer bounced clear out of the cockpit at 3,000 feet— flew back and caught the tail planes under his right arm. His arm, hooked over the tail plane, was the only thing between him and 3,000 feet of nice, blue, bumpy space. He fought his way back to the top of the tail, kicked a hole in it with his knees, and got footing enough to crawl back into the cockpit where he fell limply to the floor, a complete nervous wreck. How's that, eh? . . .

George Mosely was also in the air at the time and anxiously watched the leather-coated observer make his way back up the fuselage until he was able to dive headfirst into his seat. Mosely recalled, "Some of the other men saw it. They said he left the fuselage bodily and flew through the air for a space of five feet until he struck the vertical stabilizer that knocked him back to the fuselage."

A few days after this remarkable incident MacLeish and the rest of the navy fliers were ordered back to Dunkirk. Kenneth spent the Fourth of July in Paris and reached the naval air station the following afternoon. Three days later pilots MacLeish, Ingalls, and Judd, along with their observers, transferred to 218 Squadron for temporary duty on day bombers.

Dunkirk, 5 July 1918

Beloved,

Well, here I am again, but to be absolutely truthful, I've been spoiled. I'm not the least bit keen about going out for some reason or another. I guess it's because bombing by day as taught by the army has left a bad taste in my mouth. Crock and Eddie Judd feel the same way about it. We none of us want to go out on these machines [D.H. 9 bombers]. There is all kinds of activity in the air up here, and if I stick through the next month, I'll always be safe. The way I figure it, I get a chance to shoot down Huns, or be shot down. Everything lies in the balance, so unless you've gotten bad news by cable concerning me, I'll have passed over the danger when you get this. . . .

Dunkirk, 6 July 1918

My Beloved,

Now I have more time, so I can tell you some of the news. At present Crock, Eddie Judd, and I are up here with "Lootenant" Gates's Navy. We will only be here until Monday when we will be attached to the RAF again, a squadron of D.H. 9s this time. Isn't it funny. I will have been with three different organizations—the RNAS, the USN, and the RAF—all of this since April first. When we finish up with them we will have been trained as flight commanders. When our men and machines arrive I will be a flight commander as well as a squadron leader. Can you beat it? But that will be absolutely ideal. I will be flying all the time. It's perfectly marvelous.

Bob is here—he just arrived from London, and if you ever get your ring, you have Bob to thank for getting it to you. I had to leave it sitting at CPS & Co. safe, but I practically made all the arrangements about sending it by [diplomatic] pouch. I missed Commander [William Fuller] Gresham, and anyway, he has been torpedoed twice.

I think we'll have a rattling good raid tonight. Just my luck—I begged off going with the English until Monday because I'm so thin and weak after that spell at Clermont, and I want to catch up on food and sleep here. Well, they say the barrage has improved tenfold since I left, so it will be wonderfully interesting to watch. . . .

Dunkirk, 7 July 1918

My Beloved,

The wildest thing just happened that I ever heard of. A big seaplane had a forced landing, and our motorboat went out to pick them up. The French got there first and the motorboat was signaled to return. It got the signal and turned around. Several hours later we got word that it had been sunk by German shore batteries way up near Ostend. How under the sun do you think it ever got way up there? Doc Stevens[1] and six enlisted men are missing. If any were alive after they were hit, they will probably swim ashore and be taken prisoner. Isn't that the rottenest luck you ever heard of. Doc Stevens was my English prof up at

Hotchkiss School in 1911–12, and it was quite a coincidence that he should have been stationed at the same place with me.

Do you remember when Crock, Shorty, and I were at Ayr in the same room with an army duck named Lloyd Hamilton? Well, he's a flight commander up here in this area [Petite Synthe] in an American squadron [17th Aerosquadron]. He ran into von Richthofen's flight the day before he [von Richthofen] was shot down, and von Richthofen got their major and another man in flames from four hundred yards. Lloyd and his gang got one of the Huns. Von R.'s flight were all painted a solid color, for instance, von R.'s plane was solid red. Well, these ducks shot down the blue one. Lloyd has had lots of scraps. When von R. was shot down the Australians dressed him up and took pictures of him after he was dead. Can you beat those Australians?

Well, I must close now and see whether I can help Di out. Poor boy. He's discouraged to begin with, and the C.O. job at this station is a hard one. I'm afraid he and Bob are going to break soon, as he thinks Bob is keeping him from flying land machines. I'm not in the mood for writing. I feel more like fighting, but love you more than ever today.

1. A. M. Stevens, a 1905 Yale graduate and later Rhodes scholar, taught French, English, and German at Hotchkiss School in the period 1908–12. He survived this encounter with the German shore battery, was captured and interned, and was released following the Armistice.

Dunkirk, 8 July 1918

Bestest Beloved,

Well, the outcome of yesterday's affair was rather tragic. The two strongest swimmers, the Doc and a chief petty officer, beat the rest in, and didn't give the favoring tide quite time enough to carry them to our side of the lines. The C.P.O. came ashore behind the Hun lines, the Doc was last seen by a sniper, emerging from the water with his hands over his head in no-man's-land, directly in front of the Hun trenches, and was seen to walk right into their arms. He had evidently been shot in the head while still swimming, though that is only a report. Two poorer swimmers let the tide wash them ashore this side of the piers at Nieuport and are safe. A third man was picked up by a French seaplane. The other two probably never reached shore. When last seen they were having a rough time. To show how they [the Germans] shoot, the first shot went through the canvas canopy, the second through the superstructure, and the third through the hull.

I am going out to 218 Squadron RAF near Calais. It's a good squadron as far as the men are concerned, and I'm sure I'll have a wonderful time. Just use the same old address and I'll get the mail promptly.

We had a bird of a raid last night. One direct hit on the station, and also on a tub on the other side of the Channel which set fire to some crude oil, and attracted the Huns like flies to a sugar bowl. One Gotha was hit and you could hear it go into a spin, but I think it came out of it, because after a few seconds the motors came on again very low over the town, and it went home. Some say that was another Hun and that they heard the first one crash into the sea.

I wondered why they told me that the barrage here was better and then smiled and winked at each other. Now I know. There is a crowd of ruffians who have some movable guns and they planted one around the corner of our house. I thought at first that the Huns were dropping their eggs on us, because it was as hard to stay on the bed as it is to stay on a bucking bronco. But finally I caught the scream of a depart [outgoing shell] and guessed at what was up. It sure gave me a thrill at first.

Did you know that you might get your ring sometime before next New Year's? Well, you may. Bob is tending to it, though I'm not sure how successful he'll be. It will come all marked Red Cross and War Council and H. P. Davison, for which I expect to get severely "strafed" by Mr. Davison, but just so the ring gets there. . . .

I feel much better now than I did when I came up here, but I'm not fit yet. Of course, we'll have to train a little on D.H. 9s before we do any real work, so that will give me a chance to catch up. I weigh about six pounds less than I should, but I'm gaining fast these days.

I must close now and pack. It seems funny to be sitting here in the ruins of my old office, with broken glass, plaster, and bricks heaped a foot high on the desk, and the blue sky over my head instead of a roof! I wish this bloody war could be called off. I'm fed up with it. . . .

While Kenneth entrusted Priscilla's ring to Bob Lovett in early June, many weeks passed before it reached North America. In a letter to Adele Brown, Lovett reported, "You, of course, have heard the good news about Kennie and Priscie much before I saw Ken; and as my time is exceedingly pressed at present, would you please tell her how very happy I am. . . . You might also tell Chubbie (or is it Slim now?) that I am having the devil's own job getting her ring over to her; Kennie entrusted it to me, and I've at last got it started; barring delays, she should get it by the first week in August."

Calais, 10 July 1918

Beloved,

. . . Well, I'm here [Fretnum] at 218 Squadron. I brought rain with me, though. Somebody else furnished a nice little hole in the roof over my head, so we have a very jolly, but unnecessary, time, me and the rain. . . .

I simply can't understand why you haven't been receiving mail from me. There is only one period when you wouldn't receive many letters from me, and that was when I was on my way down to Clermont. I had loads to do then and was very worried, and didn't have anything decent to write about. I just didn't write for a few days. I'm terribly worried because these letters are my only diary. They will be so interesting to read over when we are together again, because then I can explain more and give you little details that I'm sure would interest you. . . .

The Dude [Harry Davison][1] and Alfie [Allan Ames][2] didn't sail when they got their orders, did they? It seems to me they should be over by now if they did. I was in Paris over the Fourth of July and no word had been heard from them. I just want Alfie for one night and that will be plenty. I want him in Dunkirk on a nice night with a full moon and no wind. I want to go walking with him and then have the Huns pay us a visit. Alfie is easily kidded and I think I could get at least one rise out of him. He'd do what everyone who comes up here always does. I did it. Crock, Shorty, and Di all did it. Got into their first air raid. In each case the worst for months and months, and then, though scared to death, they wouldn't get out of bed, for fear of being kidded. Alfie would walk along as if nothing were happening at all, with shrapnel falling like hail, and a bomb every once in a while. Believe me, the people in Paris can say what they want about "la Grosse Bertha" and their air raids, and the people in London can talk about theirs, but there's just one little thing, they've never been to Dunkirk during a raid and land bombardment by "Loegenboom." I've been in them all and there's nothing as terrifying as Loegenboom

at night. From the two blasts by Mournful Mary, through forty
seconds of agony that seem like ninety years, clear on through when
you're bounced out of bed by the explosion, it's terrible, that's all.
Nobody, not even the Huns, know where the shell is going to land at
that range, and all one hears is the screech through the air, that is, if
he's lucky; if he doesn't hear it he never hears anything else. . . .

*1. Harry Davison was sent overseas in July 1918, then ordered to Italy to ferry giant
Caproni bombers north across the Alps to Dunkirk. He was later attached to the Northern
Bombing Group.*

*2. Allan "Alfie" Ames, from St. Paul, Minnesota, reached naval headquarters in Paris
in July 1918, assigned to operations and intelligence duties. During August he toured naval
aviation bases in France.*

On 3 June 1918 the 82d Wing containing three squadrons, #38, #214,
and #218, was added to the Fifth Group, RAF, responsible for day and
night bombardment. On 6 July 1918 the wing moved to Fretnum immediately southwest of Calais to escape the frequent German raids. Mac-
Leish referred to one such devastating attack in his letter of 18 June 1918.
Heavy winds temporarily halted flight operations, but nothing was allowed to stand in the way of afternoon baseball.

Calais, 11 July 1918

Beloved Pam [Priscilla Murdock],

We just got trimmed 9–0 by our Bluejays. Fortunately it rained
yesterday when we were ahead 3–0, but today there wasn't a cloud in
the sky, and we had no hope.

I've never seen so much wind in my life. It's nearly time we had a bit
less, I think. It blows and blows and blows. All our buses are ready,
and so are the Huns', so there will be a merry old time when it stops
blowing. It won't do to go spitting in the Huns' face for a while,
anyway.

The rest of our gang have their orders now, and will be up this way
soon—also, your ring is being attended to—all this from a letter Bob
wrote Di. Budge, if you ever get that ring won't I be happy. It's about
the first really tangible bit of love I have sent, it seems to me. If you
look into the stone, maybe you'll see something there, Lord knows, I
left it. And on top of the stone, Budge, it will always be there as a
token of my love.

Nothing interesting to write about except that I rode a motorcycle into Calais this P.M. and nearly broke my back. The roads are fright-ful. But don't worry, dear, everything will come out all right, it's got to.

Calais, 12 July 1918

Beloved,
. . . There was a Marine Corps pilot attached to this squadron. He left today to take charge of a squadron of marines who will come up here to this sector. He's a "full-out" old scout, I'll say that much for him, and a nice fellow to play around with. If all the marines are his type, I don't think I'll mind them very much.[1]

There's the cutest little puppy named George here that you ever saw. He refuses to let me write. First he walks all over the letter, and then he attacks the pen with a growl. He's a great hound, about as large as a silver dollar, and slightly overbalanced. That is, his feet are by far the most conspicuous part of him, and his head is next. He looks (and acts) like a Mexican hairless. Only when they removed the hair from this one they removed the brains also.

1. *One of three marine squadron commanders sent to Europe in June 1918 ahead of their units and temporarily attached to British units: Douglas Roben, Roy Geiger, or, most likely, William McIlvain, who served with 218 Squadron as an observer.*

Calais, 14 July 1918

Beloved,
. . . I knew something funny was going to happen. They're going to send me over the lines on a raid without even giving me a trial flight in the machines. I've never flown anything like these buses before, so it will be their own fault if I smash up landing or don't find my way back. Usually a green pilot gets a few weeks before he goes on patrol, that is, even though he has flown the machines before. Well, it will be exciting anyway.

They got two Huns this morning, and one of the observers was slightly wounded. There is plenty to do in this sector right now.

All this mud on the paper is George again. He takes great delight in messing things up, and socks, slippers, and letters are things. A fly must look huge to George. He stalks them the way a lion stalks its game.

Bob just called up. He's over at our H.Q. at St. Inglevert.[1] I guess he's moved up from Paris for good now. I hope he has, anyway, because he can accomplish so much more up here.

George wants me to tell you that this pen wiggling around is too much for him. He says he simply must attack it. Also, he doesn't quite understand why it should make funny remarks that way. He has smelled all the letters so far, and he says they pass his olfactory censorship.

Today is the French Fourth of July [Bastille Day]. The French seem to enjoy it as much as the Americans enjoy the Fourth. I've never seen so many men with a happy "tan" on.

George has gone to sleep on my left hand so I can't maneuver enough to keep the paper still, let alone get an envelope. . . .

1. *The château at St. Inglevert served as headquarters for the navy's Northern Bombing Group.*

Dunkirk, 16 July 1918

Beloved One,

Well, my hunch was wrong. I just had a flip in these buses.[1] I'm afraid all of us are stale on flying, it holds no thrills at all. You see a man is only good at this flying game, really good, for the first six or eight months, possibly a year. I've been shifting around from pillar to post, and my best days are over until I get a few months' rest, which I'll never get, and I'll have to fly eight months before I even get two weeks.

They say there's mail for the crowd at St. Inglevert, but none for this part of the crowd. I think I'm a bit sore with the mail service myself.

Good news. Bob phoned and said he couldn't get the ring in the pouch, but Surgeon Lane, a two-and-a-half-striper, is on his way home with it, and will deliver it to Mr. Lovett's secretary[2], who will give it to you. If old "Surg" hasn't left yet, he will soon, so keep an open eye about the time you get this, if not sooner. In case you haven't it by now, you better get in touch with Mr. Lovett's secretary, I've forgotten his name, and tell him that it's coming via Surgeon Lane, who will phone him on arrival in New York, and then tell him where you'll be so he can give it to you. Bob and I aren't sure yet that you and Adele are at 690 Park Avenue [H. P. Davison's] yet.

Bob is going back to Paris tomorrow, but will be up again in a few days. Some of our buses are here, and we will only be with this squadron for three or four raids, and then we'll go down and get them. . . .

1. *During MacLeish's July stay with 218 Squadron he flew D.H. 9 day bombers, an underpowered aircraft introduced the previous December and eventually replaced by the much-improved D.H. 9a.*

2. *Lieutenant Commander Harry H. Lane, attached to navy headquarters in Paris, was ordered back to the United States in the early summer of 1918. Robert S. Lovett was a lawyer and chief executive of the Union Pacific Railroad system, with offices in New York City.*

On the morning of 16 July 1918 a group of thirteen day bombers from 218 Squadron, which included navy pilots Kenneth MacLeish and Edward Judd, attacked the mole at Zeebrugge and the German naval vessels anchored there. During a mission that lasted nearly three hours, six aircraft were hit by the heavy anti-aircraft barrage, and one failed to return to base. MacLeish's observer, Irving Sheely, later told his parents, "On my first bombing trip one of these shells burst just beneath my tail. A piece of 'scrapnel' went through the rudder. You may be sure the old boat rocked a little also." The attacking planes dropped a total of 2,200 pounds of bombs and fired 500 rounds into a salvage ship. MacLeish later reported that his four 50-pound bombs released at a height of 13,000 feet had fallen into the sea.

Dunkirk, 16 July 1918

Beloved,

Now just tell me this, aren't you pretty glad to get this letter from me? I should think you would be because I was very earnest this morning when I told you goodbye forever by mental telepathy—did you get it? Well, it was this way.

There were nine Huns behind me ready to dive. They were quite far back, but there all the same, and Archie was almost ten times as noisy and friendly as I ever hope to see him again. The air was black. Well, I got over the objective, and dropped my bombs, and then Archie hit me. It wasn't a full hit, or you wouldn't be reading this. It was under the tail of the bus. I went into all kinds of dives and gizzy-wiggles before I could get control again. I looked at Sheely and Sheely looked at me, but I don't remember that anything in particular was said. My mouth was so full of my heart that I would naturally have died if I'd opened it. I can only guess about Sheely, but he didn't say an awful lot, if he ever opened his mouth. Well, now, just as I pulled out of the dive, poppety-bang, ugh, my motor corked. Quit on me cold. I had a 30- or 50-mile wind to fly into. Just then she began to sputter and gurgle, and then she caught on five cylinders, and it took me fifty-five minutes to go thirty miles. Before I decided to make a stab at it, I looked down and there was Holland, so peaceful and green. And I remembered that prisoners of war get two months out of every three on leave, as food is scarce—and what couldn't a man do with two months' leave and no more war to excite him. But I turned to the old engine, then sort of looked up, and I've never meant any words more in my life than these: "It's my duty to go back, but it's up to you to get me there—this bloody engine won't—Amen. . . ."

Shortly after landing and grabbing lunch, MacLeish took off again for a thirty-five minute test flight on another machine, most likely to replace the one damaged in the morning's raid. The D.H. 9 bombers flown by 218 Squadron barely attained 85 mph at 13,000 feet without bombs, and 75 mph fully loaded.

Dunkirk, 17 July 1918

Beloved One,

. . . Constance Binney of *Cosmopolitan* magazine has graciously accepted a position on our wall. She looks haughtily down on Eddie Judd, looks slyly away from Dave [Ingalls], and smiles at me. I had to fight for my part of the picture, but I won it after some hot engagements. She says goodbye to us when we go on raids and "cheer ho" when we come back. Did you say you knew her? Well, cherish that little acquaintance till some naval aviators get to "blighty," will you?

George has attacked one of my spiral puttees; having nicely unrolled it all over the floor he is now busy with the other. What would you do with a curse like that? The puttee is about as big as he is, and that makes the struggle furious. . . .

I'm not on the E[arly] M[orning] P[atrol] tomorrow. I'm glad too, because the E. is quite capital. It stands for early, only it should be spelled EEEarly in this case. . . .

Dunkirk, 18 July 1918

Beloved One,

I hate to tell you about my new hunch. Well, I might as well, but don't be disappointed if it's wrong. According to my dope, if the

Huns don't show more in this offensive than they are at present, I'll be at your house for Christmas, so save a place at the table for me.

I'm simply furious! What do you think? Archie [MacLeish] has been sent home to instruct,[1] and he's gone and he didn't take your ring!!! I'll never, as long as I live, speak to him again. He's a mutt, a chump, and a pinhead of the first class. Ugh, I hate the lucky bum. Why can't I go home and instruct?

Lord, isn't that disgusting? I never have been so wild in my life. What would you do if you had such a stupid brother? I'd strangle him if I could get my hands on him. . . .

1. *In the midst of the Château-Thierry battle, Lieutenant Archibald MacLeish of the 146th Field Artillery was ordered back to the United States to serve with the 33d Field Artillery at Camp Meade, Maryland.*

Kenneth embarked on his second raid the following day, this time against the harbor, docks, and warehouses at Bruges where German work ships were attempting to salvage sunken destroyers. A total of twelve machines participated in the early-morning raid, escorted by 204 Squadron. After dropping approximately 2,400 pounds of bombs, all aircraft returned safely to base.

Dunkirk, 19 July 1918

Beloved One,

. . . I went out on another raid this A.M. and had more engine trouble.[1] I broke a valve spring just after I crossed the lines, but my motor turned up pretty well, so I decided to go ahead with it. I stayed with our formation over the objective, but dropped way, way back again coming home against the wind. I'm absolutely sick of having engine trouble when everything is against me that way. I caught aich, ee, double el all the way from the objective to the coast because I was alone. But I dodged the stuff pretty successfully. What hurts me most is that I drew a perfect bead on the factory, and due to the wind all my bombs went about four hundred yards over into a bit of nice green field. I could weep, I'm so disgusted.

On the way home I was feeling particularly "full out," so I dove towards a very famous Archie battery and opened up with my guns at 13,000 feet. Then my observer emptied a pan from his gun. He had no sooner finished than wonk, wonk, woof, old Archie began to bark. I felt like taking off my helmet to them. Lord, they are good. They only fired four or five shots, but every one of them had my exact altitude, and they were no more than fifty yards to one side. I'll have to be awfully "full-out" before I do that again.

I'm going on my last raid tomorrow, if it's a nice day. I don't know where I'll go after that, perhaps down to get our machines, and then back here to be attached to the same squadron, with our own buses. Of course, that's only a rumor, but wouldn't that be marvelous.

I wouldn't write lieutenant or try to kid me anymore about it if I were you—if there ever was a myth, that's it. I'll never get a senior-grade lieutenant's commission in this wide, wide world.

1. *Probably the undependable 230-hp Siddely Puma in-line six-cylinder engine.*

MacLeish's third and final raid with 218 Squadron commenced at 6:55 A.M. on 20 July. Eleven machines hit the Zeebrugge mole and salvage ships, dredgers, docks, and lock gates. From a height of 14,000 feet Kenneth and his observer dropped eight 25-pound Cooper bombs near the mouth of the Bruges canal, close to three dredgers and one torpedo boat.

Shortly after returning to the Fretnum aerodrome, MacLeish shifted back to Dunkirk and thence on to Paris for another stint of office duty at headquarters before reassignment to the navy's assembly and repair station at Pauillac. As usual, Priscilla was on his mind.

Paris, 24 July 1918

Dear Priscilla,

I work in an office now so I rate a typewriter, as you may have noticed. I work for Bob and my work consists of making myself look busy whenever I'm here, which is a few minutes a day when I have nothing else to do. But I love my work and I love my boss and I love Paris, so why should I moan?

Guess what I'll have to do for a job in a few days? I'll be stationed down near Bordeaux at a receiving station [Pauillac] where I am to accept and test all the new machines sent over for our squadrons up north. When I have tested enough buses or broken my neck, I can come back again.

Bob and I just rigged up a good one to put over on the family. I'll write home and tell them that they needn't worry about our [engagement] announcement, that I'm expecting you over here shortly, and that I can arrange matters without the announcement. How's that for something that will make them sit up and wipe their eyes. They think I'm kidding when I tell them there's a war on, but they will wake up to the fact that there is a war in their own front yard!

I will be in Paris until next Sunday and then I will start out for Pauillac. Ken Smith, Shorty, Di, Bob, and I all had lunch together, and we all wished that you and several others I can name were at the table with us.

Paris, 25 July 1918

Dear Priscilla,

Well, I still have my desk job as you may notice by carefully observing the contours of this epistle. I don't think it's necessary for me to stick around here much more as I find this chair very tame and not inclined to sneak off when nobody is looking.

I took Miss Guthrie [of CPS & Co.] out to dinner last night and we had a very delightful meal considering the fact that we were the only people in the whole restaurant, and that the cook must have mistaken us for Hun spies and tried to poison us! Either he poisoned us, or else I have suddenly grown too much around the middle. But no matter how mad she is at me now, she won't be so sore when she gets the bunch of sugar I wangled. . . .

Your ring will soon be on its way at last. This time I think it is final. A marine captain named Smith will take it. The ring should be in your hands by the 15th of August at the very outside, and perhaps before that if everything goes well. Of course, if the Huns want to be mean and sink the bloody ship, why then it will all be off. But if I have to buy another one, I will not buy it in Paris because all the really good stuff has been taken out of town. . . .

Paris, 26 July 1918

Hello, Crowd,

I just got a letter written by you on June 13th, and I think it is just about time that I got it, and so do you, no doubt, but you're too far away to say yes. But where under the sun do you get all that "bull" about my scrap with Colonel Rees of the RFC. I told you about the scrap we had, it was up at Ayr. But there wasn't anything so marvelous about it.

Also, speaking of that same article, I retract what I said about not getting my other half stripe. I think it may come through yet, although the recommendation has just now been submitted here in Paris.

Ken Smith is here in H.Q. with me and he likes his job about as much as I do, and feels about as useful here as I do. Last night we all had a nice "Noe" party. Bob has influenza again, or nearly has it, and Ken Smith just naturally doesn't like his job, and Doug Campbell[1] the American ace has been wounded (should be wounded) and doesn't want to go home (should go home), and he says they are going to make him go anyway, and I want to go home and can't, and Ken wishes he had the influenza or something awful so that he wouldn't have to work in that office, and a lovely time was enjoyed by all.

The main trouble with me is that I try too "gosh darned" fast with this here keyboard! You see, I'm used to one of these high-speed things and this is only a slow old affair, built about two years after Cain socked Abel over the roof. But it's easier to read than my usual scrawl, so don't argue.

1. *A twenty-two-year-old Harvard graduate, Douglas Campbell became the first air service ace in May 1918. He was wounded in early June and later returned to the United States.*

Away from the front Kenneth had more time to brood over the difficulty of conducting a romance across several thousand miles of ocean. He was especially troubled by his family's seeming lack of enthusiasm for an early marriage. It took several months of cajoling and crossed cables for them to accept the notion.

Paris, 28 July 1918

Bestest Beloved,

Well, your ring is at last on its way. The old captain lit out yesterday with it, but is going on a secret mission so it will be a few days before he sails, I suppose. I sent you a cable from St.-Inglevert on the 19th of July and I sent it via CPS & Co. It arrived in Paris yesterday after being censored by the English. I don't know whether to send it back to you or not, but I guess I will, as I know you must be worried. I have cabled Mother three times and written her several times, because at last I know what the trouble is all about, and I have straightened everything out, so that when the letters arrive in the States, which should be about August 10th, everything will be all fixed up. . . .

I am not going down to Pauillac till tomorrow night as the captain[1] just arrived from up north and there is a little work to be done before I leave. I love the way they transform pilots to office boys to ordnance officers, etc. I guess I put myself in line for some dirty work when I took that ordnance job up at Dunkirk. They seem to like the idea of letting me take over all that stuff on every possible occasion, but I don't care as I am tremendously interested in that sort of thing and although I don't know anything about such things as 500-pound bombs and signal flares it's very interesting to see how much you can make others think you know. I tell you, a slippery tongue gets you further and faster than any other asset that I know of. I am trying to grease mine up a bit.

It is perfectly fascinating to see things grow down here at H.Q. What was just an idle dream yesterday is a budding reality today, and that's how things go on. You can't imagine the satisfaction of seeing such things. It is impossible to be discouraged. The news is good from every quarter. A lot depends on the condition and workmanship of the planes of course, but I am praying that they will not be a disappointment. I only wish that Adele was as proud of Bob as we all are here. He has more ability than any other man in the whole outfit. Without him we would never get anywhere. He is perfectly marvelous. Even his commanding officer asks him if it will be all right to go out to lunch, because on one occasion he went north without telling Bob and Captain Cone gave him an awful calling down. And a good example of his ability is this. There was a stack of papers about two feet high, they were all reports. It took men who in civil life were getting about $40,000 a year two days to come to any conclusions on the reports. It took Bob just two and a half hours, and every one of the older men agreed with him on every single conclusion but one. They don't give men ability like that more than once in a million times. Bob has changed since he's been over here, and he is now easier to know than he used to be. I have really been able to understand him since I have been in Paris this time. He is one fine boy and I'll stick up for him through anything now. . . .

I lunched with Eddie Rickenbacker, the famous automobile racer and present pilot, and found him a fine sort. Johnny Wentworth, Thorne Taylor, Eddie R., and Doug Campbell[2] were all in town, so I saw quite a lot of the men who are really doing something in the army. I still am glad that I am in the navy, and they all wished they were with me! (Loud cheers!)

Well, I guess I better bring this to a close. I am getting now so that I can wiggle this thing right along. At first I was amazed to find that I had about ten fingers on each hand, and it is comforting to discover that I only have the normal number. . . .

1. *Captain Hutch I. Cone, the commander of naval aviation in Europe.*
2. *Rickenbacker and the rest were all members of the air service's 94th "Hat in the Ring" squadron.*

At the end of July Kenneth traveled south to Pauillac to assume his new duties as a test and inspection officer. The navy established the base at Pauillac on the banks of the Gironde River near Bordeaux to receive, assemble, and inspect equipment destined for its aviation forces in France. Selected by Captain Cone to be the principal air station in France, NAS Pauillac was commissioned in December 1917, and engines and aircraft began arriving the following April.

Pauillac, 31 July 1918

Belovedest,

. . . Harry [Davison] and Alfie [Ames] and the "Loot" [McDonnell] all said, "Where's your other half stripe, you're a full lieutenant?" I said get the _____ off that stuff, that I'd heard it before, and I didn't want to hear it again until there was something in it. How do they get that way? Are they trying to kid me or something?

Excuse me a minute while I light one of these cigarettes. First I smoke a Deity, and then a Bon Voyage. In the meantime my mouthful of candy, and je port.

. . . I was glad I had that lucky thing on last night. I arrived here at Pauillac yesterday afternoon; helped put out a forest fire last night, got lost in the forest, found two sailors who had become unconscious from the heat and smoke, and carried them back to a Frenchman's house, got a truck for them, and got back here at three A.M. after wandering all over France trying to find the way back. I was completely lost in the woods for an hour, of which twenty minutes was spent in water up to my waist trying to get out of a hole I fell into. But I got out finally, it was eight feet deep, and had stickers and brambles all around so that I couldn't grab onto anything to pull on. . . .

By August 1918 the base at Pauillac, established the previous year, had expanded enormously, and included a receiving barracks, assembly and repair plant, and supply depot for naval aviation forces stationed along the French coast. On this deepwater site workmen created a factory town, complete with sawmill, sail-lofts, machine shops, warehouses, hospitals, garages, and a movie theater. The training facilities at nearby Moutchic were similarly enlarged. But the recently arrived MacLeish was less interested in the activity surrounding him than in the problem of lost mail.

Pauillac, 2 August 1918

Beloved One,

I'm getting mad at this mail business around these parts. I know that there are at least three letters for me "somewhere in France," because they were at Fretnum when I left St. Inglevert, and I left there July 22d, but there isn't any sign of the mail yet.

I went over to Moutchic last night, and you have no idea how the place has changed since I was there last. Only two buildings were there then, but now there is a crowd of them. And life at Océan [a hotel in Gironde], you remember how lonely I was down there. Well, there are hundreds of people there now.

They gave quite a party. In the afternoon there was exhibition bombing and shooting from planes, one of the planes being the first "Liberty"-driven outfit[1] I have seen in the air. Then we had a slick old dinner, and after that the Blue Jackets staged a real show. They had a good boxing match, some darn good musical numbers, and some very clever vaudeville sketches. It was a big night. The funniest thing was a battle royal between some ships' cooks and some wardroom stewards. The idea was to blindfold the men and give them a tin cup for their left hand and a boxing glove for their right. They tapped the cups on the deck to let the others know where they were, and then when they met they used the gloves. There were about four on a side. It ended up between the biggest Negro I ever saw and the littlest thing I ever saw. It was a scream.

They had some movies of U.S. Navy aviation in France, and it was all of Moutchic, so it was popular to say the least. Tonight is a big night here. There is a fight between Eddie Nugent and a good boxer from one of the convoy ships. It will be a good scrap. I think Nugent is a well-known boxer, and so is the other man. Sunday there is a great old baseball game in Bordeaux. [Grover Cleveland] Alexander of the Phillies, Johnny Evers, the old Chicago Cubs star, and a whole bunch of professionals are going to play.[2] That's the only excitement. Our machines won't be taken off the ships until tomorrow anyway.

1. The first shipment of American-built Liberty motors reached Pauillac in April 1918, and the first aircraft at the end of the following month. Planes for the Northern Bombing Group arrived later.

2. Hall of Fame pitcher Grover Cleveland Alexander (1887–1950) won thirty or more games in 1915, 1916, and 1917, before embarking on a goodwill tour of American overseas bases in 1918. Second baseman Johnny Evers (1881–1947) played for the Chicago Cubs in the first decade of the twentieth century, later managed the Boston Red Sox, and was finally inducted into the Hall of Fame with the rest of the famed Tinkers-to-Evers-to-Chance double play combination.

Pauillac, 3 August 1918

Beloved,

The scrap last night wasn't very good. One man was a clever boxer, but he was too old. The other was clever and he was in perfect physical condition. The outcome was a round and a half of very fast and interesting boxing, and then old boy Fitzpatrick took the count. There were a couple of "prelims" that weren't very good, but the remarks were funny. One lad was putting it all over the other when a Blue Jacket bellowed out, "I'll bet that little guy thinks we're ALL throwing gloves at him."

To add spice to the entertainment, a very charming Red Cross lady sang a song about taking a walk with any one of us next Saturday afternoon, and after they carried off the wounded, after the rush was over, some of the boys bickered with the manager at the stage door. One offered to give him a sealskin piano for an introduction, and another a bale of bricks.

Oh, by the way, I take it all back. You were right, as usual. I have another half stripe [promotion to full lieutenant]. It was telephoned down to me and the official papers follow. Pretty soft, eh? The odd thing, according to the message, it is USN, not USNRF, but there must be some mistake, because they can't make me a regular unless I want to be one, and I'm here to state that I enlisted for four years OR the duration of the war, and when this war is over, or when I've served my other three years, I'm out!

I think I'll go over to Moutchic next Monday and stay there a couple of days to take a course on the new machine gun [Marlin] they're giving us.[1] All I know of it is which end the bullets come out of. I'd rather know some more seeing that I will have to do some fighting with them. Of course, that never bothered the people at home. They think that if you know how to load the gun, it is sufficient.

Rumor has it that the *Rochambeau* was sunk. Archie and Doug Campbell were on board. I don't believe it, so I'm not worrying. . . .[2]

1. The American-built Marlin machine gun, a belt-fed weapon firing 650 rounds per minute, was mounted on the D.H. 4 bombers shipped from the United States. The Marlin had an unfortunate reputation for jamming at inopportune moments.

2. The liner Rochambeau (which reached the United States safely) carried Archibald MacLeish home to his new assignment with the 33d Field Artillery, and a recovering Douglas Campbell stateside for other duties.

Pauillac, 6 August 1918

Beloved Pal,

I'm still wondering whether or not to murder the mail clerk in Paris, or whether to make him die slowly and with great pain. Why, I've known lots of people who get hurt for smaller things than forgetting another man is alive. I think I'll write up to Paris. I need some mail!! Very badly!! I can't see why I don't get some unless they're sending it to St. Inglevert or some other ungodly place.

Not a blessed thing was done today. The people unloaded a few of our crates at ten o'clock this morning, and we didn't see them again all day—our hangar is about two hundred yards from the dock. They couldn't make two hundred yards in seven hours, so it doesn't look like we will ever get those machines assembled. There are about thirty-six people running the operation, and only a couple of men to obey their orders—one of them (me) is on the verge of nervous prostration, and the other never obeyed an order in his life, so thirty-six people all giving orders at once doesn't faze him.

Did I tell you that Alexander and six other National and American League players and two college stars beat our bunch of "gobs" 3–0, and for seven innings the score was 0–0. Our "gob" pitcher didn't walk as many men as Alexander did, and only allowed one more hit than he did, and struck out more men. Our pitcher showed up just as well as Alexander did. . . .

Despite the preparations and energy expended, work at the Pauillac base sometimes proceeded at a snail's pace, and the movement of aircraft to the Northern Bombing Group lagged well behind schedule. Rumors of army-navy amalgamation added to MacLeish's frustrations. Such plans were discussed in Congress, but no final action was ever taken.

Pauillac, 8 August 1918

Beloved,

Did you ever hear me let out a good, long, sonorous string of honest-to-goodness cussing? Well, stick around, then, and you'll hear some, because I've got some nice green ink, and a fine excuse for swearing.

I hear that in about three months' time they are going to unite the army and navy flying corps. If they do, I get out! If I can't get out legally, I'm going to land in Holland, but I'm going to get out. I'll be————if I'll take orders from any wet, young rube fresh from the farm with about as much sense as a half-witted chicken. I consider this the greatest piece of plain, ordinary dirty work the U.S. ever saw. They even have the English working for it! I mean by they, the army, such men as Fulois and Milling who a few months ago were first lieutenants and are now generals and colonels. It's an outrage. . . .[1]

The army gets all the newspaper notoriety, and the people at home think the army is it! You would faint if I told you how many subs naval aviation has sunk, or how successfully the night bombers have dropped their bombs. You don't hear about that. It isn't our policy to toot our horns the way the army does.

I'm too mad to write a nice letter. I'm so mad I can't sleep, but I'm going to try, so good night!

1. *MacLeish's remarks about General Benjamin D. Fulois, then chief of the Air Service–Zone of Advance, and Colonel Thomas DeWitt Milling, chief of staff of the First Army Air Service, were rather off base. Both were pioneers of army aviation and compiled distinguished wartime records.*

Pauillac, 8 August 1918

Beloved,

I have made a great discovery. I have discovered how to have a quiet afternoon in France. It works (I mean the pen). Well, as I was saying, when you have two hours to spare, come down here to Pauillac and try to get a tool out of the shops. We had two little holes to drill in a piece of wood. I sent a mechanic after the drill, and he didn't come back at the end of an hour. I walked up to the office to shoot a smoke, and while there heard violent but muffled cursing. There was the mechanic with perspiration streaming from his face, slips and sheets of paper fluttering from his hands, and big, blue, juicy oaths fluttering from his lips. I didn't have self-control enough to ask him what the trouble was, but I found then that he had gone to the shop and inquired about the drill. They sent him to the stores office. At this point he had to sit down and carefully explain exactly what he meant by a drill, what it looked like, what he wanted to drill with it, how old he was, what was the color of his wife's hair, how many children he thought he had, and two or three thousand minor questions. When that was over it dawned on the man that what was wanted was one small drill. Finally, he grasped the situation, and in five minutes had the papers ready, only three sheets. From there the mechanic had to go to the supply officer, and have another inquisition as stupid as the last one. After swearing his life away and signing thirty vouchers and promises, he was directed to storehouse number two, which is down near Spain, I believe. At that point the mechanic was on the verge of death, so he dropped into the sick bay to get a shot in his arm. He arrived at number two storehouse some time after noon on August 8th and was told to sit down and rest his ears while they opened a crate to get his drill out. With surprising alacrity the young man attacked the crate, and in the years that passed, lo and behold, so great was his strength, that he was able to get a board off the crate. When the mechanic was given the drill he was relieved of several papers, told to keep others, and was also supplied with several others of the most attractive pink hue. He returned some hours later with the papers in a wheelbarrow, and the drill in a safe, guarded by a company of drilled troops. He had been "elsewhere" on his return voyage, because he broke the painful stillness of the machine shop with an exultant smile, and burst in upon us drunk, dressed up, and highly perfumed. We removed our hats while the holes were bored with the sacred drill, and tomorrow I'm going to detach a couple of working parties, get the station band, and march the drill back again.

The next time I want a tool I'm going to put the palms of both hands on a pickax, hire a mechanic who at that particular time has the tool I want out of the shop, and quietly but forcefully slay him, and remove said tool from said mechanic. This is some war. I don't know how I ever got along without wars before this. They are indispensable. Be calm, cool, and collected, this will all pass over, and I'll come out of it as soon as this present spasm wears off. Oh where, oh where has my little sense gone? You have my heart, but did you take my mind too? It won't help you any.

Kenneth's trip to Moutchic for instruction on the Marlin machine gun was both a homecoming and a revelation. The small camp hastily thrown together in the fall of 1917 had evolved into a sizable training base. The curriculum now included navigation, gunnery, signaling, airplanes, motors, ground school, and flight instruction. There were also courses in bombing and intelligence work. Twenty-three permanent officers, three dozen student pilots, and five hundred enlisted men were stationed there, along with twenty-four aircraft, a mix of HS-1s, Donnet-Denhauts, and Telliers.

Pauillac, 15 August 1918

Beloved,

I went over to Moutchic and took the course there on the Marlin gun. It was pretty good sport too, as the man over there is very good, although no dope has come over from the States on the gun. But that is natural.

Well, your ring has started. It started last Sunday or Monday, and you should have it by August 20th or 25th. I don't know what ship it went over on. Also, by that time, Father should have received my letter, and everything ought to be all fixed up for the announcement. . . .

Alfie [Ames] is leaving me today. He is on a tour of inspection of all the stations. It certainly was fine seeing him again, as he just came from you.

I heard unofficially that I just missed being sent home. Do you know, now that my own future is so dark, and since there is such a mess over here, I wouldn't mind being sent home. Judd was finally decided on. He was to have been one of my flight commanders in my squadron, except that he was in Paris at the time.

Pauillac, 17 August 1918

Beloved One,

. . . I just fall out of one job and into another, with no qualifications whatsoever. Guess what I am now. I'm chief pilot at Pauillac, and I have a nice Cadillac 8 all of my own, and three assistants, all pilots. Commander [David] Hanrahan, my Northern Bombing boss, told me that if I ever flew a seaplane again he'd kick me out of the navy. The odd part of it is that in this job I have to fly nothing but seaplanes. I have to fly every machine they assemble here to send to the stations along the coast of France. They send many, I might say, and I have to run that risk. I dodge it as much as possible, however.

Our old land hacks are almost ready now. We got one engine in today, and it should be ready to fly by Tuesday. Then life will start all over again for me. My job as chief pilot is only temporary, thank heaven. My boss returns Tuesday, and after that the lucky stiff is going back to the United States. I don't know why I say lucky, only if all that is keeping me from wanting to go back too is my sense of duty, all I can say is that I have Some Sense of Duty! I just plan to go home unless I am at the front, then I wouldn't ever want to go for all the money in the world. . . .

Kenneth's expectations of joining the Northern Bombing Group near Dunkirk as a squadron leader or flight commander were abruptly shattered in late August by news that he would soon be returned to Paris headquarters and then sent to Eastleigh on the English coast. Located four miles from Southampton, the RAF acceptance park at Eastleigh was turned over to the navy in July 1918 to be used as the staging point for the planned Northern Bombing campaign. Planes, motors, and equipment destined for the squadrons in northern France were routed through Eastleigh. The base eventually accommodated sixty officers and fifteen hundred enlisted men, and the commander after 20 July was none other than MacLeish's old C.O. from Dunkirk, Godfrey DeC. Chevalier.

Pauillac, 19 August 1918

Beloved,

Why is it that the bottom drops out of everything so regularly these days? What do you suppose the latest gloom is? I have had the most complete training that it is possible to get. I have had some very good experience in war flying. They considered me good enough three weeks ago to give me the first navy day bombing squadron, and they have so changed within that time that I seem to be worth nothing to them. They are going to send me to Eastleigh, England, to test and accept more machines!

There are hundreds of men who know more about planes and engines than I do, but who haven't the experience I have had. Why not give them that job and give me a man's job? I have come to a standstill.

I can't be happy unless I either go to the front, or home. I'm built in a funny way. As long as I'm busy on a real job, I'm as happy and good-natured as can be, but when I feel useless and have no job, oh Lord, I get so tired of doing nothing.

I think that the first D.H. [Liberty-powered D.H. 4 day bomber] will be ready tomorrow, and that will make the time pass quickly. Every hour seems like a month. I am going up to Paris and put it to them straight. If I have too much rank, why I'll get rid of some of it, but I have a right to be kept busy, even if they do want to baby me, and keep me from getting hurt. How do they know that I can't take care of myself. They've never given me half a chance to show it.

I think I'll try to get back [at NAS Dunkirk] with Di on seaplanes. If I do, well, I'll wager my daughter's hand against your vast estates that there won't be a more tickled man this side of the old Statue of Liberty. This is sort of a poor excuse for a letter. I don't really feel half as blue as I sound, and I feel better now that it's off my chest.

Kenneth's foul mood over being denied a combat role was quickly tempered by a cable from Priscilla reporting that all objections at home had been overcome and their engagement was about to be announced. He was further heartened by the presence in Paris of fellow Yale man George Mosely, with whom he had served at Dunkirk and Clermont-Ferrand. While Kenneth was unsure what the future might hold, Paris was still Paris!

Paris, 23 August 1918

Beloved,

Well, I have a desk job that may last from now till the end of the war, but I don't care in the least because I have absolutely gone off my trolley! I am so excited, I am so happy, and I love you so, and everything is going so well that you couldn't faze me with a declaration of peace. Never have I been so happy, I haven't a care in the world, and I like everybody and the weather is perfect and no one can make me mad anymore, and I can't seem to worry as for once in my life there isn't anything to worry about! How would you like to feel that way, or perhaps you do. I may have to worry a little bit, but it won't be for long, and I'll soon tell you all about it and have it off my chest.

I was ordered back to Paris five minutes after I received your angelic cable, and I had no time to get the cable off from there, and I didn't want to wait until I got to Paris as the cable wouldn't reach you till late as it was, so I cabled Miss Guthrie to send the cable to you, and she said Joy in it, and I hope you don't think I ever intended to say that word, because that's what some men say when they cover themselves with perfume. You see, I didn't know until the 21st of August that we were announcing the engagement on the 22d. So I didn't have very much time to act. But if you will forgive that one word joy, I don't have a thing in the world to worry about. Eddie Judd is going home, so I think I will go out and get something to send home to you. It probably won't be much, but it will bring a lot of love.

I haven't been able to write to you for the last few days because I have been on these wonderful French trains for the last few days and nights. I ask you, is there anything under the sun worse than sitting up for two nights and a day in a French train when the thermometer reads about 212 degrees?

I flew the Liberty [Liberty-powered D.H. 4] that we were supposed to have and it sure is a wonder. Talk about power, I haven't seen much more. She seemed very solid. She stunted beautifully too. Well, I have a million and one things to do and no time to do it in, so I will have to close now, but I'll write more tonight.

Paris, 24 August 1918

Beloved,

This is the life! Nothing to do but chase around Paris looking for thin (I started to say things, but the typewriter stopped at thin), well, things, that no one seems to know anything about. For instance, I went to see the army about a little thing and it was as bad as trying to locate the drill down at Pauillac the other day. I think I must have walked all over the building looking for some sort of advice to follow. I gave them some advice myself, which I have reason to believe they ought to follow. I think that the boss [Hanrahan] will go north soon and that PROBABLY means that I will go with him or follow shortly. There are a few things that I have to arrange before I can leave, such as seeing about maps for flying some machines up.[1] My job requires a versatile map. I am everything from a simple office boy to a navigator, by way of an ordnance man.

What do you know about the war news now? It may be slightly exaggerated, but not much. I have seen lots of people just back from the front and they all say the same thing about what is going on. I cannot convince myself that this will ever turn into a decisive military victory for the Allies, but I can't help feeling that it is the beginning of the end. . . .

1. *Possibly a reference to maps required by pilots ferrying Caproni bombers from northern Italy to the navy's bases on the Channel coast, or D.H. 4 bombers from Pauillac to Dunkirk.*

Temporary office duties in Paris made few demands, and both Kenneth and companion George Mosley found plenty of time to relax and sightsee. The previous summer Mosely, recently enlisted in the French air force, had visited La Varrenne-sur-Marne, a small village situated a few miles east of Paris. He went rowing and swimming, enchanted by the idyllic scene—a river filled with small islands so close together that the branches of the trees met overhead to form a dense canopy. In August 1918, with time on his hands, he visited the village again, this time accompanied by MacLeish. They enjoyed a remarkably tranquil respite from the pressures of war.

Paris, 26 August 1918

Belovedest,

I had the most wonderful time yesterday. George Mosely and I got on the train and rode out to a lovely spot called La Varrenne-sur-Marne. It's on the banks of the river and it's too beautiful for words. We got into bathing suits, hired a little rowboat with sliding seats and outrigged oars. It was just like a rowing shell, and then we started out to spend the afternoon. We took turns rowing until we both had so many blisters that we couldn't row anymore, and then we stopped, tied our ship to the bank, and had a glorious old swim. I never enjoyed anything so much in my life. I haven't had any real exercise for so long, and oh that water felt good. By the time we stopped rowing and swimming we must have been up by the big war—I've never rowed so far and I know I've never swum so far before. We submarined each other all the way back, during which operation I caused a drought in the Marne valley by consuming all the water in the river, so there was none to push under the bridges.

When we got back to the boat there were some French children swimming there, they seemed sort of friendly, so we ducked a couple of them to see how friendly they really were, and when they came up they asked us to dinner with a whole French family, and all I could say was "oui." I forgot all I ever knew and I didn't waste time talking or trying to talk—I just ate. The food was marvelous. George speaks "poilu" French, which is French minus all the verbs. He was in the French army for some time. And I left it all to George. There was a girl in the family, about twelve or thirteen years old, and she got a drag with me by asking me to teach her English, and by stealing some cigarettes from her father, as mine were all gone. She gave me a long farewell address. I don't know what she said except that I am supposed to go out again next Sunday. The old boy was fine. He was so pleased when he found that George had been in the French army, and that we both had been up near Dunkirk for so long. He's full out to win the war. Well, so are we! . . .

Assignment at navy headquarters in Paris also opened up a world of possibilites for nighttime entertainment, opportunities the two young fliers were eager to explore. They found the theaters of Paris quite unlike anything they had seen in New Haven, Chicago, or New York.

Paris, 28 August 1918

Beloved,

I haven't written for a while. I don't know why. I guess it's because there was nothing to write about. I've been so busy doing absolutely nothing.

George and I went over in the Montmartre the other night to a real theater. You get out and walk down a little alley, by a graveyard, and into a church. The church is very old and very quaint and it is called the Théatre Grand-Guignol. It sure is a scream to walk into a church and see all the earmarks of the same, even the carpets, and then see rather raw and always melodramatic plays. The acting, they say, is about the best in Paris.

They usually give about five plays. The other night they gave three very exciting, melodramatic plays, and two farces, and they were perfectly wonderful. You know the French people will say the most horrible things, but if they're funny, they get by. That is true even among the best of them. These two funny plays were screams, but they were for "les jeunes filles." You couldn't possibly take offense at them because they weren't vulgar and they were funny. Just as an example I'll tell you about one of them, but you must promise not to get mad at me.

The curtain rises on a household scene. A wealthy Frenchman and his wife are entertaining a very dear gentleman friend of theirs. The man and his wife are the only members of the family. The guest, wishing to be polite and carry on a lively conversation, broaches the subject of children. He says that every family in France ought to have children in it. The wife thinks the idea is fine, but the husband doesn't go for it. The subject becomes heated to such an extent that the wife leaves the room in a rage, and the two men carry it on until finally the host kicks his guest out. It is evidently a sore subject with the husband and the wife, and one that has been often discussed.

Then the wife comes back and they have an awful fight. She tells him that she has even gone to see doctors, and that it is all his fault, and she accuses him of being sterile. He simply goes wild, and in his rage he says, "Why, I have a child." Then his wife, simply enraged, says she doesn't believe it and asks for proof. So the husband shows her a letter from a woman in which she said the child would be called Henri in honor of him.

Finally the wife is reconciled, and she says she is going to adopt the child. The husband thinks she's fine and tells her how generous and magnanimous she is. So she puts on her hat and goes to get the child.

In the meantime the unwelcome guest returns, and the husband tells him all about the scrap, and how wonderfully it turned out. Then the guest, being reminded of his own past, tells of a son that HE has. The host doesn't believe it, so the guest pulls out this letter which turns out to be an exact duplicate, word for word, of the host's, except that the child is to be named Gustave. Then they fight as to who owns the kid, and finally decide that it shall be called Henri Gustave.

Pretty soon the wife returns with a sad expression, but no baby boy. That takes the wind out of the men's sails, and they ask what happened. She says that a man had come and taken the child away just a few minutes before she got there, and she reads the letter that was written to him, which was exactly like the other two, only the child is called Charles.

The curtain goes down on three utterly dejected people. It's perfectly screaming the way they play it, but it sure is raw when you think about it later, yet no one takes offense at it. The other funny play was really raw to me, it was raw because of a certain condition that exists here, and accepted by everyone, but it doesn't exist at home. It sure was awful.

The three weird plays were wonderfully done. One was about an old lighthouse keeper and his son who go crazy with loneliness and kill each other while the storm rages outside. Another is about a doctor who murders one wife and then gets another, and the ghost of the first wife kills the second. Talk about spooky! Wonderful acting.

Last night George and I went to Miss Guthrie's for dinner and she made us some deviled lobster in a chafing dish. It was the best stuff I ever tasted. We had a slick old meal crowned with Peach Cardinal. Oh boy! I was so full of wonderful food I couldn't move. . . .

There isn't a thing else to tell about. Oh, how I wish they'd let me fly. Dave [Ingalls] is up at the front with 213 Squadron [RAF] again, on scouts, having the time of his life, and instead of being with him where I belong, I'm down here doing nothing.

Though Kenneth enjoyed Paris, he longed to return to active duty, especially when informed of the exploits of his Yale friends. Companion David "Crock" Ingalls spent most of August attached to an RAF squadron flying Sopwith Camels and making quite a name for himself. Before being recalled from the front in late September, he scored five confirmed victories to become the navy's only World War One ace.

Also in late summer the Northern Bombing Group, after many delays and false starts, commenced active operations with a 15 August Caproni attack on the submarine repair docks at Ostend. The marine day bombing squadrons were also beginning to gather at Dunkirk, while the first Pauillac-assembled D.H. 4 bombers arrived in early September.

MacLeish's efforts to rejoin the fighting seemed stymied, however; all his plans and requests came to naught. He resigned himself to another stretch of duty at a support base, this time in Eastleigh.

Paris, 28 August 1918

Dearest Father,

. . . Just at present I am stationed here in Paris with nothing very much to keep me busy. I expect to be sent to England in the near future on a job which embraces a whole new set of powers. I have always been fond of machines and engines, and they are picking me for all the dirty work in connection with the arming of machines and bombs as well as installation of the far-famed Liberty engine, of which I know little, or nothing, except that it has lots of power and sounds good. I tested out an American-built machine with a Liberty engine down at Pauillac, and I was surely pleased with it. I did all kinds of stunts with it, and the plane and engine both behaved admirably. I only wish they could catch the people who are ruining the engines before they reach us and after they leave the factory. Even whole bolts are taken out of the engine, and in one instance we found that the bushing had been taken out of the bearing, so that the crankshaft would have broken if we had tried to run it in that condition.

I expect to fly up to Calais in a few days, but I don't know when I will get the chance. I am living in a perfect horror of one thing: since they gave me my last raise in rank they have not seemed to favor the idea of letting me go up to the front anymore. They say I am not to risk getting hurt, as they want me for a desk job. Isn't that about enough to drive a man to drink. They haven't given me much chance to show whether I can take care of myself or not. If I have to sit through the rest of this war without ever doing any more fighting, it will simply break my heart. I came over here to fight, and that's what I want most to do, because I can never make myself feel that I am helping to win the war while I am sitting behind a desk. But I guess that if they will give me a man's job, as they have promised, I can be fairly happy.

Give my dearest love to the family, and to the Bruce MacLeish family. Isn't it splendid that Archie got home? I am not due for a furlough until next April, and if there is any chance of doing any fighting, of course, I wouldn't come home then, as all the real sport and fighting take place in the spring. My only chance is this winter, or next winter, unless they hand me that awful desk job. In that case I don't care much if there is a war or not.

Paris, 31 August 1918

Beloved,

. . . I had a slight setback today due to the ancient fallacy of counting one's chickens before they hatch. I gathered the idea that I was to go up to the front again, and I lived on air for a day or so, then today I received orders to go to Eastleigh, England, as final test and acceptance officer for all the machines for the navy day squadrons. Di, I think, will get a day squadron, and I begged and beseeched him to let me be in it when it started at least, even though they wouldn't let me stay there very long. Then they also promised me a job with those dirty marines. They wished that one on me, as some fool marine put in a request for me as a flight commander, but I'd just as soon do it if it means I can fly.

Beloved, some day you and I are going to come over here to Paris and I'm going to show you a Paris that very few people know—the real Paris. I know the gay Paris, and I am just beginning to know a little of the real, beautiful, artistic Paris. George Mosely and I have gone out to dinner the last three nights, and each time to a place where there are no Americans, to places where one meets real Parisians. We went first to the Tour d'Argent over across the river. That is well known for its duck and soufflé fish. Then last night we went to Foyot's restaurant up in the Montmartre. I have never had such a meal, never. The maître d'hôtel took a personal interest in his guests, and he came around to talk to us. He took such wonderful pride in his food and service. And our waiter took such pride in his profession.

Then we went to a quaint little theater. The show was hopeless, but the atmosphere was wonderful. Oh, we've had some glorious times, George and I, and we've each planned to take our fiancées to Paris for a while until they get sick of it.

I am going to Eastleigh on September 4th and will probably be there for a month or six weeks. It is called the U.S. Naval Aviation Repair Base.

Tomorrow George and I are going to take Miss Guthrie out to La Varrenne, that little town on the Marne. She will enjoy it, I'm sure, because she's overworked and needs some recreation. We'll give her a good row. . . .

Paris, 31 August 1918

Dearest Family,

. . . I may get up to the front again soon, that is, after I get through at Eastleigh. I sure am crazy about day bombing, because after having been up at Dunkirk during so many raids, I took a keen and personal interest in where my bombs went, and when I cut them loose I leaned over the side with a two-foot grin to watch them, and then I said to those below, "Now, you run for a change!" And it was a satisfaction to see them explode. . . .

In early September MacLeish crossed the Channel to assume his new duties at the Eastleigh assembly and repair base. Personnel poured in faster than accommodations could be readied, and several officers boarded at hotels in nearby Southampton, rather than at the station. The presence of Godfrey Chevalier, Kenneth's commander from Dunkirk days, provided one bright note. A spark plug, Chevalier energized everyone around him. George Mosely called him "a fine fellow, full of pep and fire. I would give anything to be under an officer like him."

Eastleigh, 5 September 1918

Beloved,

Now if you were in my place, what would you do about writing a letter. There isn't any place to write one, not even a chair, and no time to write one. What shall I do?

I'm here in England and I hope that you got my cable about it. I think I'll go back to France in a day or two to get my luggage and pay accounts, and also some idea of why I was sent here. There's plenty to do here, only I seem to tread on everyone else's toes when I do it.

I think eventually that I will have a job here for a couple or three months when I come back, unless the unexpected happens, and we can talk the marines out of some machines. In that case I'll have a temporary job at the front for a while, perhaps a permanent one.

I have the old skipper here that I had over in France at Dunkirk. He's the very salt of the earth, and I'm too pleased for words, because when I used to be with him I was an ensign, but now I'm the same rank that he is, and he calls me "Ken" and we have a wonderful old time. He really is a corker and we get along well as we're both engaged, and that creates a sort of mutual understanding over here.

I'm all up in the air. If we get these machines, I shall go to the front. If we don't, I shall try to get the job of chief pilot here at Eastleigh. If I can't get that I'll be so mad I won't be worth knowing, and there it ends. I won't be able to give you any more information until I get back from France.

Kenneth's resentment of the marine aviators who had "robbed" him of the opportunity to fly day bombardment missions knew no bounds. With a chip on his shoulder, he rarely missed an opportunity to complain about their behavior and attitudes, or to provoke an argument.

Eastleigh, 8 September 1918

Beloved,

It's one of those ice-cold, rainy days that make the English Channel climate the most detestable thing on earth. If there's anything that makes me miserable, it's a day like this.

I had a big fight yesterday, but the outcome is that I know what my job is, and also who's the boss around here. I was assigned to duty, and I had just begun to get started, when along came one of those _____ , _____ marines and started giving me orders. He didn't want some of the things I wanted, and he wanted some things that I didn't want, and he proved that he didn't know anything about an airplane and that he was, like all marines, a "bull" artist.[1]

He came around and started to butt in on my work, and I asked him why there were no marines with the marine troops to [illegible] them some aerial defense, and that got him mad. Then we had it out, hot and heavy. I loathe the sight of a marine, and that only made it worse. It finally ended this way—I am final inspection and test officer, and assembly and repairs take orders from me, and from no one else. The marine captain is "nobody" and will be sent out to chase orders that have not been delivered. Nobody listens to him. He has never been over the lines, yet he's a squadron commander. That's marine stuff for you!

I am still debating as to whether I should stay here until I get a chance to fly with army men, or go over and fly with those _____ , _____ marines. The possibilities here are perfectly wonderful. I know I can make a go of it. I'm so heart and soul in this job. It's THE job that will hold my interest, because I'm so daffy on the subject of machines and engines, and this work gives me a chance to putter around the shops all day long. Next to flying, this will be THE job. I think I'd rather have it than be connected with those marines, even though I could fly with them. . . .

1. *Captain William McIlvain, a pioneer aviator, was temporarily assigned to the Eastleigh base to expedite shipment of planes and equipment to marine day bombardment squadrons in France.*

Eastleigh, 8 September 1918

Dearest Family,

. . . I am responsible for the machines that leave here for the front, and if the slightest thing goes wrong with them, I pay the penalty. With so much responsibility there is quite a bit of freedom, of course, and that is where the fun comes in. If I don't like the design of a machine, I can redesign it if it gets as bad as that. So you see, it's pretty fine putting my pet ideas about airplanes into practice. I am so sure that I can improve on the type we have here and I'm waiting with bated breath for the day when the first one is ready to try out. I figure that by refining it in some ways, strengthening it in others, and streamlining certain parts, I can get at least 5 mph more speed, and carry 20 or 30 pounds more, and still have it stronger than it was to begin with. It should be so, because on paper it shows twice as much as that, but we shall see when the time comes.

The first thing for me to do here is to get my health back. I'm a physical wreck. I have lost twelve pounds, which is quite some for me, and I am very nervous and irritable.

My future is a very peculiar proposition. This job is open to me. If I can't fly with a heavy squadron I will take it. If a navy squadron is ever organized I will surely be a flight commander, and they have promised to make me a squadron commander as soon as we get two squadrons. So the only person who knows exactly what will happen to me can't be asked.

MacLeish's weakened physical condition and uncertain future weighed heavily on his mind. While he tried to project a confident image for friends and relatives at home, some of his associates in Europe observed a different man. In early September Di Gates reported to Trubee Davison, still recuperating back in New York, that "Ken seems to have lost all interest in his work and to be thoroughly tired of flying. A nice trip to the States would be about the best thing for him. He has done an awful lot of flying and very much work since he has been over here."

Eastleigh, 9 September 1918

Belovedest,

. . . Nothing of interest to report on this front today. They sent the marine away on a wild goose chase, a chase after some instruments, and he doesn't know what they're for, so he's sure to get it wrong, which delights me greatly.

Freddy Beach left us and went over to France today,[1] and we primed him with a lovely story for the captain [Hanrahan], and if it doesn't result in our getting a squadron, I'm going to commit some suicide or something.

I spent the whole day scheming about how I was going to be able to have a machine of my own, and I think I've worked it all out now in my mind. There is one bus with a small radiator, so that it can't be put into service. I'm going to take it, take out all the machine gun business, move the tank forward, and then open up the fuselage and put in four seats. Then we can go on parties in the same machine, and also we can bring back ferry pilots with it. If I can't get it that way, why, I may have to crash it a bit on a "test," but I need that machine.

1. *After training at Clermont-Ferrand in May and June 1918, and then service with the British in July and at Pauillac in August, Freddy Beach was assigned temporary flight duty with the French naval Escardrille St.-Pol stationed near Dunkirk.*

Eastleigh, 12 September 1918

You Old Darling!

. . . I went to an English dance last night, broke a chair, tore a Lady's dress, and said "Dash!" in front of my host. You see, some harebrain suggested a game of General Post and I discovered in the course of the game that two people can't jump on the same chair without breaking same. I also learned that if you stand on a Lady's train and she walks away, you are apt to find yourself still standing on the train, with a very white and embarrassing and delicate "situation" before you. The last sentence is twice as funny as you think it is because the dress tore off at the waist, and there's some saying about the force of gravity that I forget at the moment, but I hope you won't laugh at the situation the way I did, and almost got kicked out of the house. The way I came to say Dash in front of the host was different— he asked me to screw the electric light bulb into its socket, only there wasn't any bulb and I got 100 volts right square in the socket. . . .

Eastleigh, 13 September 1918
(Friday the 13th!!!)

Beloved,

So far, so good. The only thing that has gone radically wrong today is that I lost my chance to eat dinner because Lady Swaythling called at the camp and my seat was taken by one of the party, but that's wild. I expected to bust my ruddy neck. If I can only make the grade and get upstairs without having the elevator fall down the hole, or without having the hotel burn up, I'll be tickled to pieces. After all, it's been a most successful day, considering.[1]

Captain Hanrahan will be down tomorrow, so I guess that means that I'll get kicked out of here. Every time he sees me he sends me to some new place, and after I've been there a while, he sends me away again. It's a great life, and all that, but you must pardon me if I seem to possess that "stay home" quality for a while after we're married, because the sight of a train makes me ill. I don't mind boats, because they have berths in them, but I figured it out that since I've been over here I've made twenty-four all-night trips, I've never had a berth, and I've never been in an empty compartment so that I could stretch out and sleep. . . .

Last night I went to bed at nine-thirty P.M., and about three A.M. in walked the skipper [Chevalier] and about six other officers, all drunk as lords, and all sore at me because I ditched them and went to bed. I paid the penalty. They roughhoused me, operated on my ribs, tore off my pajamas, and almost kicked me out of the hotel by making such an unearthly racket. . . .

Our skipper was on the loose the other night, too. He got home at six A.M., called out the band, and went into everyone's room, yelling "rise and shine!" and then the band played a tune. The band is part of [John Phillip] Sousa's Great Lakes Band, and it's the best I've ever heard. The skipper went away for the rest of the day, and he's a wreck now. That's what comes of ordering a man back to the States when he doesn't want to go. . . .[2]

1. The Swaythling family generously acted as unofficial hosts to the Americans stationed at Eastleigh.
2. Chevalier relinquished command of the station to Commander Bayard T. Bulmer on 22 September 1918.

Like most American servicemen, MacLeish found the news from France tremendously encouraging in September 1918. He told his parents, "The old doughboys are doing mighty well around St. Mihiel. It certainly looks as though something would break, somewhere, sometime soon."

Eastleigh, 15 September 1918

Beloved,

What a wonderful thing sleep is. I had some of it last night, so much, in fact, that I missed the bus out to the station this morning, then I felt sick for the rest of the day until I lay down this afternoon and put in another three-hour workout on the "downy," and now I feel like a new man.

They gave another dance for the American nurses here at the hotel and what do you think, one of them was good-looking. They rushed her to such an extent that I only had one look at her, but it was nice getting that.[1]

With this new draft law in effect, things must be pretty lonely at home. I've never seen so many Americans in my life, not even in America, as I've seen recently. It seems as though there must be an awfully big bunch over here, or else I'm a poor judge of numbers. If the old kaiser could see some of the sights I've seen, he'd pull in his neck and ask who got America sore at him. There are doughboys of every possible kind. Bunches of splendid young men, many of them college men, crowds of men who were "boys" in every city and town at home. Big, awkward, gawky, yet powerful farmers from the back-woods. And here and there a "weak sister" with watery blue eyes, glasses a foot thick, but with an expression that never passed over his face before. I saw a funny sight once. There was a whole crowd of little, powerful lumberjacks that stretched for blocks, and at the end of the whole line came a HUGE fat man, he was about Fatty Arbuckle's size, and even more powerful.[2] The lumberjacks were about waist-high as they bent forward under their packs, but old fatty, with a little pudgy baby face, walking along perfectly straight with his tremendous pack that didn't seem to worry him any more than a pillow would, and in addition under one arm he carried a huge duffel bag, the size of a small man, and under the other arm he carried an officer's pack and his own rifle. He walked along as though he didn't have a thing to carry, it was a scream. And when everyone laughed and cheered when he passed, he shyly blustered and his toes crossed up and got in his way.

I found out yesterday how it happened that Captain Hanrahan saw me and didn't tell me to go somewhere else. He had it all fixed to send me away, only Chevy [Lieutenant Chevalier] the skipper said that he wanted me to stay, and the old "Iron Duke" said he could keep me as long as he wanted to. I'll be here for a month or two until Di gets his group operating.

The old Iron Duke. Really, Budge, he's the most fascinating character in the navy. I've never seen a man with so much personal magnetism. He has a marvelous Irish humor, and he's always on the go. He hasn't any idea what he's doing, but he's always doing something, and he always gets balled up. . . .

Talking with the American girls last night nearly drove me frantic. Believe me, French girls are pretty, English girls are wholesome and splendid, but American girls have it on them both. And you've got it all on all American girls, and I want you. . . .

1. The management of the Southwestern Hotel arranged dances with American nurses or telephone operators whenever possible.
2. Fatty Arbuckle was an early star of silent screen comedies.

                                                    Eastleigh, 18 September 1918

Beloved,

I moved out to camp, and if there is anything on earth worse than sleeping between two blankets that have been left out in the rain for a week or so, and in a draft, well, I never heard of it. If I don't get pneumonia, I'll be lucky.

There is absolutely nothing for me to do here at present, and consequently, nothing to write about. So, if this letter is dull, don't blame me, I can't help it. . . .

I sent over to France for my old observer [Irving Sheely]. He's a good old horse, and he'll be a useful member of the flight department.

I read in the paper that the Committee on Military Affairs in the Senate voted 9–2 for a coalition of the army and navy in aviation. That looks bad, doesn't it? Well, if they unite, that will be my chance to put in for home leave. I'm going to put in for home duty as well. I'm sick of inaction. I would rather loaf at home where I can have you than loaf over here.

                                                    Eastleigh, 23 September 1918

Beloved,

Lord, it's hard to write letters in this place. There isn't a chair in camp, only one fire, and these days, no spare time.

I got a letter from Bob the other day in which he asked me to come over and take command of a night squadron, but I think the day work is better, so I'm going to hold out for that.

I was in bed for a day with a cold, but I knew that was coming sooner or later, and I still have it with me, and there's no hope of losing it until we get quarters that are fit to live in. The only thing that worries me is the tremendous number of pneumonia cases in camp. One fellow died yesterday and another is sinking now. I don't mind the cold, but I can't see getting pneumonia. . . .

By mid-September Bob Lovett had been promoted to wing commander in the Northern Bombing Group. He informed Adele Brown, "Did I tell you that I am a wing commander now? . . . I'm insufferably stuck up now, have been presented to the king." Fully aware of

Kenneth's frustration and unhappiness, Lovett used his influence to try and find a position for him in France. While MacLeish admitted that Lovett's offer of a night bombing squadron "tickled him stiff," he declined the honor, begging instead, "For the love of Pete get me out of this hole and back to 213 Squadron." Lovett then tried to secure command of a day squadron, but the response was the same. "Bob," Kenneth responded, "There's no use of trying to make a commanding officer out of me if I can't fly and fly when I want. . . . Some people are born to paint, some to write, some to lead, and some just plain 'go out and do it all by yourself.' "

Eastleigh, 25 September 1918

Beloved Pal,

I know I've got it, and I'll have to go to Denver sooner or later, so, if eventually, why not now? I think I'll take a machine and go up about 20,000 feet or so and sit there for an hour or so and see if I can't get the old Denver effect.

Did I tell you that "Chevy," the old C.O. here, was so mad at me for flying the first machine when he wasn't on the station that he nearly spit in my eye? But this morning he came around and said everything was O.K. again.

Who do you think arrived on the station today on one of these boards of inquest? "Snoot" [Graham] Brush![1] I nearly fell over backward. He is a live wire, he is the life of the board, and wins the greatest admiration wherever he goes. He sure is a wonder, and he says he's going straight home soon and getting married. The poor stiff! I nearly pushed him over. He didn't get the drift, but he won't start any of that bunk again. I only saw him for a minute or two, but it was like a breath of heaven. I almost asked him if he had a job for me in Washington, but then I remembered that there's a war on over here. . . .

1. Brush, serving with the aviation division of the Bureau of Navigation, was a member of a troubleshooting team sent to Europe in August 1918 to identify and correct the numerous delays in assembling and utilizing new aircraft.

In late September Kenneth suffered a relapse of the flu that he had first endured at Clermont-Ferrand. The Eastleigh base was hard hit by the growing epidemic. Among the other victims sent to the base hospital was Irving Sheely, MacLeish's observer. Nearly twenty men died before the epidemic ran its course.

Eastleigh, 27 September 1918

Beloved,

I finally succumbed, my feet wouldn't track, I ached all over, and I'm coughing my lungs out. I came to the hospital again yesterday. This is the second time I've had the old flu since June. That's too much. I hope this turns out to be a light case, because my lungs will be a wreck if I have it again as badly as before.

Eddie McDonnell, "Poosh" [Reginald] Coombe, and our old Huntington mechanic Bill Miller flew over from the other side [northern France] this afternoon. Poosh is going to stay a while. He wants to learn to fly day bombers, so I'm going to give him some instruction.

Dave Ingalls got another Hun! That makes three Huns and two balloons.[1] Isn't he the luckiest stiff who ever lived. How does he rate all that flying when his old sidekick has to sit here and do nothing except get sick? I'm jealous, to be perfectly frank, I'm darned jealous.

Eddie McDonnell just came in to see me. He says that the navy is going to start soon and that I will be a flight commander first and a squadron commander as soon as there are two squadrons. That's fair enough, eh?

All my love, old pal. I miss you so.

1. *Ingalls scored his last kill on 24 September over Nieuport against a two-seater Rumpler observation plane, his fifth victory in six weeks. Shortly thereafter he was ordered to duty in England.*

Eastleigh, 30 September 1918

Beloved,

. . . Did you ever have consumption? It's no fun, is it? No! I coughed so hard last night that I am black and blue from the waist up. The reason that you can't see it is because it's on the inside, and the reason that I know it is, is because everything gets black and blue when I cough.

Mr. and Mrs. [Harry] Davison went to London this afternoon, but he's coming back on Tuesday, and then we're all going to fly over and see the war and some of the boys.

The war news is slick, isn't it? The old doughboys forgot to even look at the concrete fortifications in the Hindenburg line, which are supposed to be impregnable. They just went on through.[1]

I am going to get out of the hospital this morning and test some of the machines, and then if everything is "Jake," I'll stay up, if not, I'll come back to bed. . . .

1. *On 26 September the United States First Army commenced its assault in the Meuse-Argonne region, the largest AEF action of World War One.*

Eastleigh, 2 October 1918

Beloved,

Well, it's fairly late, but I must keep up my average, especially as I'm going away tomorrow. I am going to ferry a bus over, God willing, he wasn't today! (Should be He!)

I believe the last letter I wrote you was when I was a dope fiend for three whole days, and then I got out of the hospital. Now I find that everything in my department has gone to wrack and ruin in my absence, and I think I'll go back and take some more dope, as I haven't time to either sleep or eat.

There is some slight chance that I may be able to collect a little of my baggage that I haven't seen for two or three months. What's the sense of having baggage if you aren't allowed to see it but three times a year. But then I feel so grateful to the English and French railroads if they let me have one or two pieces of baggage at the end of a trip that I really shouldn't moon about a paltry bedroll and suitcase. . . .

Three marines came over to ferry machines back.[1] It will take about one day and one night to come over by rail and fly back. They each brought a large suitcase, and one man brought a small trunk. I wonder where they expect to put all this baggage. They won't be allowed to put it in the machine, not with me around. Poor boobs, just like all marines. . . .

C'mon over, the war's fine! Bulgaria won't play anymore, and Turkey lost some of its feathers—she's next, and then Austria may stop wandering.

Cheerio, you priceless old dear.

1. *Marine pilots were busy ferrying aircraft from Eastleigh to their bases in France, preparing to commence large-scale day bombing raids. The first such attack came on 15 October against the German-held rail junction at Thielt, Belgium.*

By early October the war news on all fronts looked good. With the British advancing in Macedonia and the French in Serbia, Bulgaria sought an armistice in late September. Against the Turks, Allied troops took Haifa and Acre on 23 September. Damascus fell on the first of October. The Austrians were also falling back, as were the Germans in northern France. After four horrendous years, the smell of victory was in the air.

5

"The Last Patrol":
Kenneth MacLeish's Rendezvous
with Death

October 1918–February 1919

MACLEISH'S ELATION AT returning to front-line duty in early October was quickly tempered by news that his close friend Di Gates had been shot down on 4 October near Roulers, Belgium, and was still missing, possibly dead. George Mosely—who, with Gates, was then flying with the French naval Escardrille St.-Pol—reported that six aircraft were patrolling in formation just below the clouds when they were suddenly attacked by fifteen Germans. Gates was "with us when the attack began," Mosely recalled, "and after that no one saw him. We did everything we could to get some information regarding him, but could find nothing."

With mixed emotions MacLeish flew from Eastleigh to Dunkirk on 13 October and spent the evening visiting Bob Lovett and others at the Northern Bombing Group. Early the next morning he made a short test flight and then set off on patrol with his old Royal Air Force mates from 213 Squadron flying Sopwith Camels. In a wild melee over Belgium he scored his first aerial victory of the war. MacLeish joined a second patrol later that afternoon, a flight from which he never returned.

No one saw the young American's plane go down, though it was known that he had been actively engaged with the enemy. Despite a disturbing lack of news, many believed he might yet be found alive, and some of Kenneth's friends were heartened by rumors that a naval aviator had been captured behind the lines. Even at the end of October Bob Lovett held out hope that Kenneth would turn up in a German prisoner-of-war camp.

But the Armistice of 11 November came and went, and still there was no word. Not until the day after Christmas 1918, was the mystery solved, when Alfred Rouse, a Belgian landowner from Schoore, near Ostend, returned to his wrecked farmstead. There among the ruins he discovered the body of Lieutenant MacLeish, still wearing aviator's gloves, helmet on, chin strap secured. Two hundred yards away lay the wreckage of his airplane, shattered by machine gun fire.

The following day a party of RAF officers identified the victim, and shortly after Rouse buried the fallen aviator where he had died. He also wrote a heartfelt letter to Kenneth's mother back in Glencoe, Illinois, describing these events and expressing his deepest sympathy. Because of postwar confusion and some crossed communications, however, neither Rouse's letter nor official notification reached MacLeish's family and friends until well after New Year's 1919. Bruce MacLeish, Kenneth's older brother, informed Priscilla of her fiancé's death on 30 January. Ironically, one of the first cables of condolence came from Di Gates, who had not, after all, been killed in early October, but had crash-landed safely behind enemy lines and spent the remainder of the war in a German prison camp.

At first a stark wooden cross marked Kenneth's grave at Schoore, and later a plain headstone. On Memorial Day 1919 Kenneth's brother Norman visited the site and placed a small bouquet of flowers by the simple monument. The following year Lieutenant Kenneth MacLeish's remains were moved to a military cemetery in Waereghem, Belgium. Surrounded now by fallen comrades from a long-ago war, he lies there still.

Eastleigh, 8 October 1918

Dearest Ishbel,

Poor old Di is gone, I'm afraid. It goes hard losing him. He's always been a sort of a brother of mine, and I surely love him like one. He was last seen over Roulers in the Belgian lines, with ten or fifteen Fokker biplanes[1] and triplanes diving on him, and Di made a climbing turn and came into one of the Huns' tails.

The British say no machines were shot down that day near there, and Belgians, further north, say two machines fell, one on each side of the lines, but they won't know till today which was which, or whether they both were Huns.

I'm going up to the front Saturday, on scouts. I'm lucky! What do you say?

1. *Fokker D-VIIs, placed in service April 1918 and first flown by Manfred von Richthofen's* Jagdgeschwader *I*.

Eastleigh, 8 October 1918

Dearest Old Pal,

I haven't dared write for the last few days because I've just been hoping against hope that poor old Di would show up, but I guess that the chances are slim. Oh pal, of all the men on earth that it's hard to lose! I'm just crushed—I've never, never taken anything so badly— I've lost lots of friends, but Di was different—I've been brought up with him[1], and he's one of two men that I actually love—Arch is the other.

He had no business going out in SPADs to begin with, but his not showing up is the most mysterious thing! . . . The formation that Di was in was made up of four or five green men, Freddy Beach among them, and a French flight commander. They ran into twelve or fifteen Fokkers over Roulers. They dove away from them, and presumably the same bunch dove on them again. The formation dove again, with the exception of Di. Freddy had a Hun on his tail, so he turned as he dove, and as he looked back, he saw Di making a climbing turn onto a Hun's tail—that's the last that was seen or heard of Di. I simply can't give up hope—not yet! If any man can get out of a tight fix—Di can, and somehow I feel that he's safe. . . .

I ought to be the happiest man on earth, but with Di gone I feel pretty low. You see, Dave [Ingalls] is about fed up, so they took him back from 213 Squadron and he's coming down here to take my job, and I am going up to 213 to get some experience on scouts again. If you remember, I was out with them last spring. I only hope I can do half as well as Crock. He surely made a name for himself. He got four Huns and a couple of kite balloons, to say nothing of all kinds of trench strafing, etc.

I've done something that I think will make you happy—I did it because I love you. I passed through London, and asked them if they would send me home as an instructor after I came back from the front. They seemed pretty keen on it, too, so it may work, but don't be disappointed if it doesn't. I mean by that, don't take anything for granted.

Coming through London I saw Elsie Janis[2] in "Hullo America." It's a wonderful show. She sings a song that took my fancy:

> Give me the moonlight,
> Show me the girl,
> And leave the rest to me.
>
> Give me a little seat
> With room for two,
> Where no one else can see.
>
> Give me a shady nook,
> Where there's a babbling brook
> In close proximity.
>
> Give me the moonlight,
> Show me the girl,
> And leave the rest to me.

Frank Lynch[3], Poosh Coombe, Crock, and I are all here together. Gosh, I'm homesick. We have Frank here at the table, and we're making him write to Betty. Pal dear, I worship you, and I need you tonight. I'm blue.

1. *Gates and MacLeish had attended both Hotchkiss School and Yale together.*
2. *Elsie [Janis] Bierbower (1889–1956), a vaudeville and musical stage performer known as the "Sweetheart of the AEF."*
3. *A Yale classmate of MacLeish's from Lawrence, Massachusetts, Lynch was then serving at Eastleigh as a ferry pilot.*

Eastleigh, 9 October 1918

Dear Trubee [Davison],

The whole gang's here—Crock, Frank, Push, and myself. It's wonderful luck if you ever get near more than one of these Huntington birds. . . . Re: Di, I personally haven't given up hope, not by any means, though I suppose I should, as facts are pretty much against him.

George Mosely, Freddy Beach, Van Fleet[1], and Di were all in one flight together with two green French pilots, and apparently a "cold-footed" French flight C.O. They started on a patrol and George M. and Van Fleet came back with dud engines. The other went on. They were between [censored] and [censored] when twelve or fifteen Fokker triplanes and biplanes dove on them. The leader signaled to dive and they all dove away. Then they came back to about the same place, somewhere near Roulers, when the same bunch of Huns dove on them again. The flight C.O. signaled for a dive again. Everyone but Di dove. Freddy B. saw him last. Freddy had a Hun on his tail so he turned, and as he looked back he saw Di pull into a climbing turn and come onto a Hun's tail. . . .

I still feel sure he's all right, though I'm weakening as time passes. He's too dear a friend to lose.

1. William C. Van Fleet, born in Sacramento, California, served with the Lafayette Flying Corps, and received his American commission in August 1918. In the fall of 1918 he was attached to the Northern Bombing Group. He also flew some missions with the French Escadrille St.-Pol.

Eastleigh, 10 October 1918

Beloved Pal,

I got hold of several of our observers today for the first time in months, and they surely are in rotten spirits. They have been treated like dogs, and it's about time something was done about it. I don't know whether they can be taught to fly or not, but I think they can. If so, they will be able to get commissions. I feel guilty about them as I once had the power to get them commissions, but it fell through.

I don't know whether I'll be able to get off. The weather is persistently bad, and it looks as though it would keep on being bad for a long time. I'm crazy to get started. Bob [Lovett] nearly queered the deal once. He told the captain [Hanrahan] that he didn't think it was wise to let me go because Di went out and hadn't returned. I don't think that follows, because I trained on the buses I'm going out on, and Di had never flown that kind of bus before.

You should see the pipe Crock has. It's about ten feet long and he has to rest one end of the table or it will break his jaw. . . .

On 10 October David Ingalls assumed MacLeish's duties at Eastleigh. In a letter written to his father that evening, Ingalls reported that MacLeish was planning to fly to France on Sunday, weather permitting, though he doubted that the trip would take place as scheduled, because of the heavy rain. But thick clouds did not stop the two Yalies from having a little fun. As Ingalls recorded, "In spite of the weather, Ken took me up this morning for a joyride. It's the first time I've been up in an American machine [D.H. 4] and I am certainly agreeably surprised." Ingalls also informed Emma Guthrie at CPS & Co. in Paris that MacLeish would soon be returning to France.

Eastleigh, 10 October 1918

Dear Aunt Emma [Guthrie],

So Dave told you the news! Well, isn't it wonderful? And I have an absolutely clear conscience about the whole thing, because it all happened without a word from me. I flew a new bus over to one of the squadrons, and it happened that the captain [Hanrahan] saw me and asked me where I was going. I told him that I was on my way back, and he said, "No, you're not going back; you're going out to 213 Squadron again!" I nearly fell on his neck and kissed him. If I were not scared that he would knock me down I would have, too. . . .

Kenneth wrote his last letter to Priscilla on 11 October 1918. The following day he readied himself for a return to combat duty and on 13 October crossed the English Channel to Dunkirk.

Eastleigh, 11 October 1918

Beloved Pal,

The weather seems to be clearing, so I wouldn't be surprised if I could get off tomorrow or the next day. It surely will be a relief, although I hate to leave Crock and Frank and Poosh. I don't suppose that they'll let me stay out very long, it's just my luck not to get a chance to go out at all. I wouldn't be surprised if I couldn't, now that Bob has talked to the captain.

I had the queerest night last night! I went to bed but I couldn't sleep to save my soul! The more I got to thinking about moonlight and fall evenings, the less chance I had of sleeping. I went over every second of that night. Beloved—what a perfect night it was—one of those chilly, clear, autumn nights, and oh pal, what a moon! Wasn't it gorgeous? The whole thing seemed to foretell the future. It seemed to give me an insight into the perfect, the beautiful Love that was to be mine, yet it was stern—it seemed to indicate that the price of such a marvelous Love was very dear. It has turned out that way, hasn't it, little pal? It is such a wonderful love, yet the price is this long separation. It sometimes seems to me that it must cease soon. It can't go on this way much longer! And I feel sure that it will stop soon. I'm going out to the front to make one last try at really doing something. If the luck is with me, all well and good, if it isn't—if there aren't any Huns in the sky, or if I don't come through with a punch, then I'll give up and try my hand at something else. I'll either get Alphie [Ames] to send me home, or I'll get Snoot Brush to give me a job at home. I think I can do his kind of work. I certainly can do what Albert D[itman] is doing[1]. All my love. . . .

1. *Ditman, a native of Brooklyn, New York (b. 1884), trained with the Yale Unit and then served with the Navy Department in a nonflying capacity, visiting air stations, factories, and patrol bases in the United States.*

Kenneth MacLeish's final day at the front can be traced in the stained pages of his squadron logbook now preserved at the Public Records Office in Kew, England. He began with a fifteen-minute test flight at seven-thirty in the morning. Two hours later nineteen English planes, including Kenneth's Camel, took off for a high-altitude bombing attack against retreating German troops near Ardoye in Belgium. From a height of 10,000 feet MacLeish dropped four small Cooper bombs on the enemy below. All the Allied pilots encountered heavy opposition, and three Camels failed to return. In the melee that morning Captain Green and MacLeish destroyed a Fokker biplane, the log observing that the enemy scout was last seen "disappearing amongst the houses at Theurout."

Two hours after finishing one sortie, a second group of fifteen Camels commenced another patrol along the Channel coast. Two miles north of Dixmude they spotted eleven Fokkers at 8,000 feet and three more at 12,000. A wild scramble ensued, and several German planes were destroyed. Among the British forces, Captain Green, Lieutenant Allen, and MacLeish failed to return. The log stated that "Lieutenant MacLeish was last seen attacking about seven Fokkers single-handed." Foster Rockwell, an early member of the Yale Unit family who later served with the American Red Cross in London, summarized what little was known in a cable to Trubee Davison in New York. After that there was no further word.

T 183 JY CABLE
FROM: FOSTER ROCKWELL
LONDON, 23 OCTOBER 1918
TO: TRUBEE DAVISON
690 PARK AVENUE, NEW YORK

GATES'S MACHINE FOUND BURNED, BUT NOT CRASHED. GROUND INDICATES GOOD LANDING AND NO BURNED CLOTHING—PROBABLE PILOT BURNED MACHINE. INDI-

CATION THAT GATES IS PRISONER AND NOT SERIOUSLY
INJURED, IF AT ALL.
    MACLEISH PLANE NOT FOUND, BUT INHABITANTS SAY
NAVAL AVIATOR CAPTURED IN THAT LOCALITY. CON-
FIDENT BOTH ARE PRISONERS. WILL KEEP YOU FULLY
ADVISED. RED CROSS PRISONER BUREAU HAS THE MAT-
TER IN HAND AND WILL SEE THAT BOTH HAVE EVERY
CARE WHEN LOCATED.

Priscilla Murdock, far removed from the scene of fighting, frantically
sought word of Kenneth's fate. With few facts to work with, her friends
tried to offer hope and encouragement. Bob Lovett, especially, urged her
to wait patiently, attempting to put the best light on the available information.

Paris, 29 October 1918

Dear Chub [Priscilla Murdock, from Robert Lovett],
    I know that my cable came to you with something of a shock,
because I doubt if the [Navy] Department notifies all the interested
ones in such cases. Ken was flying with the English when he was
posted missing, and we who knew him refused to believe that anything more serious than capture had befallen him. Accordingly, when
the Huns were driven out of this area, we sent in a party to the district
in which he was driven down, and we searched for planes and interviewed the peasants near there.
    My search party had not returned when I sent the cable to reassure
you, and here are the brief facts that lead us to feel confident that Ken is
a prisoner and safe. The old woman who saw two English pilots land
said that one just burnt his machine and the other was captured before
he could finish the job. She identified the uniform of one of the airmen
as similar to that worn by one in our service, and said that the Huns
told her one officer was Canadian and the other American. She saw
both walk out of the field without limping and said one was slightly
wounded in the nose.
    Now the thing for you to do, Chub, my friend, is to wait patiently
for Ken to come home, and never for a moment doubt that we who
love him will see that everything within our power is done to make it
easier for him. If you send anything, follow my instructions carefully:
send him canned milk, crackers, chocolate (nut variety), cigarettes,
sardines. Anything in small, compressed foodstuffs will be all right.

Be careful not to send too much, only a little at a time. And put no writing on anything.

We are all in the pink and confidently looking for the big streak up here. There is no need to tell you how much I miss Kennie for you two have the same feeling, but there are few friends that I have ever cared for as much; hence consider me at your disposal in anything I may be able to do for you. A line is all you need. . . .

Even in the last week before the Armistice some hope remained. In a letter from Paris dated 3 November, Evelyn Preston commiserated with Adele Brown about the two missing aviators, saying, "It certainly is tough about Gates and MacLeish. The Red Cross is doing all they can to get news of them, and they very often have wonderful results."

But even after the fighting ended, there was no news, and the last glimmers of hope flickered out. All that remained were the nagging questions. Finally, in late December, the mystery was solved when Alfred Rouse, a landowner from Schoore, Belgium, returned to his wrecked farmstead about six miles southwest of Leffinghe. There he discovered the fully dressed body of an American naval aviator and, about two hundred yards away, his wrecked Sopwith Camel.

Rouse quickly informed the British authorities, and soon a party of officers from 213 Squadron journeyed to the site and identified the body. Not for another month, however, was this information passed on to the Americans. In the meantime Rouse wrote a letter to Kenneth's mother, Martha MacLeish, whose address he found among the slain aviator's personal papers.

Belgium, 26 December 1918

To Martha MacLeish [from Alfred Rouse],

I have the honor to fulfill a sad duty in letting you know that I discovered today at six P.M. the body of an American aviator under the following circumstances:

I had gone, assisted by M. Théo Riaison, a Flemish architect from Bruges, and M. Henri Stubbe, in the vicinity of Ostend, to investigate the damage done by the war. While clearing away the ruins of the buildings we discovered the body of a military man, with all his uniform on and buttoned, lying behind the stables of said farm. Death seems to have occurred two months before.

We immediately removed the debris we could reach about the victim and investigated to find who he was. We found—

First—A blue leather portfolio stamped on the outside with white metal letters "K. McL." On the inside it was stamped with gold letters "Lieut. K. MacLeish." This portfolio contained letters, photographs, a personal card with the name "Mr. Kenneth MacLeish" and the sum of £19 sterling, in fourteen notes of £1 and one note of £5.

Second—A disc of gilded metal marked on the back "Lieut. K. MacLeish, USNRF."

Third—A portfolio of pigskin containing his address written in ink—"K. MacLeish, etc. 4 place de Jena, Paris," and containing memoranda concerning the United States Naval Aviation Forces in foreign service, and an insurance policy to the amount of $10,000 in favor of Mrs. Martha Hillard MacLeish, 459 Longwood Avenue, Glencoe, Ill.

All these objects have been turned over to the military authority at Bruges, with the request that they be sent to you. We are holding the receipt.

I thought, Madame, that it was my duty to have the body placed in a casket and properly buried. I am sure that I have noted in accordance with the wishes of his family. The grave is on my property in the neighborhood of the spot on which the unfortunate aviator found the heroic death of a soldier. I have the honor to let you know, Madame, that I consent very gladly to authorize you to maintain gratuitously the grave, and to have placed for you, if you so wish, a suitable monument. I am entirely at your disposition to give you all the information which you could desire. Accept, Madame, my sincere expression of sympathy.

P.S. The cross on the grave would be inscribed "Kenneth MacLeish, Born the 9th September 1894, Glencoe, Ill. Found the 26th of December, 1918."

When word of Rouse's discovery finally reached American headquarters in late January, Captain David Hanrahan dispatched Lieutenant John Menzies, a Yale classmate of Kenneth's, to inspect the gravesite and make a report.

AUTINGUES, PAS DE CALAIS, 2 FEBRUARY 1919
FROM: LT. (JG) J. C. MENZIES, USNRF
TO: CAPTAIN D. C. HANRAHAN, USN
SUBJECT: INFORMATION REGARDING FINDING AND INTERMENT OF THE BODY
OF LIEUT. KENNETH MACLEISH

1. I have interviewed Mr. Alfred Rouse, solicitor and landowner at Ghiselles, Belgium, on the 28th of January 1919 concerning the finding and disposal of the body of Lieut. MacLeish who was killed in an air battle near Schoore, Belgium, on the 14th of October 1918.

2. Mr. Rouse is the owner of the farm upon which the body of Lieut. MacLeish was found and upon which his body is now buried.

3. Lieut. MacLeish's body was found in the location indicated on the accompanying sketch, laying face down on a pile of debris at the side of a small outbuilding. His flying helmet was still strapped, his coat was buttoned, and his flying gloves were still on his hands. Nothing had been removed from the body in the lines of valuables or papers. These papers and valuables have since been removed by Mr. Rouse and forwarded through proper channels.

4. I questioned Mr. Rouse concerning the condition of the body when found. The body had been lying on the ground from the 14th of October 1918 until the 26th of December 1918, and was in an advanced stage of decomposition, but the flying helmet was unpierced by bullets as was his flying coat, and upon opening the coat no trace of blood was found upon the white shirt which he wore, thus indicating that he had received no body or head wounds.

5. No trace of Lieut. MacLeish's airplane could be found within a radius of one mile from the spot on which his body was found.[1] I have searched the ground thoroughly within that radius, and there is no trace of the plane unless it is submerged in water as there is a great deal of flooded country thereabouts. There are no inhabitants in that region whom I could question regarding the location of this plane, and it is my opinion that either Lieut. MacLeish had traveled some distance from the spot where he was brought down or else the Germans removed the plane from the spot.

6. Lieut. MacLeish, at the time of his death, was flying a Camel scout machine belonging to #213 Squadron, Royal Air Force, and information regarding the flight during which he was killed may be obtained from the commanding officer of that squadron.

7. The body has been interred at the point indicated on the accompanying sketch, and is enclosed in a wooden casket. The grave was marked by a wooden cross with Lieut. MacLeish's name on it. Since then a stone has been erected on the spot and the grave may be easily identified.

8. Considering the condition of the body as it was found, and the terrain surrounding the spot, my opinion is that Lieut. MacLeish died

after reaching the ground. The spot on which the body was found was in the active battle area at that time, and he may have run into gas while attempting to get to cover or to escape.

9. I have taken several photographs of the grave and the surrounding terrain, and as soon as I have a chance to have those developed and printed, prints will be available.

10. I should take this opportunity to remark upon the extreme kindness of Mr. Rouse, indicated by his efforts in taking care of this matter, and of the two other gentlemen, namely, Mr. Théo Riaison and Mr. Henri Stubbe.

    1. Despite earlier reports that the plane was found two hundred yards away, the American search party did not find it. Perhaps the wreckage had been removed.

A few days later Captain Hanrahan, the commander of the Northern Bombing Group, wrote to Bruce MacLeish, explaining what steps had been taken thus far.

                                                             31 January 1919
To Bruce MacLeish [from Captain David Hanrahan],
    You have undoubtedly been informed by now of the fact that your brother's body was found and buried. On receipt of the information I immediately dispatched an officer to the place, had a photograph taken of his grave, and had inquiries made in regard to finding your brother's body. . . .

    One of your brother's former classmates, Lieutenant John C. Menzies, is installing today a small headstone, properly marked, which we obtained in Calais. I can assure you that everything that can possibly be done is being done, as we were all very fond of your brother. He was, without exception, the most popular man in our force, and his loss was deeply felt by us all.

    I had not given up all hope of his being a prisoner until lately when every possible avenue of search had been opened with no result. The country in which your brother's body was found is extremely bad. It is covered far and wide with bush camouflage. Its vicinity has been inundated for a large period of time. The roads were impassable until very recently.

    The body was buried in the vicinity of where it was found, which was near the village of Schoore, near a small farmhouse, just off the road between Schoore and Leke. I had been informed by the commanding officer of #213 Squadron that your brother was lost in the vicinity of Leffinghe, but this proved to be an error, the spot being about ten kilometers southwest of Leffinghe. . . . He was in a very bad fight at the time and it would appear that he was shot down and thrown out of his plane. . . .

I regret as much as you do the long interval that has elapsed before we were informed of the finding of the body. But being familiar with the poor service in this part of the world, it is not surprising that the letter written by this person [Alfred Rouse] shortly after he and his friends found your brother did not arrive at my office until practically one month later. While I hesitate to place any blame for this on the English authorities to whom this letter was evidently sent, it appears that their red tape was responsible for the delay, as a motorcycle could have carried this message to me in a few hours, as they are all familiar with the location of my headquarters. . . .

We one and all want to express to your parents our deepest sympathies in the loss of our gallant comrade who was one of the finest pilots who ever flew over the north country, and he was thoroughly unhappy with his inactivity over a long period. Not having any day squadron, I made special use of your brother, because of his all-round ability, in other duties in this organization, but he kept after me, telling me that he hoped he would be given a chance to do further work over the lines. I was specially requested to send him with 213 Squadron, RAF, as he had been with them before. He was exceedingly happy at the idea of going back with 213 and getting a chance at the Hun. Misfortune overtook him too soon. . . .

Bruce MacLeish then undertook the sad duty of officially informing Priscilla Murdock that Kenneth was dead.

TELEGRAM
30 JANUARY 1919
[BRUCE MACLEISH TO PRISCILLA MURDOCK]

CABLE JUST RECEIVED—OFFICIAL COMMUNICATION REPORTS KENNETH'S BODY FOUND AT SCHOORE, BELGIUM, WHERE IT WAS BURIED—STEPS HAVE BEEN TAKEN TO REMOVE TO MILITARY CEMETERY AT CALAIRAS—

The same day a cable of condolence arrived from Di Gates, only recently released from captivity. He had been a prisoner since being shot down on 4 October, first at Ghent in Belgium, then in Germany at Karlsruhe and Villengen. An escape attempt was foiled only a few yards from the Swiss border. Gates was finally freed on 26 November, crossed over to England in December, and returned to the United States aboard the battleship *Arkansas* in early February.

> TELEGRAM
> 30 JANUARY 1919
> [DI GATES TO PRISCILLA MURDOCK]
>
> ARCHIE JUST TOLD ME OF VERY SAD DEFINITE NEWS CON-
> CERNING KENNY—MY OWN GRIEF HELPS ME TO APPRECI-
> ATE YOURS TO SOME EXTENT—WILL RETURN TO NEW
> YORK IN MORNING FRIDAY AND AM LOOKING FORWARD
> TO SEEING YOU—MY DEEPEST SYMPATHIES.

By mid-February both Gates and Menzies had returned to New York. The departed MacLeish was much on their minds, as the following letter from Menzies to Gates makes clear.

New York, February 1919

[John Menzies to Di Gates]

I received your letter a day or so ago during a visit at home. I have been in New York most of the time since arriving from overseas and I was here when you wrote. It is too bad I was not here at the [Yale] club when you could find me. We could have had quite a talk.

I am glad that you saw "Dinty" Moore. He was with us when I went up to Ghiselles to question Mr. Rouse concerning the finding of Ken Macleish's grave. In fact, Dinty acted as interpreter as his French is considerably better than mine.

So I will assume that he told you most of what was said at the time. Mr. Rouse certainly deserves a great many thanks, for he has certainly been a very generous and painstaking gentleman throughout this affair.

I am enclosing photographs of Ken's grave and an envelope containing the address of the stonecutter whom we engaged in Calais to erect the stone. You will also find a copy of the letter which I wrote to

Captain Hanrahan. I have not sent this letter to Ken's folks as I know the official form appears cold and blunt, and the letter contains some information which I do not believe would cause anything but pain to them.

I took a great many pictures of the grave as the weather was very dud, and I hoped to get at least one or two good ones. Most of them are fair. I am sending a set to Ken's people.

I will stop now and trust to seeing you in New Haven very shortly.

Soon after receiving official notification of their son's death, the MacLeishes arranged for a memorial service to be held at Glencoe where Kenneth had grown up.

MEMORIAL ADDRESS DELIVERED BY THE REV. CHARLES W. GILKEY AT GLENCOE, ILLINOIS, 2 FEBRUARY 1919

. . . You may remember that about the time we entered the war, the *Atlantic Monthly* published a collection of very remarkable letters written by young French soldiers at the front to their families and friends; . . . Kenneth MacLeish is one of those rare spirits who live on in the hearts of us who knew and loved him, not only because of his spotless life and gallant death, but because in his own letters he has revealed what manner of man he was, what spirit and purpose sustained him in his hazardous line of service, what faith upheld him as he looked steadily into the face of death. . . .

While traveling in Europe the following spring, Norman MacLeish visited his brother's grave on Memorial Day. At first the family had planned to bring Kenneth home to be reinterred in Illinois, but Norman changed his mind, noting that "four days in that gallant, lovable country was enough to convince me. . . . I can't think of a better place for Kenney to rest. . . . At all events, Kenney won't be forgotten or lost there, and nowhere could he receive more loving care."

And finally, in December 1919 the United States paid homage to Lieutenant MacLeish. Josephus Daniels, secretary of the navy, wired Kenneth's mother that destroyer #220, then building at Philadelphia, would be named for the Yale flier. Kenneth was also posthumously awarded the Navy Cross for "distinguished service and extraordinary heroism." Four days later Ishbel MacLeish traveled down to Philadelphia from Vassar College to christen the new warship.

In the years that followed, Kenneth's friends and relatives remembered him in different ways. Colleagues in the Yale Unit toasted his exploits and devotion at their reunions. His mother published a memorial volume of her son's letters. Various family members visited Kenneth's gravesite at the Waereghem military cemetery in Belgium where he had been reinterred with so many other victims of the war. Archibald MacLeish renamed his firstborn son after the uncle he would never know. Perhaps that was one way of holding onto the memories. In a letter to his mother written on the second anniversary of Kenneth's death, Archibald observed poignantly, "As time goes by I have a strange impression that it is we who are leaving Kenney rather than Kenney who has left us. . . . I feel as each period of time goes by that the current of time and change is bearing me away from the things he and I knew together."

And what of Priscilla? After the war she returned to her parents' home, worked, visited with old friends like the Davisons, Gates, and Lovetts. She did not marry until 1927. She treasured Kenneth's letters for the rest of her life.

Index

About the Author

Geoffrey L. Rossano has been studying early military aviation since 1968. Currently teaching at the Salisbury School in Salisbury, Connecticut, he holds an undergraduate degree from Tufts University and M.A. and Ph.D. degrees from the University of North Carolina at Chapel Hill. A consulting historian to a wide range of museums and historical societies, he is also the author of *Between Ocean and Empire: An Illustrated History of Long Island* and *Creating a Dignified Past: Museums and the Colonial Revival.* He is now working on a study of American colonial maritime trade with Central America; in addition, with the aid of a U.S. Navy research grant, he is engaged in a definitive study of naval aviation in Europe during World War I.

The **Naval Institute Press** is the book-publishing arm of the U.S. Naval Institute, a private, nonprofit professional society for members of the sea services and civilians who share an interest in naval and maritime affairs. Established in 1873 at the U.S. Naval Academy in Annapolis, Maryland, where its offices remain today, the Naval Institute has more than 100,000 members worldwide.

Members of the Naval Institute receive the influential monthly magazine *Proceedings* and discounts on fine nautical prints, ship and aircraft photos, and subscriptions to the quarterly *Naval History* magazine. They also have access to the transcripts of the Institute's Oral History Program and get discounted admission to any of the Institute-sponsored seminars regularly offered around the country.

The Naval Institute's book-publishing program, begun in 1898 with basic guides to naval practices, has broadened its scope in recent years to include books of more general interest. Now the Naval Institute Press publishes more than forty new titles each year, ranging from how-to books on boating and navigation to battle histories, biographies, ship and aircraft guides, and novels. Institute members receive discounts on the Press's more than 375 books.

Full-time students are eligible for special half-price membership rates. Life memberships are also available.

For a free catalog describing the Naval Institute Press books currently available, and for further information about U.S. Naval Institute membership, please write to:

Membership & Communications Department
U.S. Naval Institute
Annapolis, Maryland 21402
Or call, toll-free, (800) 233–USNI. In Maryland, call (301) 224–3378.

THE NAVAL INSTITUTE PRESS

THE PRICE OF HONOR

The World War One Letters
of Naval Aviator Kenneth MacLeish

Designed by Pamela L. Schnitter

Set in Bembo
by TC Systems, Inc.,
Shippensburg, Pennsylvania

Printed on 60-lb. Sebago Eggshell Cream and 70-lb. Glatco Gloss
and bound in Permalin Wedgewood Buckram and Holliston Kingston Natural
with text-matching endsheets
by The Maple-Vail Book Manufacturing Group
York, Pennsylvania